MY
REVISION
NOTES

OCR

A-level

COMPUTER SCIENCE
SECOND EDITION

George Rouse, Jason Pitt and Sean O'Byrne

Boost

HODDER
EDUCATION
AN HACHETTE UK COMPANY

Every effort has been made to trace all copyright holders, but if any have been inadvertently overlooked, the Publishers will be pleased to make the necessary arrangements at the first opportunity.

Although every effort has been made to ensure that website addresses are correct at time of going to press, Hodder Education cannot be held responsible for the content of any website mentioned in this book. It is sometimes possible to find a relocated web page by typing in the address of the home page for a website in the URL window of your browser.

Hachette UK's policy is to use papers that are natural, renewable and recyclable products and made from wood grown in well-managed forests and other controlled sources. The logging and manufacturing processes are expected to conform to the environmental regulations of the country of origin.

Orders: please contact Hachette UK Distribution, Hely Hutchinson Centre, Milton Road, Didcot, Oxfordshire, OX11 7HH. Telephone: +44 (0)1235 827827.
Email education@hachette.co.uk. Lines are open from 9 a.m. to 5 p.m., Monday to Friday.
You can also order through our website: www.hoddereducation.co.uk

ISBN: 978 1 3983 2547 0

© George Rouse, Jason Pitt and Sean O'Byrne 2021

First published in 2021 by

Hodder Education,

An Hachette UK Company

Carmelite House

50 Victoria Embankment

London EC4Y 0DZ

www.hoddereducation.co.uk

Impression number   10 9 8 7 6 5 4

Year   2025 2024

All rights reserved. Apart from any use permitted under UK copyright law, no part of this publication may be reproduced or transmitted in any form or by any means, electronic or mechanical, including photocopying and recording, or held within any information storage and retrieval system, without permission in writing from the publisher or under licence from the Copyright Licensing Agency Limited. Further details of such licences (for reprographic reproduction) may be obtained from the Copyright Licensing Agency Limited, www.cla.co.uk

Cover photo © Holmessu - stock.adobe.com

Illustrations by Aptara, Inc.

Typeset by Aptara, Inc.

Printed in India

A catalogue record for this title is available from the British Library.

Get the most from this book

Everyone has to decide his or her own revision strategy, but it is essential to review your work, learn it and test your understanding. These Revision Notes will help you to do that in a planned way, topic by topic. Use this book as the cornerstone of your revision and don't hesitate to write in it — personalise your notes and check your progress by ticking off each section as you revise.

Tick to track your progress

Use the revision planner on pages 4 and 5 to plan your revision, topic by topic. Tick each box when you have:

✚ revised and understood a topic
✚ tested yourself
✚ practised the exam questions and gone online to check your answers and complete the quick quizzes

You can also keep track of your revision by ticking off each topic heading in the book. You may find it helpful to add your own notes as you work through each topic.

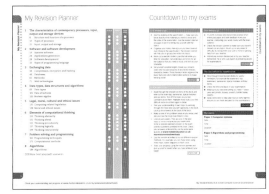

Features to help you succeed

Exam tips

Expert tips are given throughout the book to help you polish your exam technique in order to maximise your chances in the exam.

Typical mistakes

The authors identify the typical mistakes candidates make and explain how you can avoid them.

Now test yourself

These short, knowledge-based questions provide the first step in testing your learning. Answers are at the back of the book.

Definitions and key words

Clear, concise definitions of essential key terms are provided where they first appear.

Key words from the specification are highlighted in bold throughout the book.

Making links

This feature identifies specific connections between topics and tells you how revising these will aid your exam answers.

Exam skills

These summaries highlight how to specific skills identified or applicable in that chapter can be applied to your exam answers.

Revision activities

These activities will help you to understand each topic in an interactive way.

Exam practice

Practice exam questions are provided for each topic. Use them to consolidate your revision and practise your exam skills.

Summaries

The summaries provide a quick-check bullet list for each topic.

Online

Go online to find answers to the exam practice questions and try out the extra quick quizzes at **www.hoddereducation.co.uk/ myrevisionnotesdownloads**

My Revision Planner

1 The characteristics of contemporary processors, input, output and storage devices

REVISED | TESTED | EXAM READY

8   Structure and function of a processor
13 Types of processor
15 Input, output and storage

2 Software and software development

19 Systems software
24 Applications generation
28 Software development
33 Types of programming language

3 Exchanging data

44 Compression, encryption and hashing
49 Databases
65 Networks
71 Web technologies

4 Data types, data structures and algorithms

83   Data types
101 Data structures
120 Boolean algebra

5 Legal, moral, cultural and ethical issues

133 Computing-related legislation
138 Moral and ethical issues

6 Elements of computational thinking

150 Thinking abstractly
152 Thinking ahead
155 Thinking procedurally
157 Thinking logically
159 Thinking concurrently

7 Problem solving and programming

163 Programming techniques
175 Computational methods

8 Algorithms

184 Algorithms

209 Now test yourself answers

Check your understanding and progress at **www.hoddereducation.co.uk/myrevisionnotesdownloads**

Countdown to my exams

6–8 weeks to go

+ Start by looking at the specification — make sure you know exactly what material you need to revise and the style of the examination. Use the revision planner on pages 4 and 5 to familiarise yourself with the topics.
+ Organise your notes, making sure you have covered everything on the specification. The revision planner will help you to group your notes into topics.
+ Work out a realistic revision plan that will allow you time for relaxation. Set aside days and times for all the subjects that you need to study, and stick to your timetable.
+ Set yourself sensible targets. Break your revision down into focused sessions of around 40 minutes, divided by breaks. These Revision Notes organise the basic facts into short, memorable sections to make revising easier.

REVISED

2–6 weeks to go

+ Read through the relevant sections of this book and refer to the exam tips, summaries, typical mistakes and key terms. Tick off the topics as you feel confident about them. Highlight those topics you find difficult and look at them again in detail.
+ Test your understanding of each topic by working through the 'Now test yourself' questions in the book. Look up the answers at the back of the book.
+ Make a note of any problem areas as you revise, and ask your teacher to go over these in class.
+ Look at past papers. They are one of the best ways to revise and practise your exam skills. Write or prepare planned answers to the exam practice questions provided in this book. Check your answers online and try out the extra quick quizzes at **www.hoddereducation.co.uk/ myrevisionnotesdownloads**
+ Use the revision activities to try out different revision methods. For example, you can make notes using mind maps, spider diagrams or flash cards.
+ Track your progress using the revision planner and give yourself a reward when you have achieved your target.

REVISED

One week to go

+ Try to fit in at least one more timed practice of an entire past paper and seek feedback from your teacher, comparing your work closely with the mark scheme.
+ Check the revision planner to make sure you haven't missed out any topics. Brush up on any areas of difficulty by talking them over with a friend or getting help from your teacher.
+ Attend any revision classes put on by your teacher. Remember, he or she is an expert at preparing people for examinations.

REVISED

The day before the examination

+ Flick through these Revision Notes for useful reminders, for example the examiners' tips, examiners' summaries, typical mistakes and key terms.
+ Check the time and place of your examination.
+ Make sure you have everything you need — extra pens and pencils, tissues, a watch, bottled water, sweets.
+ Allow some time to relax and have an early night to ensure you are fresh and alert for the examinations.

REVISED

My exams

Paper 1 Computer systems

Date:..

Time: ....

Location: ....

Paper 2 Algorithms and programming

Date:..

Time: ....

Location: ....

Assessing A level Computer Science

As a student of Computer Science, it is important that you understand three things in relation to the A level examinations:
+ assessment objectives
+ the command words used
+ the nature of the examination papers.

> **Assessment objectives**
>
> + AO1 You should be able to demonstrate knowledge and understanding of the principles and concepts of computer science, including abstraction, logic, algorithms and data representation.
> + AO2 You must be able to apply your knowledge and understanding to the principles and concepts of computer science, including analysing problems in computational terms.
> + AO3 You must be able to design, program and evaluate computer systems that solve problems, making reasoned judgements about these systems and presenting conclusions.

Command words

REVISED

Familiarity with the relevant command words is important and helps you to avoid wasting time in the exam room, for example trying to evaluate when there is no requirement for it. The most frequently used command words in the A level papers, along with number of marks for associated questions, are:
+ **Calculate**: requires you to work out the value of something. A correct final answer, to the required degree of accuracy and with the correct units is required. Working is not always required, but there may be credit for correct working even when the answer is incorrect. (AO1, AO2)
+ **Compare**: requires you to describe the differences and similarities between two situations. (AO1, AO2)
+ **Describe**: requires you to set out the characteristics or features of something. (AO1)
+ **Discuss**: requires you to identify and expand upon points related to different aspects of the situation/system/issue, looking at both sides of the argument. (AO1, AO2)
+ **Evaluate**: requires you to reach a conclusion based on evidence for all aspects of the situation. (AO1, AO2, AO3)
+ **Explain**: requires you to provide evidence to explain how a system works or to support a proposition about a situation. In some cases, an appropriate diagram may be used to support your explanation. (AO1, AO2)

The A level exam papers

REVISED

The Computer Science A level specification is examined through two equally weighted examination papers of 2 hours and 30 minutes duration sat at the end of the course, and a programming project. **The papers are each worth 40% of the marks, with the project worth 20%.**

Paper 1 Computer systems

There will be a mix of short and long answer questions.

Questions may cover any of the content in section 1 of the specification, computer systems, which includes:
+ computer architecture (including the structure of the central processing unit, memory and storage)
+ software and its development

Check your understanding and progress at **www.hoddereducation.co.uk/myrevisionnotesdownloads**

- storing and exchanging data (including databases, networks and web technologies)
- data representation, logic and algorithms
- legal and ethical issues.

Paper 2 Algorithms and programming

There are two sections and in both sections there will be a mix of short and long answer questions.

Questions may cover any of the content in section 2 of the specification, algorithms and programming, which includes:
- computational thinking
- problem solving
- algorithms (including knowledge of key algorithms and their efficiency).

The two sections are:
- **Section A**, worth 100 marks, will contain a mixture of questions, similar in style to paper one.
- **Section B**, worth 40 marks, will be based on a scenario that contains information to be used when answering the questions that follow.

Long answer questions

REVISED ●

Both papers will contain longer answer questions worth 9 or 12 marks. These questions may require you to link a number of topics together or look at contrasting approaches.

When tackling a longer answer question:
- Read through the question carefully to ensure you understand what is being asked.
- Take a moment to consider which part or parts of the specification the question is testing you on and to plan your answer.
- If there is a scenario, make sure your answer relates the points you are making to it.
- If you are asked to discuss two approaches, make sure you pay roughly equal attention to both.
- Where relevant, ensure you give a clear conclusion.
- Make sure you use technical terminology appropriately.

Programming questions

REVISED ●

Both papers will include programming questions. These may require you to write or follow code. The code presented in the exam will be in pseudocode (with the exception of any question in paper one specifically on JavaScript).

The exam board's style of pseudocode has been used throughout this book. There is a full description of it in the appendix of the specification. It is worth taking a little time to familiarise yourself with it.

When writing pseudocode in answers, you are free to use whatever style you wish and may want to stick with one similar to the language with which you have learned to program.

You should always use sensible variable names and indentation in your pseudocode. Where the meaning of code is not immediately obvious, add comments. In some questions, there may be marks for ensuring your code is easily readable.

Programming project

REVISED ●

The project is submitted as a report, containing the details about the process of identifying, analysing, designing, developing, testing and evaluating a solution to a problem using a suitable programming language.

1 The characteristics of contemporary processors, input, output and storage devices

Structure and function of a processor

The central processing unit (CPU) carries out the instructions in computer programs. Essentially it's what makes a computer a computer! Inside a processor there are billions of transistors (effectively electronic switches). This section looks at how CPUs work and different developments in CPU technology.

> **Central processing unit (CPU)** The central processing unit 'runs programs' by continually fetching, decoding and executing instructions.

The arithmetic logic unit, control unit and registers

REVISED

The main components of the CPU are the arithmetic logic unit, control unit and registers. These are connected to the system's main memory using pathways called buses.

Arithmetic logic unit

The arithmetic logic unit (ALU) carries out the calculations and logical decisions. The results of its calculations are stored in the accumulator.

Control unit

The control unit (CU) sends out signals to co-ordinate how the processor works. It controls how data moves around parts of the CPU and how it moves between the CPU and memory. Instructions are decoded in the control unit.

Registers

Registers are areas of memory within the processor itself. They can be accessed at extremely fast speeds so can be used by the processor without causing a bottleneck. Registers in the processor that have a specific use are called special purpose registers.

> **Register** A discrete piece of memory built onto the CPU that holds a single piece of data.

The special purpose registers you need to know are listed below.

Register	Purpose
Program counter (PC)	Keeps track of the memory location of the line of machine code being executed. With each iteration of the fetch–decode–execute cycle, it gets incremented to point to the next instruction, allowing the program to be executed in sequence, instruction by instruction. The program counter can also be changed by instructions that alter the flow of control (for example, branch like BRA, BRP and BRZ)
Memory data register (MDR)	Stores the data or instructions that are to be fetched from or sent to memory
Memory address register (MAR)	Stores the address of the data or instructions that are to be fetched from or sent to memory
Current instruction register (CIR)	Stores the most recently fetched instruction, which will be decoded and executed
Accumulator (ACC)	Stores the results of calculations made by the ALU

Check your understanding and progress at **www.hoddereducation.co.uk/myrevisionnotesdownloads**

Processors may also have general purpose registers. These can temporarily store data being used rather than sending data to and from memory. (Memory data access times are slow compared to special purpose registers but still much faster than secondary storage.)

Buses

Buses are the communication channels through which data can be sent around the computer. You need to know about three buses:
1 The **data bus** carries data between the processor and memory.
2 The **address bus** carries the address of the memory location being read from or written to.
3 The **control bus** sends control signals from the control unit.

Now test yourself   TESTED ◯

1 Describe the purpose of the control unit.
2 State the names of the three buses used by the CPU.
3 State the name of the part of the CPU responsible for calculations.

Answers on p. 209

Exam tip

A common mistake is to talk about the control bus carrying *instructions* around the processor. This is not the case. Instructions are sent to and from memory via the data bus. The control bus carries the *signals* orchestrating the fetch–decode–execute signal.

The fetch–decode–execute cycle, including its effects on registers

REVISED ◯

Making links

In order to fully understand this section you need to know about the Little Man Computer instruction set. You should revisit this section after studying Chapter 2, Assembly language.

The processor works by continually fetching, decoding then executing instructions. You need to be aware of how the registers are used during the process.

Fetch

1 The contents of the PC are copied to the MAR.
2 The read signal is sent across the control bus and the contents of the MAR are sent across the address bus.
3 The contents of the memory location stored in the MAR are then sent across the data bus and stored in the MDR.
4 The contents of the MDR are then copied to the CIR.
5 The PC is incremented by one.

Decode

6 The contents of the CIR are sent to the control unit.
7 The control unit then decodes the instruction.

Execute

8 The registers can be changed in different ways during the execution phase, depending on the instruction.

For instance, if the instruction is for a memory location to be read from or written to (that is, LDA or STA), then the address stored within the instruction will be loaded into the MAR. In the case of STA, the data stored in the ACC is sent to memory. In the case of LDA, the data is loaded from memory into the ACC.

If the instruction is to carry out a calculation (that is, ADD or SUB) then the contents of the MDR and ACC are sent to the ALU and the result sent back to the ACC.

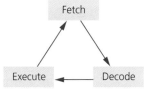

Figure 1.1 Fetch–decode–execute cycle

Now test yourself

TESTED

4 Give an example of when the contents of the ACC might be changed.

5 State the name of the bus that carries the contents of memory to the MDR.

6 Explain why the PC is incremented by 1 in each cycle.

Answers on p. 209

The factors affecting the performance of the CPU

REVISED

+ clock speed
+ number of cores
+ amount of cache memory
+ use of pipelining.

Clock speed

Processors work at incredible speeds, dictated by the clock signal. The speed of this signal, known as the clock speed, is measured in hertz (Hz).

Unit	Pulses per second
1 Hertz (Hz)	1
1 Kilohertz (kHz)	1000
1 Megahertz (MHz)	1000000
1 Gigahertz (GHz)	1000000000

Modern desktop processors tend run in the order of Gigahertz. The processor on the computer being used to write this chapter runs at a speed of 2.8 GHz. That means its processor has a clock producing 2.8 billion pulses per second.

Number of cores

A core is a processing unit within the CPU. Modern CPUs have multiple cores that can operate independently.

+ Each core is a distinct processing unit on the CPU that can run independently.
+ When multitasking, different cores can run different applications.
+ It is also possible for multiple cores to work on the same problem.
+ The more cores you have, the easier it is to run more things simultaneously. More cores also mean that tasks that can have their work shared will run more quickly.

Core A core is a processing unit within the CPU.

Cache memory A fast memory that is built on or close to the CPU and is designed to reduce the need to access RAM, which has slower access speeds.

Cache

Random access memory's (RAM's) access speed is significantly slower than the speed at which the CPU operates. To compensate for this, processors have a small amount of fast memory called cache memory:

+ Cache memory is a temporary store.
+ Cache memory is built into the processor itself, reducing the distance data has to travel to it. Data and instructions that are likely to be regularly accessed are kept in cache memory, ready for fast access.
+ By allowing the processor to access cache, the overall speed at which it operates is less likely to be limited by RAM's access speed.
+ Because cache memory is faster when it is smaller, different levels of cache are used.
+ Level one cache is the smallest and built directly into the CPU. Often each core will have its own level one cache.
+ Each subsequent cache level is larger and further away from the heart of the CPU and is therefore slower to access.
+ Modern CPUs tend to have three or four levels of cache.

Making links

Having a cache is a common concept in computing, and isn't just used in the CPU. Web browsers cache files on your computer to avoid them having to be repeatedly downloaded. You can find out more about caches in Chapter 6.

Check your understanding and progress at **www.hoddereducation.co.uk/myrevisionnotesdownloads**

The use of pipelining in a processor to improve efficiency

REVISED

The processor works by repeatedly fetching, decoding and executing instructions. If it does this one instruction at a time, then parts of the processor are potentially left sitting idle. To overcome this, using pipelining in the CPU means that different parts of the CPU performing different parts of the fetch–decode–execute cycle on a sequence of instructions. While one instruction is being executed, the next can be decoded and the one after that fetched.

> **Pipelining** When discussing a CPU, it means different parts of the CPU performing different parts of the fetch–decode–execute cycle on a sequence of instructions.

	Fetch	Decode	Execute
Step 1	Instruction 1		
Step 2	Instruction 2	Instruction 1	
Step 3	Instruction 3	Instruction 2	Instruction 1
Step 4	Instruction 4	Instruction 3	Instruction 2

This works as long as subsequent instructions can be predicted. This isn't always the case. For example, if there is a branch instruction, the CPU may not be able to tell it should fetch the instruction immediately after it, or needs to jump to a different part of the program until it is time to execute the branch instruction. If the wrong instruction is chosen to be fetched in advance, it has to be thrown away and the correct one fetched.

> **Making links**
>
> Pipelining can be seen as a more general process, not just specific to the CPU. You can read about how pipelining can be applied to other problems when looking at computational methods in Chapter 7.

Now test yourself

TESTED

7 Explain why CPUs have cache memory.

8 Explain how pipelining improves the performance of a processor.

9 Describe a situation in which more cores will improve the performance of a CPU.

Answers on p. 209

Von Neumann, Harvard and contemporary processor architecture

REVISED

A computer's architecture is the approach taken to its design. Computers with the same architecture aren't necessarily identical but will follow a specific design philosophy.

> **Architecture** When discussing computers, this refers to the approach taken in a computer's design.

Von Neumann architecture

The Von Neumann architecture has:
+ a single control unit
+ a single arithmetic logic unit
+ a single memory store that contains *both instructions and data*.

Storing data and instructions in the same memory unit and having them travel along the same bus can hold things up.

If an instruction is being read, then because memory and the data bus are in use, it is not possible to read and write data at the same time.

Harvard architecture

Harvard architecture differs from Von Neumann in that it has separate memory units and buses for data and instructions and therefore doesn't suffer from the restriction of having a single memory store.

Contemporary processors

While modern processors have many of the features of the model described at the start of the chapter, in practice, they are many times more complex. Over time, processor designers have come up with many ideas to improve performance and efficiency. A number are described below but there are many more, with new ones being developed all the time.

Simultaneous multithreading

+ A 'thread' is the sequence of instructions that have been sent to the CPU to be processed.
+ Simultaneous multithreading allows two threads to run on each core at one time.
+ The core is designed so that the part of it that fetches and decodes, the 'front end', is duplicated. This means that it is capable of fetching and decoding two threads at once.
+ As the execution part of the core is not continuously being used, it can switch between the two threads.
+ It should be noted that while simultaneous multithreading will improve performance, two cores that are not multithreading will outperform one similar core with two threads.

Out of order execution

+ In the model you have studied, each instruction is fetched, decoded then executed.
+ In reality, some instructions may take longer than others to execute, leaving other parts of the CPU idle.
+ Out of order execution allows instructions to be executed ahead of when they usually would be if the required resources are available, preventing delays. This requires the CPU to check that the instruction to be executed out of order isn't dependent on data yet to be processed.

Branch prediction

+ We have seen that one issue with pipelining is that the pipeline has to be cleared if the prediction is wrong, costing time.
+ Modern CPUs use branch prediction to try and work out where a program will go at a decision point. This reduces how often the pipeline has to be cleared, improving overall speed of execution.

Variable clock speed

+ Modern processors are able to change their clock speeds. They may temporarily be able to increase it during intensive tasks to give a performance boost
+ There is, however, a limit as to how long this can be done for before overheating means it has to return to its normal speed.
+ Some CPUs can also reduce their clock speed to reduce power consumption and extend battery life in portable devices.

Power conservation

As well as adjusting clock speed to conserve power, modern CPUs are able to shut off parts of their circuity that aren't being used at a given point in time. This might, for example, be parts dedicated to video processing. All this helps to reduce power consumption.

> **Exam tip**
>
> You may come across the term Hyper-Threading. This is the processor manufacturer Intel's proprietary name for their version of simultaneous multithreading. In an exam you should always give generic and not proprietary names. Therefore always use the term simultaneous multithreading not Hyper-Threading.

Now test yourself   TESTED ◯

10 Describe one difference between the Von Neumann and Harvard architectures.

11 Give one example of a feature a contemporary processor might have.

Answers on p. 209

Types of processor

The differences between and uses of CISC and RISC processors

REVISED

There are two main approaches to CPUs – reduced instruction set computing (RISC) and complex instruction set computing (CISC). An instruction set is the list of instructions a CPU is able to decode.

+ RISC processors have a smaller range of instructions than CISC processors.
+ The smaller instruction set means fewer transistors are needed. Therefore, they generally require less power and cost less to produce.
+ The instructions in a CISC processor may take several clock cycles to execute. RISC instructions usually take a single clock cycle, meaning they are better suited to pipelining.
+ Compilers for RISC processors tend to be more complicated, so for a given program more instructions are likely to be generated.
+ RISC processors have fewer addressing modes than CISC processors but more general-purpose registers.

> **Reduced instruction set computing (RISC)** A design approach where a CPU uses a small set of instructions. While this means a loss of some of the more specialised instructions, it allows for efficiencies in the processor design.
>
> **Complex instruction set computing (CISC)** This was a term retroactively coined for non-RISC processors. CISC processors tend to have a larger instruction set, including very specialised instructions.

Making links

Because RISC and CISC CPUs have different instruction sets, a program that runs on one type of CPU will not run on the other. This means different compilers need to be used for programs targeted to run on RISC or CISC devices. You can find out more about compilers in Chapter 2.

You should also keep in mind that just because two CPUs are both RISC (or both CISC) designs, this does not mean they necessarily have the same instruction set. The terms RISC and CISC simply describe the philosophy for the design of the instruction set.

Now test yourself

TESTED

12 State which has more addressing modes: a CISC or a RISC processor.

13 State which processor type is likely to be made of more transistors, RISC or CISC.

14 Explain why some laptop manufacturers have started to produce laptops with RISC CPUs rather than the CISC approach they have previously used.

Answers on p. 209

GPUs and their uses (including those not related to graphics)

REVISED

A graphics processing unit (GPU) is specifically designed to perform the calculations associated with displaying graphics. GPUs:

+ have instruction sets specifically designed for the sorts of calculations required in graphics processing
+ have the ability to process these pieces of data in parallel, referred to as single instruction multiple data (SIMD)
+ can either be placed on a graphics card with access to their own dedicated memory …
+ … or can be embedded within a CPU.
+ GPUs require additional software to convert CPU functions to GPU functions.

> **Graphics processing unit (GPU)** A type of processor designed with the purpose of drawing graphics on the screen.

It should be remembered that GPUs cannot themselves run programs. A computer still needs a CPU to run a program, but if there is a GPU, the CPU can pass on certain processing of data (traditionally the rendering of graphics) to it.

13

While designed for graphics (for example for gaming animation and graphic design), because of their special capabilities GPUs are increasingly being used in many other fields. Examples include:

+ modelling physical systems
+ audio processing
+ breaking passwords
+ machine learning.

Now test yourself

TESTED

15 Describe one way a GPU is different from a CPU.

16 Give an example of how a GPU might be used other than for drawing three dimensional (3D) graphics.

Answers on p. 209

Multicore and parallel systems

 REVISED

Parallel processing is when a computer carries out multiple computations simultaneously to solve a given problem. There are different approaches to this:

+ One is SIMD, where the same operation is carried out on multiple pieces of data, at one time. This type of parallel processing is often carried out by GPUs.
+ The other approach is multiple instructions multiple data (MIMD); here, different instructions are carried out concurrently on different pieces of data.

Parallel processing could take place within a single CPU by sharing computation across its cores. This is a multicore approach.

If we need a higher degree of parallelisation, then multiple CPUs (each with their own multiple cores) may be used. An example of this is a supercomputer. The top supercomputers in the world have tens of thousands of CPUs and GPUs, with millions of cores able to work on a problem simultaneously.

Some things are easy to parallelise. If we have a batch of one billion numbers to add together, it is easy to see that 100 processors could divide the workload to come to a total, quicker than a single CPU. On the other hand, if we want to work out the 10 000th term of the Fibonacci sequence, where each term is the calculated by adding the two previous terms (e.g. 0, 1, 1, 2, 3, 5, 8 …) there is no benefit to be gained by having more than one CPU. Most programs have some parts that can be parallelised and others that cannot.

The extent to which parallel processing speeds up the solving of a problem depends on how much of the problem is parallelisable. If only half of a program is parallelisable, then the best case that can be achieved by adding more processors is getting close to the program running in half the time of one processor.

Now test yourself

TESTED

17 Explain what is meant by MIMD.

18 Explain what is meant by SIMD.

Answers on p. 209

Input, output and storage

How different input, output and storage devices can be applied to the solution of different problems

REVISED ⬤

Hardware is the description given to the physical components of a computer system:

+ A computer system has a CPU and memory.
+ There is usually some form of storage.
+ There are usually devices to input data into and output information from the computer.
+ 'Peripheral' is the term given to hardware attached to and used with a computer, but that are not an integral part of it.

> **Hardware** The physical components of a computer system. For example the CPU, RAM, motherboard, mouse, monitor etc.

Input devices and output devices

+ Input devices allow data to be entered into a computer. Examples include keyboards, mice, microphones, scanners and joysticks.
+ Output devices allow information to be retrieved from a computer. Examples include printers, speakers, monitors and actuators (devices that cause movement).

Storage devices

Storage devices can use magnetic, optical or flash technology. This is covered in more detail in the next section.

To make an informed decision as to what device is best for a given scenario:

+ You need to have a good feel for how much storage is taken up by different types of files.
+ As a rough guide, documents and photographs require several megabytes, audio requires a couple of megabytes per minute and video tens of megabytes per minute. The number can vary depending on the quality and compression used. You should a look around your own computer and see how much space different files take up.

Device	Type	Capacity
CD	Optical	650 MB
DVD	Optical	4.7 GB
Blu-ray	Optical	25–100 GB
Hard disk drive (HDD)	Magnetic	1–20 TB
Solid state drive (SSD)	Flash	500 GB–5 TB
Tape	Magnetic	10–30 TB
USB flash drive	Flash	16 GB–1 TB

> **Exam tip**
>
> HDDs and SSDs can be external or internal. If the device needs to be moved between devices or stored away safely, then you should state the device is either 'external' or 'portable' (the latter can run without being plugged into a power supply). If the terms hard disk drive or solid state drive are used on their own they are usually assumed to be internal.

Now test yourself   TESTED ⬤

19 List ten different input devices.

20 List ten different output devices.

Answers on p. 209

The uses of magnetic, optical and flash storage devices

REVISED

Storage devices fall into three categories: magnetic, optical and flash.

Type of storage device	Description	Examples
Magnetic	Uses a magnetisable material. Patterns of magnetisation are then used to represent binary sequences. Magnetic storage tends to have a high capacity at a low cost. Their moving parts tend to make them unsuitable for portable devices as sudden movements can cause them to malfunction. They consume more power than flash media	Hard disk drive Magnetic tape (often used to back up servers)
Optical	Uses a laser and by looking at its reflection, determines where there are pits on a surface, which represent 1s and 0s. Optical media tend to be cheap to distribute and fairly resilient	Compact disc (CD) Digital versatile disc (DVD) Blu-ray disc™
Flash	Uses a special type of read-only memory that can be overwritten. While expensive, it can be read from and written to at high speeds and, as it has no moving parts, has lower power consumption. It is unaffected by sudden movements	USB memory stick Camera memory card Solid state drive

Now test yourself

TESTED

21 Find out and describe the storage devices your school or college uses to store and back up students' data.

22 State what type of media a DVD is: magnetic, optical or flash.

23 Explain why backups are usually carried out on magnetic media (e.g. tapes).

24 Explain why software tends to be distributed on DVDs rather than USB memory sticks.

Answers on p. 209–210

Exam tip

If an answer requires an optical medium that can be written to, ensure you use the R or RW suffix and not ROM. ROM indicates it is read-only, R means it can be written to once and RW can be written to many times. It is no use, therefore, suggesting a person backs up their computer onto a DVD-ROM.

RAM and ROM

REVISED

Primary memory is memory the CPU can access directly.

There are two forms of primary memory: random access memory (RAM) and read-only memory (ROM).

RAM:

+ is volatile (that is, loses its contents when electrical power is lost)
+ can be read from or written to (any location is accessed at equal speed to any other location)
+ stores the parts of the operating system, programs and data that are currently in use by the computer.

ROM:

+ is non-volatile (that is, retains its contents when electrical power is lost)
+ is read-only and so cannot be written to
+ is often used to store the computer's boot program.

Random access memory (RAM) A type of primary memory that the CPU uses for programs and data in use. It loses its contents when power is lost.

Read-only memory (ROM) A type of primary memory that can only be read from. It retains its contents even when electrical power is lost. It is often used to store start-up instructions on a computer.

Now test yourself

TESTED

25 State one difference between RAM and ROM.

26 State which of the following types of primary memory is volatile: RAM, ROM or both.

Answers on p. 210

Virtual storage

+ It is increasingly common for computers to make use of remote external storage, that is, storage not directly connected to the computer
+ Often this can be done in such a way that the operating system presents it to the user as part of the actual system.
+ This virtual storage may be stored elsewhere on a local area network or even in a data centre somewhere on the other side of the world.
+ This means that storage can be added to your computer without physically installing new hardware. Depending on your set-up, this storage can be automatically backed up, shared among multiple people and available anywhere in the world.
+ In order to access the storage, the computer needs to be connected to the network on which it resides, or the internet. This makes virtual storage unsuitable for scenarios in which a computer will be without a connection for extended periods.

> ### Now test yourself
>
> **27** Describe an advantage of using virtual storage over traditional storage inside a computer.
>
> **Answers on p. 210**
>
> TESTED

Exam tip

The specification requires you to be able to know how input, output and storage devices are 'applied to the solution of different problems'. It is, therefore, likely that questions on this topic will be given in the context of a scenario. You should take time to look at the scenario for clues as to what devices are most appropriate. For example, if the context requires portability you are likely to choose a storage device that uses flash storage such as an SSD (low power consumption and no moving parts) over one that uses magnetic storage such as an HDD.

Summary

Structure and function of a processor

+ The central processing unit (CPU) carries out the instructions in programs. The faster the clock speed (measured in GHz), the more instructions it can execute per second.
+ The CPU contains a control unit (CU), arithmetic logic unit (ALU) and registers. It is linked to memory by address, data and control buses.
+ Processor performance can be improved by increasing the clock speed, the number of cores and increasing the amount of cache memory.
+ Pipelining will also have a beneficial effect on the performance of a CPU.
+ Pipelining is when different parts of the CPU can fetch, decode and execute instructions simultaneously.
+ The Von Neumann architecture follows the fetch–decode–execute cycle and uses one ALU and one CU.
+ In the Von Neumann architecture, data and instructions are stored together in memory; in the Harvard architecture, programs and data are stored in separate memory units.
+ Modern processors have features to improve performance and power efficiency. These include out of order execution, branch prediction and power conservation.

Types of processor

+ Reduced instruction set computing (RISC) is an alternative processor architecture, which has a reduced instruction set. These instructions require fewer clock cycles to execute and mean that the processor requires fewer transistors to build. Non-RISC processors are referred to as complex instruction set computing (CISC) processors.
+ A graphics processing unit (GPU) is a specialist processor that is primarily designed for drawing 3D graphics to the screen, but can be applied to other tasks.
+ Parallel processing is the processing of multiple pieces of data at the same time. This could be with the same instruction being applied to all the data (single instruction multiple data, SIMD) or different instructions (multiple instructions multiple data, MIMD).

Input, output and storage

+ Input devices allow data to be entered into a computer; output devices allow computers to give out information; storage devices are used to permanently store data.
+ Storage devices can use magnetic, optical or flash storage.
+ Random access memory (RAM) is volatile and stores the programs and data in use.
+ Read-only memory (ROM) is non-volatile and is often used to store the computer's boot program.
+ Storage is often separate to the computer, located elsewhere on a network or even in a remote data centre. This virtual storage can be treated as part of the computer itself.

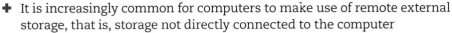

1 The characteristics of contemporary processors, input, output and storage devices

17

Exam practice

1 Explain why smartphones use flash memory.   [2]
2 Describe the purpose of the address bus.   [1]
3 Give two differences between RISC and CISC processors.   [2]
4 Describe the Von Neumann architecture.   [2]
5 Explain what is meant by a GPU.   [2]
6 State two output devices a programmer might have, justifying your choices.   [4]
7 Discuss the differences between a CPU in a smartwatch and one in a PC
   designed for gaming.   [9]

Answers available online

Check your understanding and progress at **www.hoddereducation.co.uk/myrevisionnotesdownloads**

2 Software and software development

Systems software

The need for, function and purpose of operating systems

REVISED

Operating systems are an essential piece of software in modern computer systems, managing the hardware itself and the programs running on it. Examples of operating systems are Windows, MacOS, Linux, iOS and Android.

An operating system has several roles, including to:
+ manage the system hardware
+ manage the installation and running of programs
+ manage the security of the system
+ provide a user interface.

Making links

Linux is an operating system that has many variants. This is because it is open source, meaning different groups of people have been able to take the source code and adapt it to make their own versions. You can find out more about open source software below.

Now test yourself

TESTED

1 State three roles of an operating system.

Answer on p. 210

Operating system
Software that controls the computer, manages the computer's hardware and from which other programs can be run.

User interface The means by which the computer and user interact. This could be a command line interface, where operating system commands are typed in, or a graphical user interface, where programs run in windows and the user interacts using a mouse and icons. Graphical user interfaces are far more common now than command line interfaces.

Memory management (paging, segmentation and virtual memory)

REVISED

One of the key jobs of an operating system is the management of memory.
+ When a program is run, it is retrieved from secondary storage and placed in memory.
+ Memory stores the programs and data in use by the system.

The operating system needs to ensure that:
+ memory is used efficiently – programs that are being used need to be stored in memory without space being wasted
+ data in memory is secure – most of the time, programs should not have access to other programs' data.

Storing complete programs as a single block of memory is wasteful as it means that parts of the program not being used are taking up memory, and as programs are added and removed space can be used inefficiently. For this reason, items in memory are split up. There are two ways programs and data can be split, paging and segmentation:
+ paging means memory is split up in equally sized chunks, called pages
+ segmentation is when memory is divided according to logical breaks within the program.

When a system is running low on physical memory (that is, RAM), it is able to use an area of secondary storage as virtual memory. This happens because:

Paging Where programs are divided physically into equal-sized blocks called pages (typically several kilobytes).

Segmentation Where programs are divided logically; they are split into blocks containing modules or routines.

Virtual memory The use of secondary storage as an extension of a computer's physical memory.

19

+ RAM is significantly more expensive than secondary storage.
+ Therefore a computer system will often have secondary storage that is hundreds of times larger than RAM.

Pages are swapped from main memory to virtual memory when not needed and then back to main memory when required. If a computer has to swap pages back and forth too often the computer slows down. We call this disk thrashing.

Now test yourself

TESTED

2 Describe the purpose of virtual memory.
3 Explain the difference between paging and segmentation.

Answers on p. 210

Interrupts, interrupt service routines and their role within the fetch–decode–execute cycle

REVISED

The CPU needs to know when a device needs its attention. It does this by sending a signal called an interrupt. An interrupt has a priority. Interrupts can only take processor time from tasks with a lower priority. When an interrupt is raised, the operating system runs the relevant interrupt service routine (ISR).

At the end of each iteration of the fetch–decode–execute cycle, the processor checks to see if there are any interrupts. If there are, and they are of a higher priority than the current task, the following steps are carried out:
+ The contents of the program counter and the other registers are copied to an area of memory called a stack.
+ The relevant ISR can then be loaded by changing the program counter to the location of the ISR in memory.
+ When the ISR is complete, the previous values of the program counter and other registers can be restored from the stack to the CPU.
+ If, while an interrupt is being serviced, a new, higher priority interrupt is raised, the interrupt currently being serviced is also added to a stack in memory and the new interrupt is serviced. Once this new interrupt is finished, the previous interrupt is taken off the stack and continued.

Interrupt A signal sent to a CPU to signify another process is in need of processing time.

Interrupt service routine (ISR) This is the program code that is called when an interrupt is triggered. Each interrupt will have a specific ISR associated with it. When the processor runs this ISR, it carries out the actions required to handle the situation that has triggered the interrupt.

Now test yourself

TESTED

4 Describe the purpose of an interrupt service routine.
5 Explain the significance of an interrupt having a priority.

Answers on p. 210

Making links

We examined the program counter register in Chapter 1. You will recall that its purpose is to store the location in memory of the next instruction to be fetched. Note how it is used here to point to the starting location of the ISR, meaning the CPU starts fetching, decoding and executing the code in the ISR.

For more on stacks, see Chapter 4.

Scheduling

REVISED

Modern operating systems run multiple programs at one time, known as multitasking. While it is usual today to have one user to a computer at any one time, there are still occasions where a computer has to do work for more than one user at once. An example of this might be a server giving multiple access to files.

An operating system has to ensure that each job and user gets sufficient processing time. It does this through scheduling, which is carried out by a scheduler.

Scheduling The method an operating system uses to ensure all processes get sufficient processor time.

A scheduler uses a scheduling algorithm to determine how to share processor time. The scheduling algorithms you need to know are:
+ Round robin: each process is given a fixed amount of time. If it hasn't finished by the end of that time period, it goes to the back of the queue so the next process in line can have its turn.
+ First come first served: this is just like queuing in a shop. The first process to arrive is dealt with by the CPU until it is finished. Meanwhile, any other processes that come along are queued up waiting for their turn.
+ Shortest job first: picks the job that will take the shortest time and run it until it finishes. Naturally this algorithm needs to know the time each job will take in advance.
+ Shortest remaining time: the scheduler estimates how long each process will take. It then picks the one that will take the least amount of time, and runs that. Unlike the shortest-job-first algorithm, shortest remaining time is pre-emptive. This means that if it hasn't completed after a certain amount of time, the scheduler checks to see whether any shorter processes have been added. If so, it switches to them.
+ Multilevel feedback queues: as the name suggests, a multilevel feedback queue uses a number of queues. Each of these queues has a different priority. The algorithm can move jobs between these queues depending on the jobs' behaviour.

Now test yourself

6　Describe the first come first served scheduling algorithm.
7　Describe the round-robin scheduling algorithm.

Answers on p. 210

Distributed, embedded, multitasking, multi-user and real-time operating systems

 REVISED

There are a number of different types of operating systems:
+ Distributed operating system: allows multiple computers to work together on a single task. They tend to be used in systems aimed at completing computationally intensive tasks. An example of this is rendering complex 3D animation. This workload can often be shared across a collection of computers using a distributed operating system.
+ Embedded operating system: designed to run on embedded systems rather than general-purpose computers. An embedded system is a computer that forms part of a device such as a washing machine, vending machine or a car's engine management system.
+ Multitasking operating system: can run multiple programs simultaneously. Most modern personal computer operating systems are multitasking (e.g. Windows, MacOS and Linux).
+ Multi-user operating system: allows multiple users to use a system and its resources simultaneously. It is the simultaneous aspect that is important. An operating system that allows multiple user accounts, but only one person to use the system at a time, is not classed as a multi-user operating system. Multi-user operating systems tend to be used on larger, more powerful mainframe computers able to service large numbers of users at one time. Banks and retailers are examples of organisations that use these systems, which are capable of processing large numbers of transactions while being accessed by employees and customers.
+ Real-time operating system: designed to carry out actions within a guaranteed amount of time even when left running for long periods. Usually the expected response time is within a small fraction of a second.

Autopilot on a plane is an example of a system that need to run using a real-time operating system. If the plane needs to move it is essential there is no delay!

Now test yourself · TESTED

8 Describe what is meant by a real-time operating system.
9 Describe the sort of tasks a multitasking operating system might carry out simultaneously on a student's computer.

Answers on p. 210

BIOS

REVISED

BIOS stands for 'basic input/output system'. When a computer is first switched on it looks to the BIOS to get it up and running, and so the processor's program counter points to the BIOS's memory.

While originally stored on ROM, nowadays the BIOS is often stored on flash memory so that it can be updated. This also allows settings such as the boot order of disks to be changed and saved by the user.

Making links

If you look at Chapter 1 you will see which properties of ROM made it suitable for storing a computer's BIOS.

Now test yourself · TESTED

10 Describe the purpose of a computer's BIOS.

Answer on p. 210

Device drivers

REVISED

Operating systems are expected to communicate with a wide variety of devices, each with different models and manufacturers. It would be impossible for the makers of operating systems to program them to handle all existing and future devices. This is why we need device drivers.

A device driver is a piece of software that tells the operating system how it can communicate with hardware. In the past, device drivers were often supplied on a CD-ROM with the device, but today they are often just downloaded from the internet. Sometimes the operating system can do this in the background without any intervention by the user.

Now test yourself · TESTED

11 When setting up a new printer, explain why a device driver has to be installed.

Answer on p. 210

Virtual machines

REVISED

It is possible to write a program that has the same functionality as a physical computer. We call such programs virtual machines. They have the advantage that they can be backed up and duplicated and more than one can be run at one time on a physical machine.

A common use of virtual machines is to run one operating system within another operating system. This might be because a program is needed that will not run on the host operating system or it might be because it offers a convenient way to test a program being developed on multiple platforms.

> **Virtual machine** A program that has the same functionality as, and can be used in place of, a physical machine.

Check your understanding and progress at **www.hoddereducation.co.uk/myrevisionnotesdownloads**

Making links

In the section on networking in Chapter 3, you will see that servers are computers that play an important role on a network, providing services such as file sharing, printing and email. In the past, it was usual to have a different physical machine for each server. Today you are just as likely to find one or two powerful physical machines with multiple servers inside them running on virtual machines. This has a number of benefits such as making backups easy, and being able to adjust the resources afforded to each server depending on their needs.

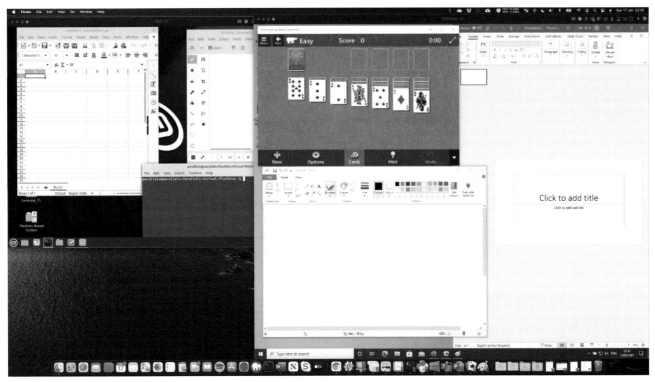

Figure 2.1 Windows 10® and Mint Linux® running in virtual machines in MacOS®

Another common use of virtual machines is interpreting intermediate code. As you will see, compilers usually convert programmers' source code into CPU readable machine code. However, with some languages, for instance Java, a compiler instead converts source code into something called intermediate code.

✚ Intermediate code is akin to an artificial machine code. Unlike machine code, it isn't designed be read by a CPU, but is a similarly efficient representation of a program and is designed to be computer readable rather than human readable.

✚ Because it is not machine code it cannot be run directly on a processor. Instead, a virtual machine is used to read the code.

✚ Any device running this virtual machine can read this intermediate code, which makes it highly portable – unlike machine code, which can only be run by CPUs for which it has been compiled.

Making links

You can find out more about compilers below.

Now test yourself   TESTED ◯

12 Explain how a virtual machine makes it possible for someone running Windows on their computer to run a program designed to run on Linux.

Answer on p. 210

Applications generation

The nature of applications and justifying suitable applications for a specific purpose

REVISED

Applications software is software that allows a user to perform a task or produce something.

Common examples of applications include:

+ word processors: used for writing letters, reports and other documents
+ spreadsheet packages: these allow a user to model complex situations, and are often used for financial calculations
+ presentation software: used to make on-screen slide shows to accompany presentations
+ desktop publishing software: used for documents where layout is important, such as newsletters
+ image editors: used to alter and amend images such as photographs
+ web browsers: allow a user to browse the World Wide Web
+ database management systems: used to run databases, which can store and search large quantities of data and present them in different ways.

There are also many other types of more specialist applications available. For instance:

+ computer-aided design packages allow engineers to build accurate designs
+ management information systems allow data to be stored and processed
+ video games provide entertainment.

All these are further examples of software applications.

> **Applications software**
> Programs that allow a user to complete a task. Examples include word processors, spreadsheet packages and presentation software.

> **Exam tip**
>
> In the exam, you may be given scenarios and asked to decide which applications would be used and what they would be used for.

> **Making links**
>
> You can find out more about databases and database management systems in Chapter 3.

> **Revision activity**
>
> It is not always obvious as to whether a database (driven by a database management system) or a spreadsheet should be used for certain tasks. As a rule of thumb, if a task requires lots of complex calculations with values that need changing, then a spreadsheet is the most suitable application. If the focus of the task is storing and organising data, then a database may be more suitable. This is not always clear-cut and there is some overlap where either system could be used.
>
> Find two examples of how your school/college might use a database and two examples of how they might use a spreadsheet package. For each example, explain why you think the particular software has been chosen.

Utilities

REVISED

Utility software is a relatively small program that has one purpose. This purpose is usually concerned with the upkeep of a computer system.

Examples of utilities include:

+ anti-malware: used to detect and remove malware on a system
+ disk defragmentation: used to rearrange where data is stored on a hard disk drive so that files load more quickly
+ backup: used to make copies of data to an alternative device or location, in case the original is damaged or lost. This can be set up to occur automatically.

> **Utility software** Small programs designed to help with the maintenance of a system. Examples include antivirus software, disk defragmentation and backup software.

Now test yourself   TESTED ◯

13 Explain the classification of software for a compression program.

14 Explain the classification of software for a desktop publishing package.

Answers on p. 210

Closed source versus open source   REVISED ◯

When software is sold commercially it is compiled to machine code. This means users can run it without having to translate it. They do not have access to the source code, that is, the high-level language code it was originally written in.

> **Source code** The program code written by the programmer, usually in a high-level language.

Closed source software

✚ Software that is only distributed as executable machine code.

✚ Most users have no need for the program's source code.

✚ It would not be wise for the company making the software to supply source code as it would mean users could amend their software and steal their work.

Open source software (OSS)

✚ Software where the source code is made publicly available.

✚ OSS grants anyone permission to amend, recompile and, if they wish, redistribute the program.

✚ This means that users can modify software to suit their needs.

✚ It also means that there is potential for anyone to play a part in the development of open source software. Examples of OSS are Linux® and OpenOffice™.

There are advantages and disadvantages of each.

✚ Open source software is usually free.

✚ Users are at liberty to amend the source code of open source software and adapt it to their purposes.

✚ Closed source software is developed by companies with lots of resources and teams of programmers. It often (but not always) tends to be more polished.

✚ Open source software can be developed by huge teams of volunteers across the world who are not constrained by the commercial considerations of the project.

✚ Open source software has the advantage that anyone can help find security holes in it but this also includes those who may exploit such failures maliciously before they are fixed.

> **Open source software** Software that has its source code freely available and grants users the right to examine, modify and share it.
>
> **Closed source software** Software distributed as executable machine code, which means the source code is kept secret.

Now test yourself   TESTED ◯

15 Explain why a program being free of charge does not necessarily mean it can be classed as open source.

16 Explain why commercial companies do not tend to make their software open source.

Answers on p. 210

Making links

There is further discussion of open source software and copyright in Chapter 5.

25

Translators: assemblers, compliers and interpreters

Machine code and translators

Computers follow instructions, represented in binary, that comprise an opcode (the instruction itself) and an operand (the data it acts on). We call this machine code. While computers only understand machine code, humans write programs in easier-to-read programming languages. To convert these languages to machine code, computers use translator programs.

Assembly code and assemblers

Machine code, being made up of just 1s and 0s, is very difficult for humans to follow. To get round this, computer scientists devised assembly code. In assembly code the opcode is represented by a mnemonic (a memorable group of letters) and the operand is represented in denary or hexadecimal. A program called an assembler is then used to convert each line of assembly code into machine code.

Assembly language and machine code are both known as low-level languages.

Compilers and interpreters

Writing assembly code is laborious; many lines of code are needed for the simplest of tasks. This led to the development of high-level languages. A high-level language is one that is more easily human-readable. Over time, many high-level languages have been created including (to name just a few): BASIC, C, C++, JavaScript and Python.

For a computer to run a program written in a high-level language, the program needs to be converted to machine code. To do this we can use a compiler or an interpreter.

Compiler

✛ A compiler takes code written in a high-level language and converts it into an executable machine code program.
✛ A compiler can take a while to perform the translation, but once the executable file is built it can be run immediately.
✛ When distributing a program, a compiled version is better: it runs quicker, does not require any additional software to run and is much harder to change than it would be if the source code was available.

Interpreter

✛ An interpreter takes each line of a high-level language program, converts it to machine code and runs it, before reading and converting the next line.
✛ An interpreter can start running the program straight away but it will run more slowly than it would if it were compiled as the interpreter has to translate each line as it is run.
✛ Interpreters can be useful during the coding and debugging process as the programmer does not have to wait for the entire program to compile: the interpreter will stop at a line if it finds an error.

> **Machine code** Instructions and data stored in binary, directly readable by the CPU.
>
> **Assembly code** A low-level language that uses single words or mnemonics to represent instructions.
>
> **Assembler** A program that converts assembly code into machine code.
>
> **Low-level languages** These are languages closely tied to the architecture of the CPU. They use the CPU's instruction set. The lowest level language is machine code, which is directly readable by the CPU. Assembly code is also considered a low-level language.
>
> **High-level languages** These are designed to be easily read by humans. They tend to use a combination of English keywords and mathematical notation. There are many high-level languages. Examples include C++, JavaScript and Python.
>
> **Compiler** A program that converts the entire high-level source code into an executable machine code file that is then executed.
>
> **Interpreter** A program that reads and executes high-level source code line by line.

Now test yourself

TESTED ○

17 Explain why a programmer might use an interpreter rather than a compiler.
18 Describe what is meant by a high-level language.

Answers on p. 210

Stages of compilation

Compilers generally work by going through the following steps:
+ lexical analysis
+ syntax analysis
+ code generation
+ code optimisation.

Lexical analysis

Lexical analysis identifies the parts that make up the program. This include the program's keywords (`for`, `while`, `if` etc.) and variables. During lexical analysis:
+ comments and whitespace are removed from the program
+ the remaining code is turned into a series of tokens (specific sequences of characters) each representing a small discrete part of the program
+ a symbol table is created to keep track of the variables and subroutines (this includes information such as data type and scope).

Syntax analysis

Syntax is the structure of a language. Just like spoken languages, computer languages have a specific structure. For example, you would usually be able to write `a = b + c` but not `b + c = a`.

In syntax analysis:
+ an abstract syntax tree is built from the tokens produced during lexical analysis
+ if any tokens break the rules of the language, syntax errors are generated.

Code generation

During code generation, the abstract code tree is converted to object code. Object code is machine code before the final step (the linker) is run.

> **Object code** When code is compiled but yet to be run through a linker, it is sometimes referred to as object code. In practice, you will often see the terms machine code and object code used interchangeably.

Code optimisation

Optimisation tweaks the code so it will run as efficiently as possible. This might mean optimising for speed of execution or optimising for using as little memory as possible.

Now test yourself　　　　　　　　　　　TESTED

19 List the stages of compilation.
20 Describe what is stored in the symbol table.

Answers on p. 210

Libraries, linkers and loaders

Libraries

Code to perform common complex tasks has often already been written (and usually compiled) and packaged as a library. This code can be reused by other programmers.

Libraries have the advantages that:
+ they save time – no need to rewrite code someone else has already written
+ they can cover complex areas that require significant expertise in an area that would be time-consuming, or unfeasible, to learn
+ a library coded in one language can be used in programs written in another language.

27

Linkers and loaders

A linker is used to combine compiled code with that from a library into a single executable file.

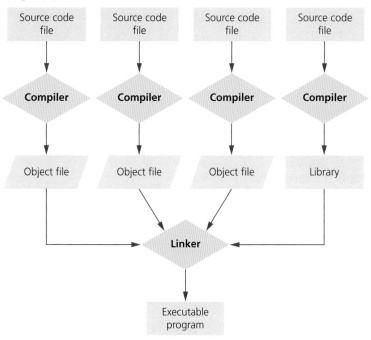

Figure 2.2 A linker combining code into a single executable program

A loader is part of the operating system and is responsible for loading a program into memory.

Now test yourself   TESTED ◯

21 Explain why programmers use libraries.

22 State the purpose of a linker.

Answers on p. 210

Software development

Large-scale mechanical engineering projects are at least as old as the pyramids. Over many centuries, best practice has developed as to how groups of people can work together towards a shared goal.

By contrast, software engineering – the process of teams working on developing programs – is a very new discipline that is only a few decades old. There has been much debate as to the best approach to take and there is, as of yet, no consensus.

This section looks at some of the methodologies that can be used for software development and their relative strengths and weaknesses.

Software development methodologies   REVISED ◯

There are a number of different ways in which software development projects can be implemented:
+ the waterfall lifecycle
+ rapid application development
+ the spiral model
+ agile methodologies
+ extreme programming

Check your understanding and progress at **www.hoddereducation.co.uk/myrevisionnotesdownloads**

The waterfall lifecycle

The waterfall lifecycle is a well-known and often criticised development model.
+ The waterfall lifecycle consists of a sequence of stages; each stage is started only after the previous one is complete.
+ It is possible to go back a stage when necessary.
+ Exact stages can vary but usually are: requirements definition, analysis, design, coding, testing, maintenance.
+ It works well where there is a clear expected output at each stage and everyone has clear responsibilities.
+ It is not suited to high-risk projects. If a problem is discovered at a later stage, a lot of work (and therefore time and money) may have been wasted.

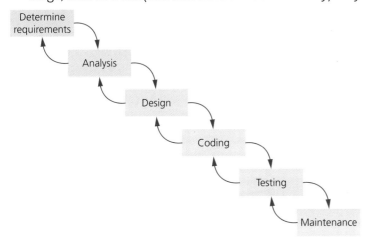

Figure 2.3 The waterfall lifecycle

Rapid application development

Rapid application development (RAD) involves the use of prototypes. A prototype is a version of the system that lacks full functionality.
+ The user is shown the prototype and gives feedback that is used to inform how the prototype is further developed.
+ This continues until the end user is happy that the prototype has all the required functionality. At this point it becomes the end product.
+ Rapid application development is well suited to projects where the requirements aren't entirely clear from the outset.
+ With continuous feedback from the client, the end product is likely to have excellent usability, though the code may not be particularly efficient.
+ It is necessary to have frequent contact with the end user.
+ It works well on small projects with small teams but does not scale well and so is less suited to large projects with big teams.

> **Prototype** An early version of a system, lacking full functionality but allowing a feel for what the final version will be like before large amounts of time are committed to its production.

```
Decide              Improve
requirements        prototype  <──────────────┐
   │                   │                  No  │
   ▼                   ▼                       │
Build    ──────►   Evaluate    ──────►   Is the
prototype          prototype with        prototype good ──┐
                   customer              enough?          │
                                                          │ Yes
                                                          ▼
                                                    Prototype
                                                    becomes final
                                                    product
```

Figure 2.4 Rapid application development

Spiral model

The spiral model is designed to try and manage risk. It consists of four stages, each forming a quadrant of the spiral that are iterated through:

1 Determine objectives: the first stage is to determine the objectives of that rotation of the spiral according to the biggest potential risks.
2 Identify and resolve risks: in the next stage, the possible risks are identified and alternative options considered. If the risks are considered too high at this stage, the project may be stopped.
3 Development and testing: the third stage allows the part of the project being worked on to be made and tested.
4 Plan next iteration: the fourth stage determines what will happen in the next iteration of the spiral.

The spiral cycle manages risk well but requires practitioners skilled in risk management.

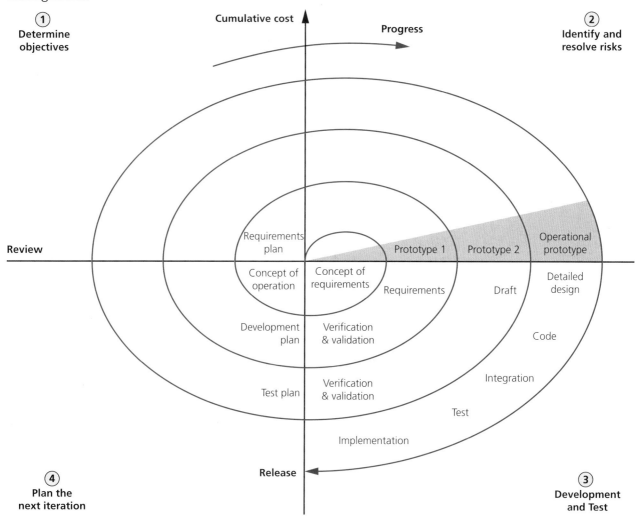

Figure 2.5 The spiral model

Agile software development

Agile software development is not a single methodology but a group of methods. These methods are designed to cope with changing requirements by producing software in an iterative manner; that is, it is produced in versions, each building on the previous one and each increasing the number of requirements it meets.

The methods focus on the quality of the software and the response to user needs. The core of the Agile philosophy can be summed up by the Agile Manifesto, which was agreed upon by 17 pre-eminent software engineers.

Check your understanding and progress at **www.hoddereducation.co.uk/myrevisionnotesdownloads**

We are uncovering better ways of developing software by doing it and helping others do it.

Through this work we have come to value:

Individuals and interactions over processes and tools

Working software over comprehensive documentation

Customer collaboration over contract negotiation

Responding to change over following a plan

That is, while there is value in the items on the right, we value the items on the left more.

https://agilemanifesto.org/

Extreme programming

An example of an agile software development methodology is extreme programming (often abbreviated to XP), a methodology that puts the emphasis on the coding itself.

✦ A representative of the customer becomes part of the team to help determine the 'user stories' (XP's equivalent of requirements and how these will be tested) and to answer questions.
✦ XP is iterative in nature – the program is coded, tested and improved repeatedly, using shorter (usually week long) iterations than RAD.
✦ Each iteration in XP produces a version of the system (albeit lacking some of the requirements) with code of a good enough quality to be used in the final product.
✦ XP uses pair programming. This is when code is written with two programmers sitting next to each other, one writing the code and the other analysing what is being written, and then switching roles at regular intervals.
✦ Programmers are encouraged to regularly 'refactor' code, that is, make it more efficient without changing what it does.
✦ Every programmer is responsible for the entire system.
✦ With such an emphasis on programming, the quality of the final code is likely to be very high.
✦ The client needs to be able to commit to having a representative working with the team.

Now test yourself

TESTED ◯

23 Describe the purpose of the prototype in rapid application development.
24 List the stages of the waterfall lifecycle model.
25 Describe the spiral model.

Answers on p. 210–11

The relative merits and drawbacks of different methodologies and when they might be used

REVISED ◯

Methodology	Advantages	Disadvantages	Suited to
Waterfall	Clear responsibilities at each stage Possible for different parts of the team to be geographically remote	If requirements change halfway through the project (or have been previously misinterpreted), previous stages have to be repeated, delaying the project	Large projects with static requirements

Methodology	Advantages	Disadvantages	Suited to
Rapid application development	The user's experience is prioritised. Can be confident the end product meets the user's needs	Little attention is paid to the efficiency of the program. Does not scale well. Can overrun initial budgets due to being an agile approach	Smaller projects where there is ready access to an end user
Spiral	Prioritises risk management and can handle changes in requirements. Suitable for high risk applications	Requires practitioners experienced in risk management and can be a long and expensive process	Large, high-risk projects without tight time constraints
Agile methodologies	Adapts to user's needs, resulting in a final system tailored. to meet their requirements	Continual collaboration is needed between the software developers and end users. Hard to determine timescale and outcomes early on	Projects where the initial requirements are hard to determine from the outset and in which the end user can play an active role in the development process

Now test yourself

TESTED

26 Describe the factors you would consider when choosing between the waterfall lifecycle and rapid application development for a software project.

27 State the disadvantages of Agile development.

Answers on p. 211

Writing and following algorithms

REVISED

Algorithms are sets of instructions that can be followed to perform a task. They are at the very heart of what computer science is about. Often software developers may wish to share algorithms with each other without writing the actual programs. This may be to avoid getting bogged down with the rules of a language or because they are familiar with different programming languages.

There are a number of ways algorithms can be described, including:

+ bulleted lists
+ flowcharts
+ pseudocode.

Computer scientists tend to express algorithms in pseudocode.

When reading algorithms, the best approach is to follow them through in the same way a computer would. When doing this with pseudocode, have a pen and paper at hand to keep track of the variable values.

> **Pseudocode** A way in which algorithms can be written using 'pretend' code. Unlike a real high-level language, there are no strict rules as to how pseudocode needs to look, but it should be understandable to someone familiar with programming (though perhaps in a different programming language to the writer).

Exam tip

Programming questions in the exam use pseudocode. To avoid any confusion there is a guide to the pseudocode style that will be used in the exam in the back of the Specification. You should ensure you are familiar with this well in advance of the exam.

Note that while the exam board limit themselves to using their pseudocode style, you are under no such restriction when answering questions. The meaning of your written pseudocode must, however, be understandable to the examiner. Do be cautious of creating lines of code that magically solve a given problem (even if they exist in the language of your choice.) For instance, if a question gives 4 marks for showing the largest number in an array called numbers, you are unlikely to get much credit for writing a solution in pseudocode such as:

```
print(max(numbers))
```

Making links

When looking at computational thinking in Chapter 6, you will reflect more on how algorithms are written and the techniques that can be used in creating an algorithm.

Now test yourself   TESTED ◯

Now test yourself   TESTED ◯

28 Follow the pseudocode below and explain what it does:

```
numbers = [… Array of 10 Random Numbers …]

pos = 0

for i = 1 to 9 //i goes from 1 to 9 inclusive

    if numbers[i] > numbers[pos] then

        pos = i

    endif

next i

print(numbers[pos] + " at " + pos)
```

29 Write an algorithm in pseudocode to determine if a word has more vowels or more consonants in it.

Answers on p. 211

Revision activity

Using a high-level language of your choice write:

1 A working version of the pseudocode shown in question 28.

2 A working version of your answer to question 29.

Types of programming language

Need for and characteristics of a variety of programming paradigms

REVISED ◯

A **programming paradigm** is the approach a programming language takes to defining a program.

Initially all programming was carried out in low-level languages, that is, those that are directly linked to the architecture of the CPU. Machine code and assembly language are both low-level languages.

In assembly language:

✚ Mnemonics (memorable letter sequences) are used in place of machine code instructions.

✚ The set of instructions varies from processor to processor, meaning that assembly code written for one processor will not necessarily work on another.

✚ Low-level languages offer a high level of control, meaning instructions can be carefully selected to reduce memory consumption and ensure best performance.

For the A-level course you have studied the Little Man Computer assembly language.

High-level languages that use English and mathematical notation are much easier to read and write. A few lines of high-level code may be the equivalent to tens of lines of assembly code. As we saw when looking at compilers and interpreters, high-level code can be run on any CPU architecture by using a compatible translator.

Making links

More on compilers and interpreters can be found earlier in this chapter.

33

A number of high-level paradigms have developed over the years, where different languages have adopted different fundamental approaches. Common high-level paradigms include:

+ **Procedural**: a language where instructions are given in sequence. These instructions can be grouped into subroutines that can be called throughout the program. Examples of procedural languages include BASIC, C, Python and Pascal.
+ **Object-oriented**: a language in which the solution is represented by objects that interact. Examples of object-oriented languages include Java and C++.
+ **Functional**: a function, in mathematics, takes in one or more values and returns a value, for example `double(4)` returns 8, and `highestCommonFactor(36,24)` returns 12. In functional programming, a description of the solution to a problem is built up through a collection of functions, some of which are used to define other functions. Examples of functional programming languages include Haskell and ML.
+ **Declarative**: a language where the characteristics of a solution are stated, rather than stating *how* the problem is solved. Examples of declarative programming languages include Prolog and SQL.

> **Making links**
>
> In Chapter 7 you will look at backtracking. Prolog is a declarative language that uses backtracking to find a solution according the criteria stated in the program.

While most problems can be solved by most languages, it is often the case that the solution to a problem is more easily represented and solved by a particular paradigm.

> **Now test yourself** TESTED ○
>
> 30 Explain why different programming paradigms exist.
>
> 31 Explain why SQL can be considered a declarative language. (You may wish to refer to Chapter 3 to look at SQL.)
>
> **Answers on p. 211**

Procedural languages

REVISED ○

In procedural programming, we give the computer instructions on the steps we want it to go through to solve a problem.

+ These instructions are given in sequence.
+ Selection is used to decide what a program does when certain conditions are met.
+ Iteration (i.e. loops) dictates how many times it does it.

In procedural programming, programs are broken down into subroutines called procedures and functions. These can then be combined to form a solution.

If all this seems familiar, that's because procedural is the paradigm used for most programming questions in the exam.

> **Now test yourself** TESTED ○
>
> 32 Discuss whether the programming language you have studied for the A level course can be considered procedural, justifying your decision.
>
> **Answer on p. 211**

Assembly language and the Little Man Computer instruction set

Machine code uses binary sequences to represent instructions (opcodes) and data on which they act (operands). Rather than having to remember which binary sequence represents which instruction, assembly code allows us to use mnemonics to represent these sequences.

As each assembly code instruction represents a machine code instruction, assembly code programs can often be much longer than their high-level equivalents.

Each processor family has its own assembly language instruction set. In this course you will be using the Little Man Computer instruction set. (The 'Little Man Computer' is a hypothetical machine used to teach the principles of assembly language programming.)

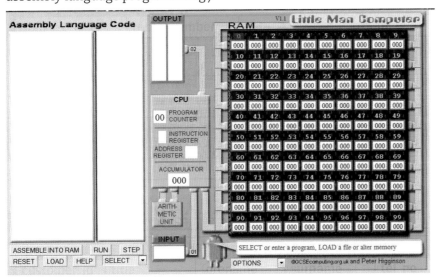

Figure 2.6 Online Little Man Computer simulator

Little Man Computer (LMC) uses 11 instructions.

Mnemonic	Instruction
ADD	Add
SUB	Subtract
STA	Stores value from the accumulator to memory
LDA	Loads value from the memory to the accumulator
BRA	Branch always
BRZ	Branch if zero
BRP	Branch if positive
INP	Input
OUT	Output
HLT	End program
DAT	Data location

Exam tip

You must be familiar with all of the LMC mnemonics and their functions.

Making links

When running a program, LMC demonstrates the fetch–decode–execute cycle, covered in Chapter 1.

Now test yourself

33 Describe what the LDA instruction does.

Answer on p. 211

TESTED ○

Each line of an LMC program can have up to four parts: a label, the mnemonic, the data and a comment.

The label is used to identify a line so it can be branched to elsewhere in the program:

```
thisLine ADD 3
```

thisLine is a label; the program can jump here with the code:

```
BRA thisLine
```

A label is also used to give a name to a memory location when used with the DAT instruction.

`attempts DAT 5`

puts the value 5 in a memory location called `attempts`.

Example

The following program takes in a number and doubles it.

```
        INP
        STA num
        ADD num
        OUT
        HLT
   num DAT
```

It works as follows:

1	INP	A number is input (and stored in the accumulator): 2
2	STA Num	The contents of the accumulator are stored in the memory location labelled num.
3	ADD Num	The contents of num are added to the accumulator.
4	OUT	The contents of the accumulator are output.
5	HLT	The program ends.
6	num DAT	A location in memory is labelled num.

You will notice that the line num DAT is last but is needed earlier. The memory location num is allocated when the program is assembled into memory, before the program is run.

Revision activity

You will recall from Chapter 1 that in the Von Neumann architecture data and instructions are stored together in memory as binary. The CPU has no way of knowing which are which, other than relying on the program counter to point to the next instruction. For this reason all data is stored at the end of the LMC program, after the HLT instruction, so it cannot accidentally be read as program code.

To see what would happen otherwise, consider the following simple program, which takes in a number, stores it in memory and outputs it.

```
        INP
        STA num
        OUT
        HLT
num DAT
```

Now try the following amended version with the DAT instruction moved.

```
        INP
        STA num
num DAT
        OUT
        HLT
```

Try running the program three different times with the following inputs and see if you can explain why the program's behaviour changes each time.

901

101

000

Check your understanding and progress at **www.hoddereducation.co.uk/myrevisionnotesdownloads**

TESTED ◯

Now test yourself

34 Write an LMC program to triple a number.

35 Write an LMC program that takes in a number and subtracts 1 from it.

Answers on p. 211

The branch instructions are used for selection (BRP and BRZ) and iteration (BRA, BRP and BRZ).

Selection

REVISED ◯

Example

Here is an example of selection.

This program outputs 0 if a number less than 10 is entered and 10 if any other number is entered.

```
start       INP
            SUB ten
            BRP tenOrMore
            LDA zero
            OUT
            BRA end
tenOrMore   LDA ten
            OUT
end         HLT
ten         DAT 10
zero        DAT 0
```

Now test yourself

TESTED ◯

36 In a high-level language of your choice, write a program equivalent to the one in the previous example.

37 Write a program in LMC that takes in a number and trebles it if it is less than 100, otherwise it doubles it.

38 Explain the difference between the BRA, BRZ and BRP instructions.

Answers on p. 211–12

Iteration

REVISED ◯

We can perform condition-controlled iteration and count-controlled iteration.

Example

This program demonstrates condition-controlled iteration by asking for a number until one less than 10 is entered:

```
start       INP
            SUB ten
            BRP start
            HLT
ten         DAT 10
```

Notice how the BRP instruction is used to loop back round to the start if the number is greater than ten (the result is positive when 10 is subtracted from entered number).

Example

This program demonstrates count-controlled iteration by counting down from a number input to zero.

```
start           INP
takeOneOff      OUT
                SUB one
                BRP takeOneOff
                HLT
one             DAT 1
```

Now test yourself

39 Write an LMC program that keeps asking for a number until one greater than 10 is entered.

40 Write an LMC program that takes in a number and outputs the number 1 that many times.

Answers on p. 212

TESTED

Modes of addressing memory

REVISED

There are different ways of accessing memory in low-level languages; we call this memory addressing. In LMC we have referred to memory locations by using names (defined with the DAT instruction). This is known as symbolic addressing. You need to know about four other kinds of addressing: direct, indirect, indexed and immediate.

✦ Direct addressing: the address given is the location of the data to be used. With direct addressing, LDA 43 means 'load the contents of location 43 into the accumulator'. LMC uses direct addressing.

✦ Indirect addressing: the address given is the memory location that holds the location of the data. If memory location 43 contains the value 119 then, using indirect addressing, LDA 43 means 'load the contents of location 43 (119) into the accumulator'.

✦ Indexed addressing: the value given is added to the value stored in the index register to give the memory location. With index addressing, if the index register contains the value 100 then LDA 43 means 'load the contents of location 143 into the accumulator'.

✦ Immediate addressing: the address given is not actually an address but the required value. LDA 43 would mean 'load the value 43 into the accumulator'.

Memory addressing
In assembly language there are different ways of referring to locations. We refer to these as different modes of memory addressing.

Index register The index register holds a value that is added to the operand of an indexed addressed instruction, to give the memory address that is to be accessed.

Example

Here are the contents of 12 memory locations:

Location	Contents
0	43
1	
2	3
3	8
4	6
5	
6	9
7	
8	
9	12
10	
11	54
12	32

Example

Using the memory contents above, `LDA 6` loads the following values into the accumulator for each type of addressing:

Addressing mode	Value in accumulator after LDA 6
Direct	9
Indirect	12
Indexed (5 in the index register)	54
Immediate	6

Now test yourself

41 Describe the difference between direct and indirect addressing.

42 Explain which is quicker to execute, an instruction using direct addressing or an instruction using immediate addressing.

Answers on p. 212

 TESTED

Object-oriented languages

REVISED

Object-oriented programming allows a program to solve problems by programming objects that interact with each other. Classes are templates made to create objects. Objects have their state represented by variables called attributes and their functionality defined by subroutines called methods.

Example

The code below contains the class House. It contains its attributes and methods (including a constructor). The main program then creates an object called myHouse of the type House, with a red door, 2 floors and a garden.

```
class House
        private doorColour

        private floors

        private garden


    public procedure new(givenDoorColour, givenFloors,
    givenGarden)
        doorColour = givenDoorColour

        floors = givenFloors

        garden = givenGarden
    endProcedure


    public procedure changeFloors(givenFloors)
        if givenFloors > 0 then

            floors = givenFloors

        endif
    endProcedure


    public procedure changeDoorColour(givenColour)
        doorColour = givenColour

    endProcedure
endclass


//Main Program
myHouse = new House("Red", 2, true)
```

Class A template used to define an object. It specifies the methods and attributes an object should have. In the following example, House is the class.

Object An instance of a class. In the following example, myHouse is an object.

Attribute Variables contained within and associated to an object. In the following example, doorColour, floors and garden are all attributes.

Method A subroutine associated with an object. In the following example, changeDoorColour and changeFloors are methods. Additionally, new is a special type of method called a 'constructor'. Constructors define how an object is created. In the example below, and in OCR pseudocode, constructors are always given the name new.

Revision activity

Implement the code in the previous example in an object-oriented language of your choice.

You will notice in the previous example that the attributes are private (meaning they cannot be accessed from outside the class) and the methods are public. By the attributes being private they cannot be altered from outside the class in ways we do not want. For example, someone cannot set the number of floors to –1. Instead we allow private attributes to be changed via public methods such as `changeFloors`. We call this encapsulation.

Now test yourself   TESTED ◯

43 Describe what is meant by a class and an object.

Answer on p. 212

A major feature of object-oriented programming is inheritance. This is where a class inherits the methods and attributes of a parent class as well as having its own.

Worked example

This example shows a class `Bungalow` which inherits from the class `House` and then an instance of a bungalow called `myBungalow` being created with a blue door, no garden and a porch. In the example, the class `Bungalow` inherits all the methods and attributes of the class `House`. However, it also has its own attribute `Porch` and method `changePorch`. (We will assume in our hypothetical example only bungalows have porches!)

Note the line `super.new(givenDoorColour, 1, givenGarden)` in the constructor. This calls the constructor from the `House` class. The remainder of the bungalow's constructor then carries out the parts specific to a bungalow.

```
class Bungalow inherits House

    private porch

    public procedure new(givenDoorColour, givenGarden,
    givenPorch)

        super.new(givenDoorColour, 1, givenGarden)

        floors = 1

        porch = givenPorch

    endprocedure

        public procedure changePorch(newPorch)

            porch = newPorch

    endprocedure

endclass

myBungalow = new Bungalow("Blue", false, true)
```

We will often want to treat objects of different classes (e.g. houses and bungalows) in the same way. Perhaps we have an array called `buildings` composed of houses and bungalows. If we want to change the door colour of everything inside the array to blue we can do this from the main program invoking a method from the `House` class. Because `Bungalow` has inherited all the `House` methods, the following is valid code and is an example of polymorphism:

```
for i = 0 to 99

    buildings[i].changeDoorColour("Blue")

next i
```

> **Encapsulation** Ensures private attributes can only be amended through public methods. This prevents objects being manipulated in unintended ways.
>
> **Inheritance** The ability for a class to inherit the methods and attributes of a parent class. Its 'child' class can have its own methods and attributes and override the methods of its parent class.

> **Polymorphism** Meaning 'many forms', polymorphism is the ability for objects of different classes to be treated in the same way. For example, the same method may be applied to objects of different classes.

Check your understanding and progress at **www.hoddereducation.co.uk/myrevisionnotesdownloads**

If any of the classes that inherit from House have their own method called changeDoorColour this will be used instead of the version in the House class. This is called overriding.

Another example of polymorphism is method overloading. Overloading is where a class has multiple methods of the same name but each with different patterns of parameters. (The parameters can vary by quantity and data type.) The correct version of the method is then selected according to the arguments passed to it.

Overriding This is when a subclass has a method of the same name (and pattern of parameters) as its parent class. The child class version is always used over that of the parent class: it is said to 'override' the parent's method.

Method overloading This is when a class contains two or more methods of the same name but that differ in the pattern of the arguments they take and/ or the type of data they return. The compiler then chooses the correct version according to the values being passed or being expected.

Example

```
class Robot

    //greet version one takes a string

    public procedure greet(name)

            print("Greetings " + name)

    endprocedure

    //greet version two takes a string and an integer

    public procedure greet(name, times)

        for i = 1 to times

                print("Hello " + name)

        next i

    endprocedure

endclass
```

If we have an object of type Robot called robo, then the line robo. greet("Betsy") will select the first method as the argument being passed is just one string, matching version one. This means it will print Greetings Betsy

On the other hand, the line robo.greet("Hamish",3) will select the second method as the arguments match version two (i.e. a string and an integer). This means it will print:

```
Hello Hamish

Hello Hamish

Hello Hamish
```

Note that it would not be valid code to have two methods of the same name, in the same class, expecting the same pattern of parameters.

Now test yourself

TESTED ◯

44 Create a class called Mansion that inherits from House. It should have the additional attribute Fountain that denotes whether or not it has a fountain. The changeFloors method needs to be overridden so no mansion can be given fewer than two floors.

Answer on p. 212

Exam tip

Object-oriented programming appears both in paper one and paper two so it is worth investing some time to ensure you are confident writing code in this style.

41

Summary

Systems software

+ Operating systems manage system hardware, manage programs being installed or run, provide an interface for the user and manage security.
+ One of the jobs of an operating system is memory management. Memory can be split logically into segments or into equal-sized pages. When physical memory is full, pages are stored in virtual memory on a secondary storage device.
+ Checks are made for interrupts at the end of each fetch–decode–execute cycle. Interrupts are used to get the processor to attend to something other than its current task. An interrupt can only take over from a lower priority process.
+ Scheduling is used to ensure all jobs get processor time. Scheduling algorithms include: round robin, first come first served, shortest job first, shortest remaining time and multilevel feedback queues.
+ There are number of different types of operating systems: multitasking, multi-user, distributed, embedded and real time.
+ The BIOS is used to help boot the system.
+ A device driver is a program that allows the operating system to control hardware devices.
+ Virtual machines are programs that perform the function of a physical computer. Two of the main uses are to run an operating system inside another and to run intermediate code.

Applications generation

+ Applications software allows users to perform different tasks; the most suitable application depends on the task, the user and the computer system being used.
+ Utilities are programs designed to keep a computer system running efficiently. Examples include antivirus and backup software.
+ Closed source software does not allow users to view or modify source code. Most commercial software is closed source.
+ Open source software allows users to view and modify their source code.
+ Compilers, interpreters and assemblers are all types of translator programs.
+ An assembler converts low-level assembly code into machine code.
+ A compiler converts code in a high-level language into an executable machine code file.
+ An interpreter converts and runs high-level code line by line.
+ Compilers work through the following stages: lexical analysis, syntax analysis, code generation and code optimisation.
+ Libraries are pre-written bodies of code that can be used by programmers.
+ Linkers combine different pieces of compiled code, including from libraries, into a single executable compiled code.
+ Loaders load a program into memory.

Software development

+ The waterfall lifecycle involves one stage being completed after another. A stage is only started when the previous one is complete.
+ In rapid application development a prototype is produced. The user evaluates it and the feedback is used to improve it. This process is continued until a final product is produced.
+ The spiral model takes an iterative approach centred on risk. The biggest risks are identified and resolved in each iteration.
+ Agile software development is a set of methodologies that work well with potentially changing requirements. One of these agile methodologies is called extreme programming.
+ Extreme programming uses techniques such as pair programming and refactoring to produce high-quality code. A user works with the development team throughout the process.
+ Algorithms can be written as flowcharts, as bulleted lists or in pseudocode.
+ Pseudocode does not have a particular syntax but it must be written so that someone familiar with programming can understand its meaning.

Types of programming language

+ Programming paradigms are the approaches programming languages take to how programs are structured in order to solve problems.
+ There are two main paradigms: high-level and low-level languages.
+ High-level languages use a mixture of English and mathematical expressions and are machine independent.
+ Low-level languages use the instructions available to a specific processor and therefore only work on machines with that processor architecture.
+ An example of a low-level language is assembly language.
+ High-level languages can be split into further paradigms: procedural, object-oriented, functional and declarative.
+ Procedural languages include Python and C.
+ Object-oriented languages include Java and C++.
+ Functional languages include Haskell and ML.
+ Declarative languages include SQL and Prolog.
+ There are four different ways to access memory: direct, indirect, indexed and immediate.
+ Object-oriented programming is a paradigm that breaks a problem down into a series of objects that interact.
+ Classes are templates that define the attributes and methods (subroutines) of these objects.
+ Inheritance allows a class to inherit all methods and attributes of a parent class (as well as having its own).
+ Encapsulation is the practice of keeping attributes in a class private so they can only be accessed through public methods.
+ Polymorphism is the ability to use the same code to process different objects according to their type.

Check your understanding and progress at **www.hoddereducation.co.uk/myrevisionnotesdownloads**

Exam practice

1 Explain how an operating system deals with physical memory being full. [2]
2 Explain what happens when an interrupt is generated. [4]
3 Explain why a self-driving car may use an operating system that is both embedded and real time. [4]
4 Describe a disadvantage of the shortest-job-first scheduling algorithm. [2]
5 Describe a disadvantage of running a program on an operating system on a virtual machine rather than directly on an operating system running on a physical machine. [2]
6 State what is meant by a utility. [1]
7 Explain why a company might choose to use closed-source software. [2]
8 Explain the similarities and differences between a compiler and an assembler. [2]
9 Explain why programmers might use an interpreter. [2]
10 Describe what happens in the lexical analysis stage of compilation. [2]
11 State what a loader does. [1]
12 Explain how extreme programming is likely to lead to high-quality code. [3]
13 Explain why the spiral model would be a better choice than the waterfall lifecycle model for a high-risk project. [4]
14 A company wishes to produce a set of office applications that they aim to sell for a number of different computer systems. Discuss why using a high-level language for this project would be far more suitable than a low-level language. [9]
15 Write an LMC program that outputs the numbers 1 to 100. [3]
16 a) Describe an advantage of direct addressing over indirect addressing. [1]
    b) Describe an advantage of indirect addressing over direct addressing. [1]
17 A library stock-control system is being developed in an object-oriented language. Describe how inheritance might be used in this program. [2]
18 Explain why encapsulation is considered best practice when using object-oriented programming. [1]
19 Write a class called `Dog`.
    a) It should have the attribute `Colour`. [1]
    b) It should have a constructor and the method `changeColour`. [2]
    c) Use encapsulation to ensure the only colours the dog can be changed to are black, brown, white or grey. [3]
20 The code below shows a class called `Student`. The class contains the student's name and an array with the names of the subjects the student studies:

```
class Student
        public name
        private Array subjects
        public procedure new(gName, gSubjects)
                name = gName
                subjects = gSubjects
        endprocedure
        public procedure foo()
                for i = 0 to subjects.length-1
                        print(subjects[i])
                next i
        endprocedure
endclass
```

    a) Explain how you would encapsulate the attribute `name` [2]
    b) Suggest an appropriate name for the method `foo` [1]
    c) Write the method `takesComputerScience()` which returns `true` if the student studies "Computer Science" and `false` otherwise. [3]

Answers available online

Compression, encryption and hashing

Lossy versus lossless compression

REVISED

Compression is the process of making files smaller by representing them using less data. This reduces the space they take up on a storage device and means they are quicker to transmit over a connection.

When compressing data, there are two approaches: lossy and lossless.

Lossy compression

+ In lossy compression information is removed.
+ It is usually used on image, video and sound files.
+ Changes may include removing frequencies of sound that the human ear is unlikely to perceive or changing very similar colours (ones the human eye would not notice as different) to the same colour.
+ The version of the file that has been compressed may look/sound identical to the original but at a bit level (i.e. the 1s and 0s that make it) it will be different.
+ The higher the compression ratio (i.e. the smaller the file has been made), the more it will be noticeably different from the original.
+ Examples of files that use lossy compression are JPEG, MP3 and MP4.

Lossless compression

+ In lossless compression no information is removed.
+ This means the original file that is reconstructed from the compressed version will be bit for bit the same as it was before compression.
+ Lossless compression is used when no information can be lost, for example in documents and program files.
+ Lossless compression tends to result in less impressive file size reductions than lossy compression.
+ Examples of files that use lossless compression are ZIP and PNG.

Now test yourself

1 Explain what is meant by file compression.

2 Name a lossy and a lossless file type for images.

3 Give one advantage of each of the file types you gave.

Answers on p. 212

TESTED

Run-length encoding and dictionary coding for lossless compression

REVISED

Two methods of lossless compression are run-length encoding (RLE) and dictionary coding.

Run-length encoding

This makes use of redundant data, so that if a data item occurs multiple times consecutively, the item is stored once in an index along with the number of repetitions. For example, the series of letters:

AAAABBBBBCCCAAABBBBBBBCCBBBBBAAA

could be represented using run-length encoding as:

4A5B3C3A7B2C4B3A

This needn't just be limited to textual representations. For example, it could be the number of adjacent pixels of the same colour in an image.

Dictionary coding

RLE performs well on data with large numbers of consecutive identical chunks, but not on other data. On English text it would be ineffective.

For instance, if we simply take the word HELLO, using RLE this becomes 1H1E2L1O Our 'compressed' output is larger than our original input.

A different approach is dictionary coding. There are many variations of this compression algorithm, but the central idea is the same. An index is built where each data item is recorded along with an index reference. The compressed file then consists of the dictionary plus the sequence of occurrences.

Reference	Data
1	if
2	you
3	are
4	not
5	fired
6	with
7	enthusiasm
8	will
9	be

A message can be constructed by supplying the dictionary and the words used, that is:

1234567289567

While this example has been shown using English text, dictionary coding can be performed at a bit level (i.e. on binary) and therefore can be applied to any data. The algorithm simply needs to determine the most frequently occurring bit patterns and ensure they are added to the dictionary.

> **Now test yourself** TESTED
>
> 4 Use RLE to compress the following sequence:
>
> AAABBBBBAAAAAAAAAAABBABBBBBB
>
> 5 Explain whether the quote below is best compressed with run-length encoding or dictionary coding:
>
> *Now this is not the end. It is not even the beginning of the end. But it is, perhaps, the end of the beginning.*
>
> Winston Churchill
>
> **Answers on p. 212**

Symmetric and asymmetric encryption

Encryption is the process of making data unreadable to third parties.

Historically, simple methods such as the Caesar cipher were used, where letters are displaced by a known amount, for example a displacement of 4 would produce the following look-up table:

Plain text letter: ABCDEFGHIJKLMNOPQRSTUVWXYZ
Cipher text letter: EFGHIJKLMNOPQRSTUVWXYZABCD

The initial message, or plaintext, HELLO becomes encrypted message, or cipher text, LIPPS

The key is the number 4.

> **Encryption** The process of making data unreadable to third parties.
>
> **Key** A value that needs to be provided to encrypt/decrypt data.

With only 26 possible keys the Caesar cipher was considered insecure many centuries ago and a modern computer could crack it in literally less time than it takes to blink an eye. Modern encryption algorithms are much more complicated but the principle remains the same:

+ Apply the encryption algorithm to the original data using the key and encrypted data is produced.
+ The recipient applies the decryption algorithm using the key to get the original unencrypted data.
+ The encryption algorithm can (and should be presumed to be) known by anyone but the key must be kept secret between the sender and receiver.

Figure 3.1 shows the encryption process and Figure 3.2 shows the decryption process.

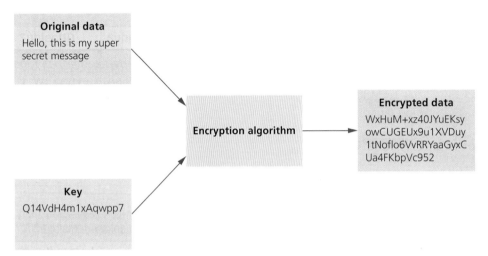

Figure 3.1 Encryption

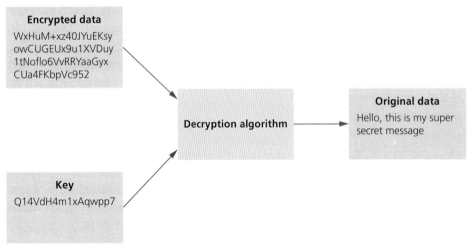

Figure 3.2 Decryption

You will notice we have used the same key to encrypt and decrypt the data. When algorithms use the same key for encryption as decryption it is called symmetric encryption. While this is fine if you are encrypting data you are storing away from prying eyes, it causes a problem if you wish to send this data to another person.

If you are sending encrypted data to another person, the problem arises as to how to send them the key. We cannot simply encrypt the key as that then requires another key, and we face the same problem. If there were a guaranteed secure way of sending the key we might as well just send the message that way.

Symmetric encryption
Encryption where the same key is used to encrypt and decrypt data.

Check your understanding and progress at **www.hoddereducation.co.uk/myrevisionnotesdownloads**

In these cases we use asymmetric encryption. In asymmetric encryption:

+ A public key is used to encrypt data.
+ This public key can be freely distributed.
+ The encrypted data can only be decrypted with a private key (which has to be kept secret).

This works because the two keys are related using some clever mathematics. In practice, asymmetric encryption takes a lot of computing power. It is common for asymmetric encryption to be used when two parties agree on a shared secret key that can then be used for symmetric encryption (which is just as secure but requires less computation power).

> **Asymmetric encryption**
> Encryption where one key (the public key) is used to encrypt data and another (the private key) is used to decrypt it.

Exam tip

When reading about encryption you may see the terms plaintext and ciphertext used. Before computers, encryption was almost always applied to written text, so plaintext refers to the original, unencrypted text and ciphertext refers to the encrypted text. Computers use algorithms that perform encryption at a bit level (i.e. to the 1s and 0s), meaning it can be applied to any data. It is therefore more accurate, in terms of computer encryption, to refer to encrypted and unencrypted data rather than plaintext and ciphertext.

Now test yourself

TESTED ◯

6 Explain why symmetric encryption would not be suitable for transferring credit card details over the internet.

7 Give one possible use of symmetric encryption.

Answers on p. 212

Hashing and its uses

REVISED ◯

A hash function is one that takes in any amount of data and gives a fixed-sized output, regardless of the size of the input.

Properties of hash functions

As well as having a fixed-sized output, a hashing algorithm should have the following properties:

+ Irreversibility: they should be one-way functions. That is, it should be impossible to calculate what data was put into the hash function given its output. This property of irreversibility is particularly useful when it comes to passwords, as we will see later. To ensure hash functions are truly irreversible, similar inputs should not give similar outputs.
+ Determinism: a hash function should be deterministic, meaning the same input will always give the same output.
+ Collision resistance: a collision is when two or more inputs give the same outputs. It is impossible to have no collisions as there are endless possible inputs and a limited number of outputs. A good hashing algorithm should, however, reduce the chance of collisions by ensuring all outputs are equally likely.

> **Hash function** A function that takes in data of any size and returns a fixed-length output.
>
> **Irreversibility** The property such that an output of a process cannot be used to derive the original input.
>
> **Determinism** The property that a process with the same inputs will always give the same output.
>
> **Collision resistance** The property that different inputs giving the same output occurs as infrequently as possible.

Example

One hashing algorithm is called SHA-256. SHA-256 takes in data and returns a 256-bit value that is usually represented as 64 hexadecimal digits. There are a few things to note from the example.

+ The first is that despite there only being one letter difference between `hello` and `hullo`, the outputs are completely different.
+ The other is that no matter how much bigger the input gets, the output still remains the same length.

Input	Output
hello	2cf24dba5fb0a30e26e83b2ac5b9e29e1b161e5c1fa7425e73043362938b9824
hullo	7835066a1457504217688c8f5d06909c6591e0ca78c254ccf17450d0d999cab0
hello, this is an example of data going into a hash function.	bb32d5eff798673675276be4706dc60fac01c077ebacf20efd0540e5ee7fdb1b

While the examples we have looked at have hashed text, the hashing algorithm works at a bit level (on the 1s and 0s that make up the data). This means they can be used on any data on a computer not just text.

Uses of hashes

Passwords

Passwords used to authenticate users when accessing systems need to be stored in a database. If that database were to get hacked, the passwords would be exposed.

For this reason, good systems will store a hash of the password rather than the password itself. When the user comes to log in:
1 The password they enter is hashed and compared against the stored hash.
2 If they are the same, the password is correct and they are granted access.

If the system is hacked, only the hashes are available and, as they cannot be reversed, the hacker is unable to get access to the passwords themselves.

If you ever forget your password and a website is able to tell you what it is, rather than offering a reset, it is likely it is not using hashing and probably not very secure!

Proof of state

Sometimes we want to prove that data hasn't changed over a period of time. One example of this is when law enforcement seize computers for an investigation. They need to prove that the contents of the computers haven't been changed from the time they were taken into custody. To do this they:
1 Take the contents of the entire secondary storage system and hash them.
2 This hash is then recorded.
3 If anyone questions whether the evidence has been tampered with, the system can be hashed again.
4 If so much as one bit of data has changed the hash will be different.

Another example is when software is made available to download on the internet. A hash of the file is often shown next to the download. The user can then hash their file when it has downloaded to confirm the download has been successful and the file has not been altered in any way.

Hash tables

Hash tables are a data structure designed for fast access of data. Each piece of data is stored using a key. For example, if users are being stored, the key might be their username. The key is hashed in a way that it is transformed into a memory location. When the programmer needs to retrieve data, they hash the key again to get the location in which the data is stored. This allows data to be accessed far more quickly than other data structures, where it may have to be searched for.

> **Making links**
>
> For more details about hash functions see Chapter 4.

> **Making links**
>
> Hash tables are covered in more detail in Chapter 4.
>
> It is the use of hashing that allows well-organised hash tables to have a constant lookup complexity O(1) (using Big-O notation). You can find out more about this in Chapter 8.

Check your understanding and progress at **www.hoddereducation.co.uk/myrevisionnotesdownloads**

Revision activity

There are lots of online hash calculators.

1 Find out what the SHA-256 algorithm output is for `Computer Science`. Try the values `hello` and `hullo` and verify you get the same output as shown previously.

2 Compare the output of the input `Laptop` for the following hashing algorithms: SHA-1, SHA-256, MD5.

Now test yourself   TESTED ⬤

8 State what features make a good hashing algorithm.

9 Explain how hashing can be used to prove a document hasn't been amended over a period of time.

Answers on p. 212

Databases

Introduction   REVISED ⬤

A database is a structured, persistent store of data.
+ Structured means it is organised in a logical way so the data it holds can be accessed and manipulated.
+ Persistent means that the data is held for as long as it is required.

A database is usually organised in terms of tables, records and fields.
+ A field stores a single piece of data. A field has a specified data type (e.g. Text, Number, Boolean). Fields are represented by columns on a table, and for that reason are sometimes referred to as columns.
+ A collection of fields composing an entry in a database are called a record. Records are represented by rows in a table and as such are referred to as rows (or, sometimes, tuples).
+ A complete set of records are called a table.

> **Database** A structured, persistent store of data, organised so that it can easily be accessed, managed and updated.

Field

customer_id	title	forename	surname	tel_no
26335	Mr	Asim	Khan	0131 496 0556
26336	Mrs	Helen	Rosen	0121 496 0600
26337	Dr	James	Montague	0113 496 0743

Table — Record —

Figure 3.3 The elements of a database

Most computer systems make use of databases. This is because databases make it convenient and fast to:
+ access data
+ update data
+ search for data
+ present data in a usable way.

Making links

Later in this chapter you will look at web technologies including server and client-side processing. Databases often form an integral part of this model. When you visit an online shop, the server-side code reads a database to generate the page based on your previous purchases. The generated code is then sent across the internet to your browser where the page is displayed.

49

Flat-file and relational databases

Flat-file databases

Simple databases can be made as lists in a single table, like in a spreadsheet. These are called flat-file databases. They are of limited use. They are fine for small amounts of data but can quickly become cumbersome if more complex data needs to be stored. One issue is that they are also prone to data redundancy.

Data redundancy means the same data is stored in different locations. This is a bad thing because not only does it waste storage space, but when updates occur, if all the instances of a data item aren't changed, there will be inconsistencies.

The simple example in Figure 3.3 is a flat-file database.

Relational databases

Because of the limitations of flat-file databases, different database models have been designed. One of the most widely used of these alternative models are relational databases.

Relational databases:
+ are based on two or more tables
+ one field in each table exists in another table
+ tables are linked using primary keys and foreign keys
+ each table is based on an entity
+ an entity is anything about which we store data, for example customer, invoice, stock item.
+ an entity has attributes that are characteristics of the entity, for example customer_name, student_id, subject_level – these become fields in a table
+ there is no rule about the order of rows in a table. When order is required, indexes are added
+ there is no rule about the order of columns.

> **Flat-file database** A database in which all data is stored in a single table.
>
> **Data redundancy** The unnecessary duplication of data in a database. When updates occur, all the instances of a data item must be changed. This leads to errors and also wastes storage space.
>
> **Relational database** A relational database consists of multiple tables linked together. Each table usually represents a 'thing' or an entity and the links are their relationships.

Now test yourself

TESTED

10 What are the three key structural elements of a database?

11 Explain the difference between a flat-file and a relational database.

12 State one advantage that relational databases have over flat-file databases.

Answers on p. 213

Primary and foreign keys

Each record in a table needs to be uniquely identifiable. In order to ensure this is the case we use a primary key.
+ A primary key is a field in a table that is unique for every record.
+ In other words, if a field is a primary key, no two records should have the same value.

Sometimes there may be a natural candidate for the primary key. For example, a database of cars may use the registration plate as no two cars can have the same registration.

Often this is not the case however, and a primary key field is created by assigning a number that increases by one for each record, to act as an identifier.

> **Primary key** A field that has a unique value for every record in a table.

Worked example

The extract of the `Booking` table below is from a database for a hotel.

room_number	date	room_type
101	21/03/2021	double
310	22/03/2021	single
250	22/03/2021	double

None of the fields in this table could be a primary key:
+ a room will be booked many times, meaning that room numbers will be duplicated in the database
+ there will be multiple bookings on each date
+ many rooms are single or double.

In this case the easiest solution is to add an identifier field `booking_id`.

booking_id	room_number	date	room_type
6348242	101	21/03/2021	double
6348243	310	22/03/2021	single
6348244	250	22/03/2021	double

In order to create a link between two tables, we use the primary key of one table as a field in the second table. Where this primary key appears in the second table, it is known as a foreign key.

> **Foreign key** The primary key of one table being used as a field in another table, creating a link.

Worked example

The same hotel database has a `Customer` table as shown below. You will notice that it has `customer_id` as its primary key.

customer_id	title	forename	surname	tel_no
26335	Mr	Asim	Khan	0131 496 0556
26336	Mrs	Helen	Rosen	0121 496 0600
26337	Dr	James	Montague	0113 496 0743

If we want to link a customer to a booking this can be done by adding the `customer_id` primary key field from the `Customer` table as a foreign key field in the `Booking` table.

booking_id	room_number	date	room_type	customer_id
6348242	101	21/03/2021	double	26335
6348243	310	22/03/2021	single	45335
6348244	250	22/03/2021	double	36587

We can see from the tables above that Mr Asim Khan has booked room 101 on 21/3/2021.

Note: there are various conventions for identifying primary and foreign keys. Usually the primary key is underlined and the foreign key overlined, but you will sometimes see variations on this. For example, primary keys in bold and foreign keys in italics.

Now test yourself

TESTED ◯

13 Explain why `surname` would not make a good primary key in a database.
14 Explain how tables are linked in a relational database.

Answers on p. 213

Secondary keys and indexing

Sometimes we may wish to search by a field other than the primary key. In order to speed this up, a database can create an index. Just like the index of a book, it stores the locations where each value occurs. This saves every record from having to be checked.

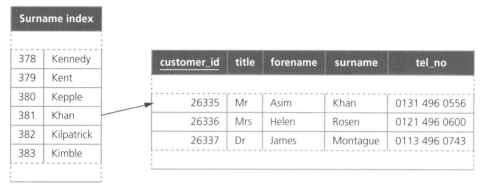

Surname index	
378	Kennedy
379	Kent
380	Kepple
381	Khan
382	Kilpatrick
383	Kimble

customer_id	title	forename	surname	tel_no
26335	Mr	Asim	Khan	0131 496 0556
26336	Mrs	Helen	Rosen	0121 496 0600
26337	Dr	James	Montague	0113 496 0743

A field that is likely to be searched and therefore indexed is known as a secondary key.

Indexes take up extra space but speed up searching.

Taking the Customer table, it is likely that customers will be searched by surname. Therefore surname would make a suitable secondary key.

> **Secondary key** A field by which records are likely to be searched and is therefore indexed.

Now test yourself   TESTED ◯

15 Explain why date_of_booking would make a good secondary key in a database hotel database.

16 State one advantage and one disadvantage of indexing a field.

Answers on p. 213

Entity-relationship modelling and normalisation

When thinking about relational databases, it is useful to be able to visually represent our ideas. We can do this by considering the entities (the objects represented by tables) and the relationships (links between these objects). These are shown in diagrammatic form using entity relationship diagrams.

There are a variety of different variations of entity-relationship diagrams. The type used in the exam uses 'crow's foot notation'.

> **Entity-relationship diagram** A diagram showing the tables, which hold the entities and their links, or relationships within a relational database.

It is called this because some of the links between the tables are reminiscent of crows' feet, see the figure opposite.
+ Entities are represented in boxes.
+ Relationships are represented by lines with either a single line (representing one) or a prong (representing many) at either end.

This gives us three types of relationships.

One-to-one relationships

These are where each instance of an entity connects to a single instance of another entity.

In the example below, each employee has one set of pay details and each set of pay details belongs to one employee.

One-to-one relationships are useful when you want to have different security settings for different tables.

In our example, all departments in a business can access the Employee table whereas only the Accounts department will be able to access the PayDetails table.

Employee ——————— PayDetails

One-to-many relationships

These are when each single instance of one entity is linked to many instances of another entity.

In the example below, each customer can place many orders but each order only belongs to one customer.

One-to-many relationships are a good way of avoiding data redundancy. By linking these two tables (rather than having one big orders table), we avoid the need to duplicate customers' details with every order they make.

(One-to-many relationships can be many-to-one depending on the order of the tables.)

Many-to-many relationships

These are when multiple instances of one entity may be linked to multiple instances of another entity.

In the example below, each order has many items and each item can be ordered many times.

This is very hard to implement in practice and therefore many-to-many relationships are avoided.

We can get rid of many-to-many relationships by placing an intermediary entity between the original entities. This intermediary table just contains its own primary key and the two primary keys of the other tables as foreign keys.

In our example, the intermediary table would contain order_id and item_id as foreign keys.

To be able to ensure there is no redundant data when representing our data in such a manner, we use a process called normalisation. This process in covered on page 57.

Now test yourself   TESTED ◯

17 State the likely relationship between the database tables Manufacturer and CarModel

18 The tables Book and Author have a many-to-many relationship. Use an entity-relationship diagram to explain how this could be resolved.

Answers on p. 213

Methods of capturing, selecting, managing and exchanging data

Capturing data

In order to get written data into a database, there are different approaches depending on the data being captured. Sometimes there is no alternative but to type it in directly.

Increasingly it is possible to use computer-based forms, for example on a website, where data can be entered directly.

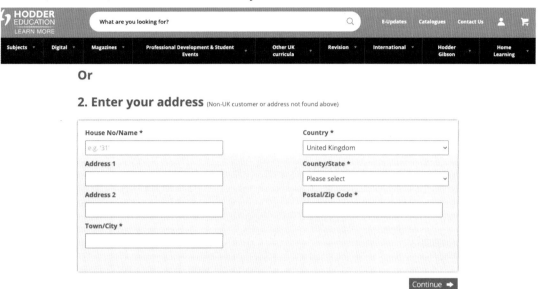

Figure 3.4 A website form

If data is being collected from printed forms, then there are two possible methods to capture it.

✚ Where the data consists of choices from a range of options, optical mark recognition (OMR) can be used. This is where a computer identifies where areas of a form have been shaded in.

> **Optical mark recognition (OMR)** A data input method that recognises the positions of marks made on paper.

Q1 [A]   [B]   [C]   [D]

Q2 [A]   [B]   [C]   [D]

Q3 [A]   [B]   [C]   [D]

Q4 [A]   [B]   [C]   [D]

Figure 3.5 An example of the use of optical mark recognition is when capturing data from multiple choice exams

✚ Optical character recognition (OCR) can be used to convert images of typed documents into readable text. This can be used if data on printed documents needs entering into databases, and when speed cameras scan car number plates.

> **Optical character recognition (OCR)** A data input method that converts images of text to machine editable text.

Numerical data can sometimes be automatically collected using sensors, for example measuring temperatures in a location at different points in time. Sensors normally measure analogue data, which will need converting into digital data using analogue-to-digital converters (ADCs).

Selecting and managing data

Between the database itself and the program or person using it, there is a layer of software known as the database management system. The DBMS ensures the database is manipulated in a consistent way while ensuring integrity and security. Examples of DBMSs include:

✚ MySQL
✚ Microsoft Access
✚ PostgreSQL.

DBMSs tend to offer one of two main methods of selecting and managing data within a database:

✚ Structured Query Language (SQL)
✚ Query by Example (QBE).

> **Structured Query Language (SQL)** A language used to find and manipulate data within a database.

SQL is a language used for selecting and updating data within a database. It is covered in more detail on page 60.

Check your understanding and progress at **www.hoddereducation.co.uk/myrevisionnotesdownloads**

With QBE, the user has a graphical interface into which required fields can be dropped, as well as allowing the user to set up conditions to filter the results.

Example

A QBE from Microsoft Access is shown below, used to select the telephone numbers of all customers with the surname *Khan*.

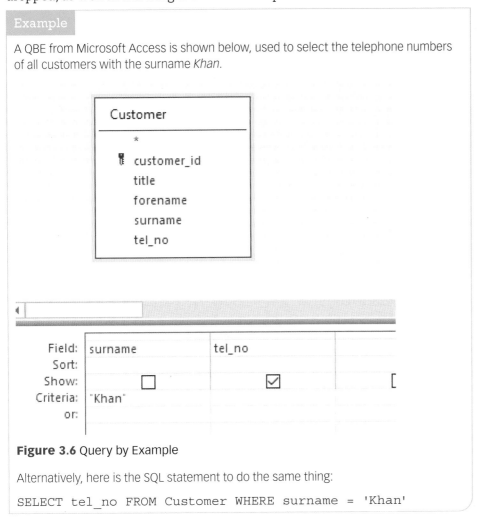

Figure 3.6 Query by Example

Alternatively, here is the SQL statement to do the same thing:

```
SELECT tel_no FROM Customer WHERE surname = 'Khan'
```

Exchanging data

In order to exchange data, it is preferable to use standard data format. There are a number of examples of these:

+ SQL can be used to transfer data between systems. A database management system (DBMS) can generate a sequence of SQL instructions that, when run on a receiving DBMS, will create the relevant tables, relationships and insert the data.
+ Comma-separated value (CSV) files are a simple way of exchanging data. In a CSV file each field can be separated by a comma.
+ eXtensible Markup Language (XML) is a markup language that uses tags to designate what different things within a document are. In the case of a database, each record could be enclosed within tags, and inside those each field enclosed within further tags.
+ JavaScript Object Notation (JSON) is a format that represents things as objects (which can contain other objects). In the case of a database, each record is an object that can contain an array of objects that represent the fields. JSON is particularly useful when sending data to a JavaScript program, for example on a web page, as JavaScript can read the data directly.

Database management system (DBMS) Software used to control a database, overseeing amendments to its structure, and used to access and amend the data itself.

55

Making links

Later in this chapter when we look at web pages you will come across another markup language called HTML. On first glance HTML and XML look very similar but while HTML is used to designate the different parts of a web page, XML is used for designating different parts of data within a larger structure.

You will also explore JavaScript more in the web technologies section of this chapter. The paradigm that is object-oriented programming is covered in Chapter 2. JSON is an example of how JavaScript and object-oriented programming can be used together.

```
INSERT INTO `Customer` (`customer_id`, `title`, `forename`, `surname`, `tel_no`)
VALUES
        (26335,'Mr.','Asim','Khan','0131 496 0556'),
        (26336,'Mrs.','Helen','Rosen','0121 496 0600'),
        (26337,'Dr.','James','Montague','0113 496 0743');
```

Figure 3.7 Extract of SQL file being used to transfer data

```
"customer_id","title","forename","surname","tel_no"
26335,"Mr.","Asim","Khan","0131 496 0556"
26336,"Mrs.","Helen","Rosen","0121 496 0600"
26337,"Dr.","James","Montague","0113 496 0743"
```

Figure 3.8 Extract of CSV file being used to transfer data

```
<row>
    <field name="customer_id">26335</field>
    <field name="title">Mr.</field>
    <field name="forename">Asim</field>
    <field name="surname">Khan</field>
    <field name="tel_no">0131 496 0556</field>
</row>

<row>
    <field name="customer_id">26336</field>
    <field name="title">Mrs.</field>
    <field name="forename">Helen</field>
    <field name="surname">Rosen</field>
    <field name="tel_no">0121 496 0600</field>
</row>

<row>
    <field name="customer_id">26337</field>
    <field name="title">Dr.</field>
    <field name="forename">James</field>
    <field name="surname">Montague</field>
    <field name="tel_no">0113 496 0743</field>
</row>
```

Figure 3.9 Extract of XML file being used to transfer data

```
"row": [
  {
    "field": [
      {
        "name": "customer_id",
        "#text": "26335"
      },
      {
        "name": "title",
        "#text": "Mr."
      },
      {
        "name": "forename",
        "#text": "Asim"
      },
      {
        "name": "surname",
        "#text": "Khan"
      },
      {
        "name": "tel_no",
        "#text": "0131 496 0556"
      }
    ]
  },
  {
    "field": [
      {
        "name": "customer_id",
        "#text": "26336"
      },
      {
        "name": "title",
        "#text": "Mrs."
```

Figure 3.10 Extract of JSON file being used to transfer data

Now test yourself

TESTED ◯

19 Describe how a school might use OMR to capture attendance data for its registers.
20 Describe how CSV files store data.

Answers on p. 213

Normalisation to third normal form

When building a relational database, it is important we avoid redundant data, that is, data that is unnecessarily repeated. Redundant data means space can be needlessly wasted and can cause inconsistencies if one version is updated and not the other.

In order to avoid redundant data we use a process called normalisation. For the course you need to know the first three stages of normalisation. There are others but these apply to very specific circumstances and are less frequently used in the real world.
+ We refer to data after the first stage as being in first normal form.
+ We refer to data after the second stage as being in second normal form.
+ We refer to data after the third stage as being in third normal form.
+ Before any normalisation, data is referred to as being in unnormalised form (UNF).

> **Normalisation** The process of changing the structure of a relational database to remove the potential for data redundancy.
>
> **First normal form (1NF)** Data after the first stage of normalisation. It must have a primary key, no repeating fields and all of them atomic.
>
> **Atomic** A field that cannot be broken down into multiple smaller fields.

First normal form

A database is in first normal form (1NF) if:
+ Data in every field is atomic (it cannot be split down into smaller pieces of data).
+ No fields repeat.
+ Every record has a primary key.

The table below contains data about students in a college. It includes the subjects they take, their teacher for each subject and that teacher's staff code (used for emails etc.).

Name	Address	Subject1	Teacher1	T1Code	Subject2	Teacher2	T2_Code	Subject3	Teacher3	T3_Code
Alison Jones	12 Queen Street, Milton Keynes, MK17 8FF	Computer Science	Mr Pitt	JJP	Biology	Mr Simons	KRS	Economics	Dr Shah	FS
Sunil Patel	6 High Street, Milton Keynes, MK44 1BY	Biology	Mr Simons	KRS	German	Miss Lambert	NWL	Chemistry	Ms Brooks	CBB
Fraser Hanson	134 Somerfield Lane, Milton Keynes, MK3 7QR	Computer Science	Mr Pitt	JJP	French	Miss Lambert	NWL			

We know it's unnormalised and not in 1NF as:
+ There is no primary key.
+ The subject field is repeated.
+ The fields Name and Address are not atomic as they can be logically split down further.

Name and Address not being atomic means searching can become more complex. If we just want to search for students who live on a particular street, we would need to build more complex queries than we would if the street was stored in its own field.

Having a repeated subject field makes queries for subjects more complex. A query to find all students who do maths requires three fields to be checked. Not every student takes a third subject yet space is put aside for this. What about if a student wishes to take a fourth or fifth subject?

To normalise to first normal form we shall:
+ add a primary key StudentID to the three records
+ remove the repeating fields, creating a new record for each subject
+ ensure all the fields are atomic by breaking down the fields Name and Address.

For simplicity, we will assume in this college no student ever has more than one teacher per subject and so every student will only have each subject in one of their records.

StudentID	Forename	Surname	HouseNo	Street	Town	Postcode	Subject	Teacher	Teacher_Code
1201	Alison	Jones	12	Queen Street	Milton Keynes	MK17 8FF	Computer Science	Mr Pitt	JJP
1201	Alison	Jones	12	Queen Street	Milton Keynes	MK17 8FF	Biology	Mr Simons	KRS
1201	Alison	Jones	12	Queen Street	Milton Keynes	MK17 8FF	Economics	Dr Shah	FS
1542	Sunil	Patel	6	High Street	Milton Keynes	MK44 1BY	Biology	Mr Simons	KRS
1542	Sunil	Patel	6	High Street	Milton Keynes	MK44 1BY	German	Miss Lambert	NWL
1542	Sunil	Patel	6	High Street	Milton Keynes	MK44 1BY	Chemistry	Ms Brooks	CBB
1677	Fraser	Hanson	134	Somerfield Lane	Milton Keynes	MK3 7QR	Computer Science	Mr Pitt	JJP
1677	Fraser	Hanson	134	Somerfield Lane	Milton Keynes	MK3 7QR	French	Miss Lambert	NWL

The field StudentID can no longer be the primary key on its own as it may appear multiple times. Therefore a composite key is formed using StudentID and Subject. A composite key is one that is made from a combination of two or more fields.

By moving the data into the table as shown we can now consider the data to be in at least 1NF: every record has a primary key, all fields are atomic and no fields repeat.

Second normal form

In order to be in second normal form (2NF):
+ The database must meet all the requirements of 1NF.
+ Every field must only depend on all of the primary key.

The second point only applies to tables with composite keys. Every field that is not part of the composite key should depend on all parts of the composite key. In other words, it should not be possible to determine what a field is by looking at only one of the fields in the composite key.

This is not the case with our table in 1NF as it is possible to determine the student's name and address purely from the StudentID, regardless of the subject.

We can solve this by creating a SUBJECT table and a TAKES table, moving fields from the original table into these two new tables, and forming some new primary and foreign keys.

Composite key A primary key made of two or more fields. While on their own they may not be unique, each record's combination of them will be.

Second normal form (2NF) Data after the second stage of normalisation. In 2NF, all data is in 1NF and has no field depending on only part of the primary key.

STUDENT

StudentID	Forename	Surname	HouseNo	Street	Town	Postcode
1201	Alison	Jones	12	Queen Street	Milton Keynes	MK17 8FF
1542	Sunil	Patel	6	High Street	Milton Keynes	MK44 1BY
1677	Fraser	Hanson	134	Somerfield Lane	Milton Keynes	MK3 7QR

Check your understanding and progress at **www.hoddereducation.co.uk/myrevisionnotesdownloads**

TAKES

TakesID	StudentID	SubjectID
1	1201	1
2	1201	2
3	1201	3
4	1542	2
5	1542	4
6	1542	5
7	1677	1
8	1677	6

SUBJECT

SubjectID	Subject	Teacher	Teacher_Code
1	Computer Science	Mr Pitt	JJP
2	Biology	Mr Simons	KRS
3	Economics	Dr Shah	FS
4	German	Miss Lambert	NWL
5	Chemistry	Ms Brooks	CBB
6	French	Ms Brooks	CBB

Notice the notation for primary and foreign keys, and how we have avoided having a many-to-many relationship between Student and Subject.

Now our database:
+ still meets all the rules of 1NF
+ plus every field in each table depends only on each primary key.

Therefore we know the database is now in 2NF.

Third normal form

In order to be in third normal form (3NF):
+ The database must meet all the requirements of 2NF.
+ No field must depend on any field other than the primary key.

The second point means it should not be possible to tell what the value of a field should be by looking at any field other than the primary key.

This is not the case in our SUBJECT table. It is possible to determine the name of the teacher from the teacher code, which is not the primary key. This can be resolved by creating a TEACHER table

> **Third normal form (3NF)**
> Data in a relational database after the third stage of normalisation. In addition to being in 2NF, every field depends solely on the primary key and no other field.

SUBJECT

SubjectID	Subject	Teacher_code
1	Computer Science	JJP
2	Biology	KRS
3	Economics	FS
4	German	NWL
5	Chemistry	CBB
6	French	NWL

TEACHER

Teacher_Code	Teacher
JJP	Mr Pitt
KRS	Mr Simons
FS	Dr Shah
NWL	Miss Lambert
CBB	Ms Brooks

Now every field in each table depends only on each primary key and so our database is in 3NF.

Now test yourself

TESTED

21 State the requirements for data to be considered in 2NF.

22 Here is a preliminary design for a database to store stock details and handle orders in a shop.

```
stock_number, stock_name, number_in_stock, supplier_ref,
supplier_name, supplier_email, order_number,
order_date, order_quantity
```

Normalise this database into 3NF.

Answers on p. 213

Exam tip

A mnemonic used to help remember normalisation is:

The key, the whole key and nothing but the key.

The key: 1NF requires a primary key (plus atomic data and no repeating fields).

The whole key: 2NF requires all fields to depend on all of the primary key.

And nothing but the key: 3NF requires that no field should depend on any other field aside from the primary key.

SQL

REVISED

SQL is a language used for communicating with databases when selecting or changing data. The SQL commands you need to know for the exam are:

+ SELECT ... FROM
+ WHERE
+ LIKE
+ AND and OR
+ DELETE
+ INSERT
+ DROP
+ JOIN

SELECT ... FROM

SELECT and FROM are used to retrieve specified fields from a specified table:

SELECT field(s) FROM table;

For example:

SELECT forename FROM Customer;

selects all the forenames of the customers in the Customer table.

SELECT forename, surname FROM Customer;

selects the forenames and surnames from the Customer table.

If all the fields are required, the * wildcard is used. For example:

SELECT * FROM Customer;

selects all the fields from the Customer table.

Check your understanding and progress at **www.hoddereducation.co.uk/myrevisionnotesdownloads**

WHERE

WHERE is used to filter the results that are returned.

        SELECT forename FROM Customer WHERE surname = 'Khan';

Note you can use the Boolean operators AND and OR as well as the comparison operators >, <, <= and <=.

Note that 'not equal to' in SQL is <>.

        SELECT customerID from Customer WHERE points > 100 AND
        level = "Platinum";

LIKE

LIKE is used with WHERE to select fields that match a given pattern. It is used with the % wildcard which represents 0 or more characters. For example:

        SELECT Name, Abbreviation FROM States WHERE Name LIKE
        'New %';

This selects the names and abbreviations of all states with a name that starts with 'New':

New Hampshire	NH
New Jersey	NJ
New Mexico	NM
New York	NY

To show the role of the % wildcard, consider the following:

        SELECT Name, Abbreviation FROM States WHERE Name LIKE '%o';

This would give:

    Colorado

    Idaho

    New Mexico

    Ohio

DELETE

DELETE is used to delete records.

DELETE FROM Customer WHERE forename = 'Jason';

deletes all records from Customer where the forename is Jason.

INSERT

INSERT adds records into a table.

INSERT INTO Customer (forename, surname, phone_number)

VALUES ('Jason', 'Pitt', '0131 496 0680');

This adds the details of customer Jason Pitt.

Insert can be used to add more than one record at once.

INSERT INTO Customer (forename, surname, phone_number)

VALUES ('Jason', 'Pitt', '0131 496 0680'),

('George', 'Rouse', '07700 900502');

DROP

DROP is used to delete whole tables.

```
DROP TABLE Customer;
```

Removes the Customer table from the database.

JOIN

JOIN is used to combine information. It selects data every time it finds a match between the two specified fields.

For instance, for the following tables:

SUBJECT

SubjectID	Subject	Teacher_code
1	Computer Science	JJP
2	Biology	KRS
3	Economics	FS
4	German	NWL
5	Chemistry	CBB
6	French	NWL

TEACHER

Teacher_Code	Teacher
JJP	Mr Pitt
KRS	Mr Simons
FS	Dr Shah
NWL	Miss Lambert
CBB	Ms Brooks

```
SELECT Subject.Subject, Teacher.Teacher

FROM Subject

INNER JOIN Teacher ON Subject.Teacher_Code = Teacher.Teacher_Code;
```

This SQL statement matches the Teacher_Code entries in the table Students to the Teacher_Code entries in the table Teacher and then displays the corresponding data from the two fields Subject and Teacher.

This means it selects:

Computer Science	Mr Pitt
Biology	Mr Simons
Economics	Dr Shah
German	Miss Lambert
Chemistry	Ms Brooks
French	Miss Lambert

Note the use of the table names with dot notation when specifying the fields (e.g. tablename.fieldname). This not only helps readability but is especially important if the two tables have any fields with the same name.

Exam tip

In your reading around the topic you may see there are several types of JOIN statement:

    LEFT JOIN

    RIGHT JOIN

    INNER JOIN

    OUTER JOIN

For this course you only need to know about the INNER JOIN, which is the default if the word JOIN is used on its own.

Now test yourself   TESTED ◯

23 A database has the following tables and fields:

CUSTOMER

CustomerID, Forename, Surname, TelephoneNumber, BonusPoints

BOOKING

BookingID,CustomerID , RoomNumber, BookingDate

  a) Write an SQL statement that gives the forename and surnames of all customers in the database.
  b) Write an SQL statement that gives the forename and surnames of all people in the table Customer who have a Birmingham telephone number (starts 0121) and have over 1000 bonus points.
  c) Write an SQL statement that gives all the rooms and booking dates booked by customers with the surname Smith.
  d) Write an SQL statement to add the customer Joshua Stevenson with the telephone number 029 2018 0606.
  e) Write an SQL statement that removes the customer table.

Answers on p. 213

Referential integrity   REVISED ◯

Referential integrity is when a DBMS ensures that a change isn't made to one table that would impact data stored on another table. For example, in a school database, referential integrity would prevent a teacher being removed from the database if there are classes to which they are linked.

In this case, Miss Lambert cannot be deleted as she teaches two classes.

> **Referential integrity**
> Guaranteeing the consistency of a database by ensuring no record points to another record that doesn't exist.

Subject

SubjectID	Subject	Teacher_Code
1	Computer Science	JJP
2	Biology	KRS
3	Economics	FS
4	German	NWL
5	Chemistry	CBB
6	French	NWL

Teacher

Teacher_Code	Teacher
JJP	Mr Pitt
KRS	Mr Simons
FS	Dr Shah
NWL	Miss Lambert
CBB	Ms Brooks

Now test yourself

24 Explain what impact a lack of referential integrity might have in a hotel's database.

Answer on p. 213

TESTED ◯

Essentially, referential integrity ensures:
+ a record cannot be deleted if its primary key appears as a foreign key on another table
+ a value cannot be entered into a foreign key field if there isn't a corresponding primary key value.

Transaction processing, ACID, record locking and redundancy

REVISED

Transaction processing and ACID

Most processes carried out by programs using a database require a number of actions to take place in the database. For example, if in a bank £50 is transferred from Person A to Person B:

+ the first action is to remove £50 from person A's account
+ and the next action is to add £50 to person B's account.

These collections of actions to perform a task are called transactions.

Care has to be taken when transactions occur to ensure the data within the database remains valid. To help ensure this, transaction systems should adhere to the ACID properties: atomicity, consistency, isolation and durability.

+ Atomicity: a change is performed or not performed. Half-finished changes must not be saved.
+ Consistency: databases have sets of rules (called constraints) that must be adhered to by all the data they contain. (For example it might be that values representing percentages all add up to 100, or that values representing money in an account never go below 0). Transactions should never leave a database in a state where any of these rules are broken.
+ Isolation: a transaction must not be able to be affected by a different transaction. Unless it can be guaranteed not to affect the running transaction, any new transaction is locked until the change is committed, then the new transaction is released. In other words, transactions can only run at the same time if the end result is the same as if they were run one after the other.
+ Durability: once made, transactions cannot be lost. Changes must be written to storage in order to preserve them.

> **Transaction** A group of actions in a database creating a unit of work.
>
> **ACID** Atomicity, consistency, isolation and durability are concepts that underpin database transactions.

Record locking

It is usual for databases to be accessed by multiple people at any one time. This can cause issues if people are trying to simultaneously access the same record. One person could accidentally overwrite the other person's change.

Record locking avoids this by preventing anyone accessing a record in use by another person.

Redundancy

A redundant system is one that duplicates the work of another. Where a database is crucial for the operation of a business, it is typical to have a second copy of the database (called a mirror database) stored on a different server. If the primary server with the database fails, the mirror can quickly be switched to, preventing loss of service. This is an example of redundancy.

> **Mirror database** An identical instance of a database kept on a separate server.

> **Exam tip**
>
> Be careful not to get confused with redundant data (unnecessarily repeated data in a database), which is a bad thing, and database redundancy (duplication of database resources to prevent downtime), which is a good thing.

> **Now test yourself**
>
> TESTED
>
> 25 Explain what is meant by a transaction that adheres to the ACID properties.
> 26 Explain why a bank might have two identical copies of their database running simultaneously.

Answers on p. 213

Check your understanding and progress at **www.hoddereducation.co.uk/myrevisionnotesdownloads**

Networks

Characteristics of networks and the importance of protocols and standards

Protocols are rules that define how devices communicate with each other. They allow different devices to make sense of the data they receive and transmit. They only work if both devices understand the protocol.

In the early days of computing, different systems would have their own sets of protocols. This would mean that you were often limited to only connecting devices by the same manufacturer.

As networking became more widely used, with devices from a range of manufacturers being connected, having standardised protocols became more important.

> **Protocol** A set of rules for communication between devices.

> **Now test yourself**   TESTED
>
> 27 Find out and explain what the following three protocols are used for:
>   a) HTTPS
>   b) DHCP
>   c) UDP
>
> **Answers on p. 213**

The internet structure

Protocol layering and the TCP/IP stack

At its most fundamental level, the internet consists of a vast number of data packets travelling around the network at very high speeds. For this to happen, each data packet has layers of further data added to it.

+ Layering is the principle of dividing a complex system into separate slices of functionality. It is common in computing systems as well as other aspects of life such as engineering.
+ Layering allows the creation and maintenance of parts of a system without having to take the whole system into account.
+ Networks use layering with protocols.
+ Protocols on each layer communicate only with the layers above and below. This means that a protocol on any layer can be changed for another protocol providing it receives and passes on data in same manner.

> **Layering** The principle of dividing a complex problem into separate, independent sub-problems.

The most commonly used protocol layers are Transmission Control Protocol/Internet Protocol (TCP/IP) stack (named after two of its protocols). The stack consists of four layers:

+ application layer
+ transport layer
+ internet layer
+ link layer.

Layer	Purpose	Examples
Application	Concerned with production and reception of data. Packages data and passes it to the transport layer	HTTP, HTTPS, IMAP, DNS
Transport	Concerned with making and breaking connections via routers	TCP, UDP
Internet	Concerned with providing links across different network types. Essential feature of the internet that allows interoperability between all connected systems	IPv4, IPv6
Link	Passes data to the physical network. It can work with any media such as copper wire, optical fibre and wireless	Wi-Fi, Ethernet

In order to send a data packet, it gets passed down the stack, starting with the application protocol, and each protocol adds its own additional necessary data. This is known as encapsulating the previous data.

Once the data packet has arrived at its destination, it is passed back up the stack and each protocol removes the relevant data (decapsulates).

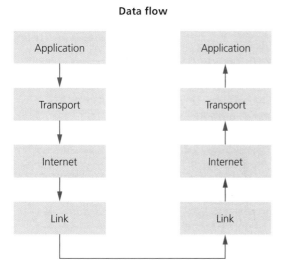

Figure 3.11 The four layers of the TCP/IP stack

DNS

Everything on a network connected to the internet is identified by an IP address. There are two systems of IP addresses the widely used: IPv4 and its successor IPv6 (there was no IPv5).

✚ IPv4 is made of four 8-bit numbers, usually represented in denary (e.g. 69.172.201.167).

✚ IPv6 is made of eight 16-bit numbers, usually represented in hexadecimal (e.g. 57f9:a6cf:44df:5411:2a1e:43f8:d7f:6bce).

We request resources on the internet by asking for a named address, such as: https://www.hodder.co.uk/a-level/computer-science

The named address is called its uniform resource locator (URL).

URLs include domain names, essentially the website's name – in this case hodder.co.uk. Domain names are constructed from a hierarchy.

> **Exam tip**
>
> Do not confuse the encapsulation of data along the stack with encapsulation in object-oriented programming (see Chapter 2). These are two totally different things.

> **Uniform resource locator (URL)** The main part of a website address e.g. hodder.co.uk

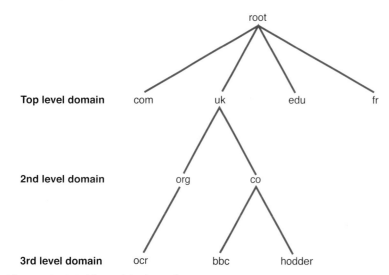

Figure 3.12 A hierarchical naming system

Check your understanding and progress at **www.hoddereducation.co.uk/myrevisionnotesdownloads**

We use URLs as they are easier to remember than IP addresses. However, a web browser needs to know the IP address of a website in order to retrieve information from it.

The domain name system (DNS) converts URLs to IP addresses. The system uses a series of servers that act like address books, matching URLs to their IP addresses.

Domain name system (DNS) is a method that computers use to find the correct IP addresses given the URL

When looking up the IP address of a URL:
1 First your computer checks its local cache to see if the IP address has previously been found.
2 If it doesn't have a copy of the IP address, it checks one of the root servers. Root servers are the highest level of servers in the DNS that hold the locations of all the top-level domain servers.
3 If the root server doesn't have a copy, it points to a server matching the top-level domain (TLD) such as .com, .uk or .org
4 These may point to second level domains (e.g. .co.uk).
5 Finally comes the authoritative name server that holds the IP address of the server being sought. This is sent back to the browser so it can visit the site.

Once the address is found, as it gets passed back to each server the address is cached so it can be found more quickly next time.

> **Making links**
>
> DNS keeps a copy of the IP addresses it has found at every server it's passed back along. This local copy is a cache. Caching is looked at in more detail when looking at computational methods in Chapter 6.

LANs and WANs
REVISED ◯

Most networks can be considered LANs or WANs.

LANs

+ Local area networks (LANs) are networks over a defined and limited location.
+ It could be a room, a building or a campus.
+ Their infrastructure is owned by the organisation that uses it, and the organisation is also responsible for its upkeep.

WANs

+ Wide area networks (WANs) cover a large geographical area.
+ Typically, they consist of interconnected LANs at different sites, connected by some form of telecoms link, which is normally provided by a separate company.
+ The internet can be considered a WAN.

Circuit and packet switching
REVISED ◯

Circuit switching

In traditional landline telephone systems, when one caller wanted to make a call to another a connection was created just for the duration of the call. This is called circuit switching.

In computer networks, circuit switching is the establishment of a physical connection between two communicating entities. It provides an exclusive dedicated channel.

The channel remains open for the duration of the communication session.

Circuit switching A pathway for the data is set up in advance of communication and then data is sent across it. The pathway is closed after transmission.

Circuit switching has three phases:

1 connection established
2 data transferred
3 connection released.

Circuit switching ties up a link so that when in use, other entities cannot use it. It is suitable when there is a need for intensive data transfer.

In reality, modern fast broadband transmissions make circuit switching less important.

Packet switching

Most networks make use of packet switching. Packet switching divides a message into data units called packets. A packet of data is a standard unit, whose makeup is decided by the network protocol.

Typically, a data packet contains the following data items.

> **Packet switching** Packets of data are sent across a network. They may take different routes and are reassembled by the receiver.
>
> **Data packet** Data is broken down into chunks called packets when sent across a network.

Header				Payload	Trailer	
Source address	Destination address	Packet sequence number	Protocol	Data	Checksum	End of packet marker
(The IP address of the device the packet is from)	(The IP address of the device the packet is going to)	(The order of the packet in the sequence)	(The type of protocol being used)	(The data itself being sent)	(A calculation used for error checking)	(Denotes the end of the packet)

Packets are sent across a network by whichever routes are available or most efficient. They may arrive in a different order to which they were sent. The receiver uses the sequence number to reassemble them into the original message.

> **Exam tip**
>
> When communicating over a circuit switched network, computers will still usually use packets. Do not be led to the misconception that packets are only used with packet switching.

Packet switching doesn't tie up large chunks of a network, making it perform better for multiple users. It is also part of what helps to make the internet reliable. If one route is unavailable, there are always others. This is one of many examples of how redundancy can boost reliability.

> **Now test yourself** TESTED
>
> 28 Describe the purpose of the link layer in the TCP/IP model.
>
> 29 In question 27 (page 65) you found out about three protocols: HTTPS, DHCP and UDP. State which layer of the TCP/IP stack each of the protocols belongs to.
>
> 30 State two differences between a LAN and a WAN.
>
> 31 Produce a DNS hierarchy diagram that would accommodate the following URLs:
>   a) www.stanford.edu/
>   b) www.princeton.edu/BarkingDogArt
>   c) www.cmu.edu/
>   d) www.cam.ac.uk/
>   e) www.worcester.ac.uk/
>
> 32 Explain how packet switching benefits all users of a network.
>
> 33 Explain why a connection using circuit switching is likely to have a constant quality whereas one using packet switching may not.

Answers on p. 213–14

Network security and threats

Security is an important part of network design. Users of a network could potentially access data they aren't entitled to. If that network is connected to the outside world via the internet, it means it can be vulnerable to hacking by anyone around the world.

Firewalls

A firewall is used to protect a network by monitoring traffic going into and out of the network from the outside world.

Firewalls:
+ are usually hardware devices (especially on big networks) but can be implemented as a software application
+ inspect packets of data entering and leaving a network
+ can block these packets according to a set of rules
+ can be configured to restrict access to certain sites or file types.

Proxies

Just like a firewall, proxies (or proxy server) sits between a network and the internet. Initially their purpose was to allow all the computers on a LAN (with their different IP addresses) to communicate with the internet. Modern routers are now able to do this. Proxies are still used, however, as they have a number of other functions:
+ Caching: proxies can keep copies of data that has been downloaded from the internet. Once the proxy receives a request for a file or website from the internet, a copy is stored on the proxy. Every subsequent person who requests the same file can get their copy directly from the proxy. This is quicker for the users and keeps down the bandwidth being used on the internet connection. The downside is that the file or website on the proxy might get out of date.
+ Logging and monitoring traffic: like a firewall, a proxy can monitor data going into a network. They can keep logs of all traffic in and out.
+ Security: external users are unable to see or access devices inside the network – their only contact is with the proxy.
+ Privacy: proxies can be external to a network and used to fetch web pages. As far as the website is concerned, the request comes from the proxy and therefore it is the proxy's IP address that is logged on the website, not that of the user.

> **Making links**
>
> Proxy servers are one of many examples in computer science where caching is used. You can find out more about caching in Chapter 6.

Encryption

Encryption is the process of making data unreadable to a third party. It has to be decrypted (by someone with the key) in order to be read. Encryption is very important and it can be used in two ways on a network:
+ Stored data can be encrypted so it cannot be read by anyone who may gain unauthorised access to a private network. (This would usually be done using symmetric encryption.)
+ Data is often encrypted during transmission. This is especially important if transmission is taking place across public communications channels or using wireless technology. (This takes place using asymmetric encryption.)

> **Making links**
>
> Encryption was covered in more detail earlier in this chapter.

> **Hacking** The process of gaining unauthorised access to a computer system.
>
> **Firewall** Software or hardware that can inspect and block incoming and outgoing network data.
>
> **Proxy** A server that sits between a network and the internet, through which internet data requests are made.

3 Exchanging data

> **Now test yourself**
>
> 34 Describe the function of a firewall.
>
> **Answer on p. 214**
>
> TESTED

Network hardware

Specialist hardware has to be used to build a network.

Network interface card

+ A network interface card (NIC) allows a computer to connect to a network.
+ Most modern computers have the NIC built into the motherboard.
+ Depending on the type of NIC, it connects a computer to a network via the Ethernet protocol (a wired connection) or the Wi-Fi protocols (a wireless connection).

Router

+ This is a device to connect networks to the internet.
+ It receives and forwards data packets to the correct IP address.
+ When directing packets to the next device, it uses a table or an algorithm to decide on the route.

Hub

+ This device connects other devices together to form a network.
+ It broadcasts all data to all possible destinations.
+ The correct destination will accept the data.

Switches

+ This device connects other devices together to form a network.
+ It has a number of physical ports.
+ It keeps track of the addresses of devices connected to each port.
+ It directs data only through the port to which the destination device is connected.

Wireless access point

+ A device that is connected to a wired network and then provides a wireless signal.
+ Other devices can then use wireless to connect to a Wi-Fi network.
+ Devices can connect from distances of up to about 100 metres.

Transmission media

+ Most networks use cables to connect devices.
+ For short distances, copper cables are used as they are cheap to implement.
+ For longer distances, fibre optic is used as it carries signals across a greater distance and has a greater data capacity than copper wire.
+ Increasingly, wireless connections are made using radio waves for part of the network. This allows great flexibility but is slower than physical cable and poses different security threats.

Now test yourself

TESTED

35 Describe the purpose of a network interface card.

36 Explain the difference between a switch and a router.

37 Give one advantage and one disadvantage of a network using Wi-Fi.

Answers on p. 214

Client–server and peer to peer

Most networks are constructed on the client–server model. This means that one, or usually many, high-end computers act as servers. Servers provide services to the users, or clients, including:

+ file storage and access
+ printing
+ internet access
+ security features such as logins and audit trails.

Client–server is usually the favoured model because:

+ client computers need not be powerful and can therefore be cheaper
+ it makes it easier to make data and software accessible from anywhere in the network
+ banks of servers can be combined to make best use of their potential
+ separate functionality can be devolved to virtual servers or physical servers.

> **Virtual server** A server that exists as a virtual machine, rather than a physical device dedicated to the task.

Making links

See Chapter 2 for more information about virtual machines.

With a peer-to-peer approach, each computer on a network has an equal status.

+ It is generally a cheap way of implementing a network.
+ It is a popular way on the internet to pass files between users without the need to go through servers.
+ Peer to peer is a useful way to make use of distributed computing to promote collaborative working.
+ However, it is not a very common way to set up a network.

> **Distributed computing** A collection of computers working together on a single task.

Now test yourself

TESTED

38 In the early 2000s, peer-to-peer systems over the internet were a common way for illegally copied material to be spread. Discuss why such networks were hard to regulate.

39 Explain why most LANs favour a client–server model over peer to peer.

Answers on p. 214

Web technologies

HTML, CSS and JavaScript

HTML

Hypertext Markup Language, or HTML, is used to define web pages. It is not a programming language but, as the name suggests, a markup language.

HTML works with tags that are used to denote what parts of the page represent. Most tags have an opening tag (e.g. `<html>`) and a closing tag (e.g. `</html>`).

Tags can contain attributes that modify what the tag contained within them does. For example, in the tag `<img src="foo.jpg">`. `src` is an attribute.

The entirety of an HTML document is usually enclosed in `<html>` tags.

Within the HTML there is a `<head>` tag that stores information about the page and a `<body>` tag that contains the content of the page:

```
<html>
        <head>
        </head>
        <body>
        </body>
</html>
```

The title of the web page is usually stored within the head tags. This is the title of the page that appears in the browser.

```
<title>My Title</title>
```

The tags h1, h2 and h3 are used for different levels of heading.

```
<h1>This is a heading</h1>
<h2>This is a subheading</h2>
<h3>This is a level further down</h3>
```

This is a heading

This is a subheading

This is a level further down

Paragraphs are contained within the `<p>` tag.

```
<p>This is a paragraph in HTML</p>
```

The page can be divided into blocks using the `<div>` or divider tags.

```
<div>This is a divider</div>
```

Numbered lists are written using `<li>` tags. They are put between `<ol>` tags for an ordered (numbered) list.

```
<ol>
    <li>Apple</li>
    <li>Banana</li>
    <li>Cherry</li>
</ol>
```

1. Apple
2. Banana
3. Cherry

Bullet points are also written using `<li>` tags but between `<ul>` tags for an unordered (bulleted) list.

```
<ul>
    <li>Apple</li>
    <li>Banana</li>
    <li>Cherry</li>
</ul>
```

- Apple
- Banana
- Cherry

Check your understanding and progress at www.hoddereducation.co.uk/myrevisionnotesdownloads

Hyperlinks are created with the `<a>` (standing for anchor) tag. The attribute `href` defines where the link leads to.

```
<a href="https://www.hoddereducation.co.uk">Hodder Website</a>
```

<u>Hodder Website</u>

> **Exam tip**
>
> In the exam you may be asked to write some HTML or explain what some HTML does. The only way to get good at this is through practice. Try making a website for one of the topics you are revising.

Now test yourself

40 Describe the purpose of the `<div>` tag.

Answer on p. 214

TESTED

Images can be inserted with the `<img>` tag. Note that `<img>` does not have a closing tag. Images use the following attributes:
+ `src` to define where the image is stored
+ `alt` to state what text should display if the image cannot be shown
+ `height` and `width` to state the dimensions of the image on screen in pixels.

In this case, the image called myPicture.jpg is stored in the same folder as the web page:

```
<img src="myPicture.jpg" alt="A picture of me!" height="90" width="160">
```

Here the image myPicture.jpg is in a folder called images:

```
<img src="images/myPicture.jpg" alt="A picture of me!" height="90" width="160">
```

In both cases the image is associate with the text 'A picture of me!' and the images will be displayed as 90 pixels high by 160 pixels wide.

> **Making links**
>
> The majority of images on the web are JPEGs and PNG files. Photographs tend to be JPEGs due to the high levels of compression. Simpler images such as logos tend to be PNGs as they do not fare so well with JPEG's lossy process.
>
> Keeping image sizes low is important as less data needs to be transferred, meaning pages load more quickly.

Forms to collect data are created using the `<form>` tag. They contain `<input>` tags to allow data to be entered.

The input tag uses the `type` attribute to state what type of input it is. The only two types you need to know for the exam are `text` (for a textbox) and `submit` (for a submit button).

```
<form>

<p>Subject Name: <input type="text" name="subjectName"></p>

<p>Subject Code: <input type="text" name="subjectCode"></p>

<input type="submit">

</form>
```

The `name` attribute is also used so the inputs can be referred to in JavaScript or server-side code.

Cascading Style Sheets

Originally any formatting on a web page was denoted using HTML. A wide range of tags were used for setting fonts, colours and so on. It became apparent that it would be desirable to separate the styling of a web page from its structure. Cascading Style Sheets (CSSs) were created to take on the job of styling pages.

To specify a styling in CSS you need a property and a value.

The statement

```
color: red;
```

denotes that the colour of text should be red, where `color` is the property and `red` is the value.

You need to know the following CSS properties.

Property	Meaning	Example
`background-color`	Specifies the background colour of an element. Usually used on `<body>` tags to change the background colour of the whole page, or with `<div>` tags to change just part of it	`background-color: LightGreen;`
`border-color`	Specifies the colour of the border (borders tend to be used on div elements).	`border-color: DarkBlue;`
`border-style`	Specifies the style of a border. Options include: dotted, dashed and solid. If not specified, the border style is none by default and therefore no border is shown	`border-style: Dotted;`
`border-width`	Specifies the width of the border in pixels	`border-width: 3px;`
`color`	Specifies the colour of text within an element	`color: #2566A1;` `color: Green`
`font-family`	Specifies the font of the text. While the exact font can be specified, this relies on it being installed on the end-user's computer. Instead, or additionally, the 'family' name is often given so the nearest match can be selected if exact font is unavailable. (Examples of families include serif, sans-serif and monospace)	`font-family: monospace;`

`font-size`	Specifies the size of the font. Size can be given in a number of ways including:
	
	em: the number of times bigger it is than the standard font on the page
	
	px: pixels
	
	%: the percentage of the size it is of the standard font on the page
		`font-size: 3em;`
		`font-size: 11px;`
		`font-size: 150%`

`height`	Specifies the height of an element (usually a div). Usually given in pixels or as a percentage of the element it is within	`height: 500px;`
`width`	Specifies the width of an element (usually a div). Usually given in pixels or as a percentage of the element it is within	`width: 80%;`

Colours can be specified in a number of ways. The most common are named colours and hexadecimal colours.

Named colours are those that have been assigned a name in CSS. You use them by just writing their name. There are 140 standard colour names that are supported.

```
border-color: DarkRed;
```

Hexadecimal colours are made up of a red, green and blue value, each between 0 and 255. With each red, green and blue having 256 possible values (0–255) there are 16.7 million (256^3) colours.

For convenience, these numbers are written in hexadecimal (e.g. 255 is FF), each using two digits. A hash symbol (#) is used to denote a number is in hexadecimal. A full amount of red, green and blue is white (#FFFFFF) and the absence of any is black (#000000).

```
border-color: #E255B7;
```

Check your understanding and progress at **www.hoddereducation.co.uk/myrevisionnotesdownloads**

Examples of hexadecimal colours:

Colour	Hex value
Black	#000000
White	#FFFFFF
Pure Red	#FF0000
Pure Green	#00FF00
Pure Blue	#0000FF
Cyan	#00FFFF
Yellow	#FFFF00
Magenta	#FF00FF
Light Sea Green	#20B2AA
Dark Slate Blue	#483D8B
Grey	#808080
Dark Orange	#FF8C00

Exam tip

Remember that in CSS colour is spelt the American way as *color*.

Similarly, grey is spelt as *gray*.

Making links

See Chapter 4 for a full description of how hexadecimal numbers are calculated.

Exam tip

If asked to set a border, always include the style. Without the style it is assumed to have a style of none and as such nothing will show. If no style is hinted at in the question, then solid is a safe bet.

CSS can be applied directly within an HTML tag using the `style` attribute. For example:

```
<div style="color:red; background-color:gray;">
```

If a style is to be applied to all tags across a page this can be done using the tag name and curly braces {}. For example:

```
h1{
        color: darkblue;
        font-size: 2em;
}
```

This means all text in `<h1>` tags should be dark blue and twice the size of the standard text on the screen.

Sometimes you might only want to apply formatting to one particular tag on a page. To do this we use identifiers. Identifiers are denoted in CSS with the hash (#) sign followed by the name they are given.

```
#important{
        color: red;
        font-family: sans-serif;
}
```

To show which tags it is to be used on, the `id` attribute is used:

```
<h2 id="important">Warning</h2>
```

An identifier can only be used once per page. If you want to use the same formatting a number of times on a page, a class is used instead. Classes in CSS are denoted by a full stop (.) followed by the name they are given:

```
.sideNote{
        font-size: 0.8em;
        color:gray;
}
```

```
<div class="sideNote"> CSS is for styling and HTML is for
structure</div>
```

It is possible for a tag to have a class and an identifier.

```
<div class="sideNote" id="important">Client-side and should
never be used to try and enforce security.</div>
```

The text in this divider is 0.8 of the usual size (from the sidenote class) and in a sans-serif font (from the important id). As both try to define the colour, the colour from the id is used (red) as this is specific to only this tag so must be of a higher priority.

Any CSS that defines all instances of a tag, classes and identifiers can be embedded within an HTML page within the `<style>` tags. For example:

```
<style>

.sideNote{

        font-size: 0.8em;

        color:gray;

}

#important{

        color: red;

        font-family: sans-serif;

}

</style>
```

This is far more efficient than applying CSS to each HTML individually. However, larger websites have many separate pages of HTML. Instead of having to add CSS within `<style>` tags for each page, it is often preferable to store the CSS externally in a file, which can then be linked to the HTML using the `<link>` tag:

```
<link rel="stylesheet" href="myStyles.css">
```

This tag has two attributes:
+ `rel="stylesheet"` states that a stylesheet is being linked to
+ `href` gives the name/location of the style sheet, in this case `myStyles.css`

JavaScript

As stated earlier, HTML is not a programming language. If we want to program things to happen within a page (for example checking whether data being entered is valid), we need to use JavaScript.

JavaScript can be embedded within an HTML document using `<script>` `</script>` tags, or stored in a file and linked to using the `src` attribute in a script tag. For example:

```
<script src="validationCode.js"></script>
```

Below is the bubble sort algorithm written in pseudocode and then JavaScript:

Pseudocode

```
set swapMade to true

while swapMade is true

        swapMade = false

        for position = 0 TO listLength-2 //i.e. the last but one
        position

        if list[position] > list[position + 1] then

                temp = list[position]
```

> **Exam tip**
>
> When an HTML element has more than one CSS statement for the same property, remember the CSS more specific to that element will always override any more general CSS. CSS in a style attribute will override an identifier and an identifier will override a class. This is the *cascading* part of CSS.

> **Now test yourself**
>
> 41 Describe how CSS can be used to make a red, dashed border, 5 pixels thick.
>
> 42 Explain the difference between a class and an identifier.
>
> **Answers on p. 214**
>
> TESTED

Check your understanding and progress at **www.hoddereducation.co.uk/myrevisionnotesdownloads**

```
            list[position] = list[position + 1]

            list[position + 1] = temp

            swapMade = true

        endif

endwhile
```

JavaScript
```javascript
function bubbleSort(list)
{
   var swapMade = true;
   while(swapMade)
   {
      swapMade=false;
      for(var position=0; position<list.length-1; position++)
      {
         if(list[position]>list[position+1])
         {
            var temp = list[position];
            list[position] = list[position+1];
            list[position+1] = temp;
            swapMade = true;
         }

      }

   }
   return list
}


var myData = [4,7,1,3,9,8];
var sorted = bubbleSort(myData);
document.write(sorted);
```

It should be easy to equate most of the code to its pseudocode equivalents. It is worth taking a quick look at the for loop, especially if you are not familiar with languages that use this style.

```
for(var position = 0; position<list.length-1; position++)
```

`var position = 0;` start the for loop creating a variable called `position`, set to 0.

`position<list.length-1;` keep it running as long as position is less than the length of the list – 1

`position++;` add one to position each time. (`position++` is the same as `position = position+1`)

Getting data from the user in JavaScript is usually done via a form. You are not expected to know how to do this from memory in an exam.

Output can be given in three ways:

1 An alert box that pops up on the screen:
```
alert("This is an alert box");
```

2 Writing directly to the page. This appears on the page in the same location the JavaScript is written.
```
document.write("This is written directly to the web page");
```

3 Changing the contents of a tag. For this the tag needs an identifier. If we have the div:

`<div id="theTagID"> </div>`

Running the code below changes the contents of that div to `Written to element`:

`elementWeAreWritingIn = document.getElementById("theTagID");`

`elementWeAreWritingIn.innerHTML = "Written to element";`

This would result in a change to the HTML:

`<div id="theTagID">Written to element</div>`

This JavaScript code can be contracted to:

`document.getElementById("theTagID").innerHTML = "Written to element";`

> **Exam tips**
>
> You will be expected to carry out the same programming techniques in JavaScript as you can in pseudocode (`if`, `while`, `for` etc.). However, you will not be expected to remember the exact details of JavaScript syntax, and will not be penalised for minor inaccuracies in syntax.
>
> You will not be expected to use JavaScript for object-oriented programming or file handling.

> **Now test yourself** TESTED ◯
>
> 43 Explain the roles HTML, CSS and JavaScript play in web pages.
>
> 44 Look at the binary search algorithm in Chapter 8. Implement it in JavaScript.
>
> **Answers on p. 214**

Search engine indexing

REVISED ◯

The World Wide Web has grown at a phenomenal speed. Initially people used online directories as guides to which sites to visit but the number of websites on the web increased exponentially. There were under 3000 websites in 1994, over a quarter of a million in 1996 and nearly two and a half million by 1998. Today the number is in the billions. It quickly became apparent that using a directory approach wasn't sustainable and search engines were created.

Search engines work by creating an index of words that appear on pages. The index is not dissimilar to the one at the back of this book, but rather than storing page numbers it will store the address of the page the word appears on and its location on the page. They use programs called spiders (or web crawlers) that visit a web page and index the words that are on the page. They then follow one of the links on the page to go to the next page to be indexed. Occasionally they will jump to a random page to avoid getting trapped on a group of pages that only link to each other.

When a search term is entered, the search engine will look for pages that contain all the words entered.

> **Search engine** A website used to find other websites. Users type in search terms and are given lists of web pages that match them.
>
> **Spider/web crawler** A program that visits websites adding terms from them to a search engine's index.

> **Now test yourself** TESTED ◯
>
> 45 Describe what is meant by a search engine spider.
>
> 46 Explain how a search engine would determine whether a web page is about *computer mice* and not *field mice*.
>
> **Answers on p. 215**

PageRank algorithm

In the days before the Google search engine, finding things on the internet was a hit and miss affair. Search engines existed but they worked by using the content of a page to determine how relevant it was.

Stanford University students Larry Page and Sergey Brin invented an algorithm that takes a different approach. This PageRank algorithm was so successful they based their company, Google, around it. PageRank works by looking at the number of links pointing to a particular page and the number of links going out from it. A page with many links pointing to it is likely to be important, as people have taken the time to link to it. This is used to generate a weighting for a page, called its PageRank, which is used to order the pages returned by the search engine.

The algorithm is recursive; it uses the existing PageRank of pages as part of the calculation for their new PageRank. It continually updates the PageRank of pages, not only taking into account the number of inbound links but also the PageRank of the pages providing those links.

These days all search engines use variants of PageRank to determine the importance of pages.

The details of the PageRank algorithm are given below for reference. For the exam you only need to know the previously described principles of how it works – not the details:

$$PR(A) = (1 - d) + d\ (PR(T1)/C(T1) + ... + PR(Tn)/C(Tn))$$

where:

PR(A) is the PageRank of page A

PR(Ti) is the PageRank of pages Ti, which link to page A

C(Ti) is the number of outbound links on page Ti

d is a damping factor, which can be set between 0 and 1.

> **PageRank algorithm** An algorithm that determines the importance of web pages, taking into account the number of incoming links a page has and the PageRank of the pages those links come from.

Exam tips

You need to know the principles of the PageRank algorithm but not the equation.

When talking about indexing and PageRank it is easy, in an exam, to fall into the trap of talking about Google. Although Google pioneered many of these techniques and is by far the most used search engine, you must remember in an exam context you should always use generic names and not brand names. Therefore, always write about *search engines* and not *Google*.

Now test yourself

TESTED ◯

47 Describe the purpose of the PageRank algorithm.

48 Site A and Site B both have 30 sites linking to them. Explain why Site A might have a much higher PageRank than Site B.

Answers on p. 215

Server and client-side processing

REVISED ◯

With any interaction between a user (client) and a server on the internet, data can be processed at either end. Client-side processing is normally carried out by JavaScript code within the web browser.

The usual process when accessing a web page is:
1 The browser requests a page from the server.
2 The server runs its scripts (and often queries a database) to produce the web page to send back.

3 The browser receives the page from the server, renders the HTML and CSS and runs any client-side scripts as needed.

When using client-side processing:
+ web traffic is reduced
+ there are fewer delays as the server does less processing
+ data can be validated before being sent to the server.

However, client-side scripts can be turned off or amended by the user. Therefore, we also need server-side processing where:
+ scripts can access databases located on the server (it would be insecure to give this access to the client)
+ it must be guaranteed that a script will be run in the way intended and cannot be amended or circumvented by the client.

Now test yourself TESTED

49 Describe an advantage to website owners of using client-side scripting.

50 Describe a disadvantage to website owners of using client-side scripting.

Answers on p. 215

Summary

Compression, encryption and hashing
+ Compression is the process of representing files in such a way that they take up less storage space.
+ Lossy compression means some date is sacrificed, making it an inexact but good enough representation of the original.
+ Lossless compression means the original data is preserved perfectly in the compression process.
+ Lossy compression tends to produce better rates of compression.
+ Run-length encoding is one form of lossless compression where data is represented alongside how many times it consecutively occurs. For example, 4R3T in RLE is RRRRTTT
+ Dictionary coding is another form of lossless compression where frequently occurring values are stored in a dictionary and replaced with the smaller value they are linked to.
+ Encryption is the process of making data unreadable to a third party.
+ Data is encrypted by applying a key to an encryption algorithm.
+ Symmetric encryption means the same key is used to encrypt and decrypt data.
+ Asymmetric encryption uses a public key to encrypt data and a private key to decrypt it.
+ Hashing is the process of turning a piece of data into a fixed-size value.
+ A hashing algorithm should be irreversible, that is, it should not be possible to determine the input from the output of a hashing algorithm.
+ A hashing algorithm should be deterministic, that is, always give the same output for the same input.
+ It should be unlikely that two inputs, when hashed, give the same output.
+ Hashing is used for storing passwords and proving data has not been changed.

Databases
+ Databases are persistent organised stores of data.
+ They comprise fields, records and tables.
+ A flat-file database stores all data in a single table.
+ Relational databases store data in multiple tables linked by primary and foreign keys.
+ A primary key is a field that uniquely identifies a record.
+ A foreign key is the primary key of one table appearing in another to create a link.
+ A secondary key is a field that is indexed so it can be searched.
+ The structure of relational databases can be shown in entity relationship diagrams.
+ Entities can be linked with one-to-one, many-to-one and many-to-many relationships.
+ Data can be captured in a number of ways including manual entry, OCR and OMR.
+ Data can be exchanged using a number of file types including XML, CSV and JSON.
+ Normalisation is the process of removing redundant data from a database to ensure consistency and avoid redundant data.
+ First normal form ensures there is a primary key, no repeating fields and atomic data.
+ Second normal form ensures all fields depend on the whole of the key.
+ Third normal form ensures all fields depend only on the primary key.
+ Structured Query Language is a language used for manipulating data in databases.
+ SELECT ... FROM ... WHERE is used to extract data.
+ LIKE is used for matching fields with similar values.
+ DELETE is used to delete records.
+ INSERT is used to add new records.
+ DROP is used to remove tables.
+ JOIN combines data from two tables.
+ Comparison operators and Boolean operators AND and OR can be used with SQL statements.

Check your understanding and progress at **www.hoddereducation.co.uk/myrevisionnotesdownloads**

- Referential integrity is used to ensure that no record points to another that doesn't exist.
- Transactions should adhere to the ACID principles:
    - atomicity: either complete or fail, never half complete
    - consistency: they never move the database into an invalid state
    - isolation: never run alongside transactions that might affect it
    - durability: changes cannot be lost.
- Record locking prevents more than one person amending a record at any time.
- Redundancy in a database system is having an identical copy of the database that can be used if the first one fails.

Networks

- Protocols are rules for communication between devices. They allow devices to have an agreed way of communicating over a network.
- Protocols on a network are layered, allowing the protocol in each layer to be easily changed.
- Most modern networks use the Transmission Control Protocol/Internet Protocol (TCP/IP) stack comprising of the layers: application, transport, internet and link.
- Domain name system (DNS) is the system that looks up IP addresses matching the URLs of web pages.
- A local area network (LAN) is used to describe a network that extends over a small geographical area
- A wide area network (WAN) is used to describe a network that extends over a large geographical area, and is often comprises interconnected LANs.
- Circuit switching sets up a connection in advance, then data is sent across it.
- With packet switching, data is broken into packets and sent across a network. Packets may arrive out of order and are reassembled by the receiver.
- Networks have to be protected so unauthorised people cannot gain access.
- Firewalls sit on the edge of a network and filter traffic going to and from it and the internet.
- Proxies act as an intermediary between a network and the internet. They can be used for caching data downloaded from the internet so network users can access it locally.
- Sensitive data should be encrypted when being stored on or transferred across a network.
- Specialist hardware is needed to build a network. This includes: network interface cards, routers, hubs, switches, wireless access points and transmission media.
- Network connections are usually copper cable, wireless or fibre-optic cable.
- In the client–server model, devices are connected to servers that provide services such as files.
- In a peer-to-peer network all devices on the network share responsibility for services.

Web technologies

- Web pages are built using a combination of HTML, CSS and JavaScript.
- HTML specifies the structure of the page using tags.
- You need to understand the tags: `<html>`, `<link>`, `<head>`, `<title>`, `<body>`, `<h1>`, `<h2>`, `<h3>`, `<img`, `<a>`, `<div>`, `<form>`, `<input>`, `<p>`, `<ol>`, `<ul>`, `<li>`, `<script>`
- You need to understand the attributes: `src`, `alt`, `height`, `width`, `href`, `type="text"`, `type="submit"`
- CSS specifies the styling of a page.
- You need to understand the following CSS: `background-color`, `border-color`, `border-style`, `border-width`, `color`, `font-family`, `font-size`, `height`, `width`.
- CSS can be placed as an attribute in an HTML tag, within `<style>` tags or as an external .css file.
- Styling can be applied to types of tags, identifiers (e.g. #menu) and classes (e.g. .introbox).
- Identifiers can only be used once per page, whereas classes can be used multiple times.
- JavaScript is used for programming on a web page, allowing interactivity.
- It can be contained within `<script>` tags in a separate file.
- Search engines are indexes of words that appear on web pages, and use spiders/web crawlers to continually visit and index pages.
- The PageRank algorithm determines the order in which search engines return results.
- The PageRank algorithm estimates the importance of a page by counting the number of other pages that link to it, taking into account those pages' PageRank too.
- PageRank is a recursive algorithm.
- Processing can take place in the browser (client side) or on the server.
- Client-side processing reduces the strain on the server but can be circumvented by the user.

Exam practice

1. Describe how a file may be compressed with lossless compression techniques. [4]
2. Identify two situations where lossy compression is not acceptable. [2]
3. State the difference between symmetric and asymmetric encryption. [2]
4. Describe how hashing differs from encryption. [4]
5. Explain why it is preferable for a system to hash users' passwords rather than encrypting them. [4]
6. Discuss to what extent speed of execution is a desirable feature of a hashing algorithm. [4]
→

7   A veterinary practice needs a database to administer its clients and their animals, and has the following requirements:
    + store data about clients
    + store data about clients' pets
    + keep track of vaccinations given
    + allow reminders about when their pets' vaccinations are due to be sent to clients by text message.

    The database includes the following fields:
    + `Client_Name`
    + `Client_Address`
    + `Pet_Name`
    + `Pet_Date_of_Birth`
    + `Pet_Animal_Type`
    + `Vaccination_Type`

    a) Identify two fields in addition to those listed above that will be needed in order to fulfil fourth requirement.   [2]

    When in third normal form, the database includes the tables: `Client`, `Pet` and `Vaccination`.

    b) State what fields would be in the table `Client`.   [4]

    c) Produce an entity relationship diagram to show the structure of the normalised database. You may add any extra tables that are needed but shouldn't assume any data is required other than that needed for the stated requirements.   [6]

    d) Produce an SQL statement that would produce a list of clients in London who own dogs.   [4]

8   Explain the difference between redundant data in a table and a database system having redundancy.   [4]

9   Define the meaning of referential integrity.   [2]

10 **a)** In terms of a database, explain the term transaction.   [2]

    b) Explain where record locking might be needed in the performance of a database transaction.   [2]

11 Explain why having common sets of protocols is an advantage to computer users.   [3]

12 State the names of the layers of the TCP/IP model.   [4]

13 Describe the process DNS uses to point a browser to the IP address of a website when a user enters its URL.   [5]

14 Describe how packet switching is used to send a file across a network.   [5]

15 Explain how packet switching handles the possibility that the receiving device may receive packets out of order.   [3]

16 Discuss the precautions that can be taken to protect data on a network against unauthorised access.   [9]

17 Explain why data sent wirelessly needs to be encrypted.   [3]

18 List the hardware that would be needed to connect five stand-alone computers and a printer to a network.   [3]

19 Explain why it is easier to keep data secure on client–server model, rather than peer to peer.   [3]

20 Explain what role a CSS file has on a web page.   [4]

21 Describe the difference between the <ol> and <ul> HTML tags.   [2]

22 Write the CSS to make all text in <h2> tags green and in a sans-serif font.   [3]

23 SQL injection involves entering SQL into a field on a website to gain access to that website's database. Justify whether checks for SQL injection code should be carried out server side or client side.   [4]

24 Discuss what happens in a search engine when a user enters a search term.   [5]

25 Discuss how HTML, CSS and JavaScript can be used to improve the accessibility of a site.   [9]

Answers available online

4 Data types, data structures and algorithms

Data types

Different data types are stored and processed in different ways. This means we have to tell the computer what type data is so that appropriate facilities for processing and storing are made available.

Primitive data types

REVISED

The main data types we use are:

Type	Description	Example
Integer	Whole number values with no decimal part	6, –12, 9, 143
Real/floating point	Numbers with decimal or fractional parts	12.3, –18.63, 3.14
Boolean	One of two values	true or false
Character	Single letter, digit, symbol or control code	S, g, 7, &
String	A string of alphanumeric characters	'hat', 'Fg7tY6', '%7&*j'

Representing positive integers in binary

REVISED

+ Computers use switches (transistors) to store and process data and these switches have just two states, either 1 (on) or 0 (off). 1 and 0 are the two numbers in the binary number system.
+ This means that, in a computer, all data – numbers, characters, sounds and images – are represented in binary.
+ Denary is a base-10 number system whereas binary is a base-2 number system.
+ When we write a number in binary, we use a similar approach to writing numbers in denary but the column headings are based on 2 rather than 10.

> **Denary** A term that describes the number system based on 10, often called decimal.

Starting on the right with the 1s column, as we move left through the columns the place value of each column is multiplied by 2 each time:

$128 = 2^8$	$64 = 2^6$	$32 = 2^5$	$16 = 2^4$	$8 = 2^3$	$4 = 2^2$	$2 = 2^1$	$1 = 2^0$

The conversion from binary to denary is straightforward: add the column values together for every column containing a 1 in the binary number.

> **Worked example**
>
> The binary number 1101101 in denary.
>
> | 128 | 64 | 32 | 16 | 8 | 4 | 2 | 1 |
> |-----|-----|-----|-----|-----|-----|-----|-----|
> | | 1 | 1 | 0 | 1 | 1 | 0 | 1 |
>
> We write down the column value for each column with a 1 in it then add them up.
>
> 64 + 32 + 8 + 4 + 1 = 109

To convert an integer from denary to binary:

✦ For each column value, starting with the most significant bit (MSB), we decide if it is smaller than or equal to our decimal number.
✦ If it is smaller or equal to, we record 1 in the table, and subtract that column value from the original decimal number. We then check if that new number is smaller than the next column value.
✦ If it is not smaller, we check the new decimal number against the next column and so on.

We continue this process until we are left with the 1s column.

> **Most significant bit (MSB)** The bit position in a binary number having the greatest value, or the left-most bit. For an 8-bit binary number this will be the left-most bit with value 128.

Worked example

To convert 97 into binary:

Is 128 smaller than 97? No, so we record 0 in the 128 column.

128	64	32	16	8	4	2	1
0							

Is 64 smaller than 97? Yes, so we record 1 in the 64 column and subtract 64 from 97.

The new number is 97 − 64 = 33

128	64	32	16	8	4	2	1
0	1						

Is 32 smaller than 33? Yes, so we record 1 in the 32 column and subtract 32 from 33.

The new number is 1

128	64	32	16	8	4	2	1
0	1	1					

We now check against 16, 8, 4 and 2 and record 0 in each of those columns.

128	64	32	16	8	4	2	1
0	1	1	0	0	0	0	

We are left with 1 so we record 1 in the 1 column.

128	64	32	16	8	4	2	1
0	1	1	0	0	0	0	1

We do not need to write down the leading 0s so 97 in decimal is 1100001 in binary.

> **Exam tips**
>
> Check your answer by converting the binary back to decimal – in this case 64 + 32 + 1 = 97.
>
> With practice you will be easily able to do this in your head, but if there are marks for working show the key stages, and *always* check your answer.

Now test yourself

TESTED ◯

1 Convert the following binary numbers to denary:
   a) 10000010
   b) 11000001
   c) 11011000
   d) 10110

2 Convert the following denary numbers to 8-bit binary values:
   a) 140
   b) 68
   c) 200
   d) 148

Answers on p. 215

Check your understanding and progress at **www.hoddereducation.co.uk/myrevisionnotesdownloads**

Representing negative numbers in binary

Sign and magnitude

This approach follows the convention we use to represent negative denary numbers: a sign, '+' or '–' followed by the number (or magnitude).

To do this we have to use the MSB to indicate the sign:
+ a '0' represents a '+'
+ a '1' represents a '–'.

> **Magnitude** Refers to the size of a value and does not take into account the sign, for example the magnitude of both 15 and –15 is 15.

This changes the headings for our columns in an 8-bit binary number to:

sign	64	32	16	8	4	2	1

Worked example

Write –29 and +33 in denary in sign and magnitude binary.
+ To store –29 as a sign and magnitude binary number in 8 bits:
  1 set the sign bit to 1 to represent '–'
  2 store the binary equivalent of 29 in the remaining 7 bits.

sign	64	32	16	8	4	2	1
1	0	0	1	1	1	0	1

+ To store + 33 as a sign and magnitude binary number in 8 bits:
  + set the sign bit to 0 to represent '+'
  + store the binary equivalent of 33 in the remaining 7 bits.

sign	64	32	16	8	4	2	1
0	0	1	0	0	0	0	1

Now test yourself

TESTED

3 How would we store the following denary values in sign and magnitude format in 8-bits?
   a) 45
   b) 125
   c) –125
   d) –68

Answers on p. 215

Two's complement

+ While we are used to dealing with a sign and a magnitude, the processing to handle this is quite complex for a computer.
+ A more effective approach is two's complement.
+ In the two's complement approach, instead of storing a sign bit in the MSB, we store a negative value equivalent to the magnitude of that column. In 8 bits the MSB would be equivalent to –128.

This changes the headings for our columns in an 8-bit binary number to:

–128	64	32	16	8	4	2	1

Worked example

Write –37 in denary in two's complement binary.
+ To store –37, we store a 1 in the MSB, representing –128, then we add the positive value to represent the difference between –128 and –37 into the remaining 7 bits.

1   128 – 37 = 91
2   91 in binary is 1011011
3   hence, –37 in two's complement is:

–128	64	32	16	8	4	2	1
1	1	0	1	1	0	1	1

To store a positive integer we put a 0 in the MSB and store the number in the remaining 7 bits.

Worked example

55 stored in 8 bits in two's complement form is:

–128	64	32	16	8	4	2	1
0	0	1	1	0	1	1	1

There is a method for converting a negative integer into two's complement form.

For an 8-bit number:
1   write down the magnitude of the number in binary (including leading 0s)
2   change all the 0s to1s and all the 1s to 0s (1's complement)
3   add 1.

1's complement A simple process for a computer: it simply turns all 1s to 0s and 0s to 1s.

Worked example

To convert –87 to two's complement form in 8 bits:

The magnitude of –87 =	87
87 in 8-bit binary =	01010111
1's complement of 87 =	10101000
Add 1in binary =	10101001

Now check the answer:

–128 + 32 + 8 + 1 = –87 ✓

So, –87 in two's complement in 8 bits is: 10101001

Now test yourself   TESTED

4   Convert the following denary numbers to 8-bit two's complement binary values:
    a) 56
    b) –72
    c) –3
    d) –80
5   Convert the following two's complement 8-bit binary values to denary:
    a) 00101000
    b) 10111100
    c) 11001111
    d) 10000111

Answers on p. 215

Check your understanding and progress at **www.hoddereducation.co.uk/myrevisionnotesdownloads**

Addition

Adding binary numbers is similar to adding in denary.

When we add 1s together we generate a carry to the next column.

There are four possibilities:

Sum	Write down	Carry to the next column
0 + 0	0	none
1 + 0	1	none
1 + 1	0	1
1 + 1 + 1	1	1

Worked example

1011 + 1111

```
        1    1    1    1
  +     1    1    0    1
      1 1    1    0    0
      1 1    1    1
```

So 1111 + 1101 = 11100

Check by converting back to denary

15 + 13 = 28 ✓

> **Exam tip**
>
> It is always worth taking a few moments to check the result of the binary addition by converting it to denary.

Another example using 8-bit binary numbers.

Worked example

11010101 + 11101001

```
      1   1   0   1   0   1   0   1
  +   1   1   1   0   1   0   0   1
      1   0   1   1   1   1   1   0
  1   1                   1
```

We have a carry into the ninth column, but we can only represent 8 bits, so it is lost.

+ The result will not fit into 8 bits.
+ This is called overflow and means the result will be incorrect.

Converting to denary, using the 8 bits available, we get 213 + 233 = 190, which is clearly incorrect.

+ Overflow errors can generate further logical errors in a program because the result is not as expected.
+ This may lead to incorrect results from the program.
+ The program may crash if it cannot deal with the overflow digit.

> **Now test yourself**
>
> 6 Complete the following binary additions:
> a) 110011 + 11101
> b) 100010 + 100111
> c) 111000 + 11110
> d) 111011 + 101010
>
> **Answers on p. 215**
>
> TESTED ⬤

Subtraction

Subtracting numbers is also similar to the way we subtract in denary. With base 10 if the number we are subtracting from is smaller than the number we are subtracting, we borrow 10 from the next column:

Worked example

What is 135 – 47?

		~~12~~	15	We borrow 10 from the next column
		2		We now need to borrow another 10
~~1~~	~~3~~	~~5~~	
–	4	7	
	8	8	

In binary subtractions we use exactly the same approach but, if required, we borrow 10 from the next column, remembering 10 in binary is 2 in denary.

Worked example

What is 46 – 11 in binary?

46 in binary is 101110

11 in binary is 1011

				0	1	10	We borrow 10 from the next column
					~~10~~		Now this is 0 we borrow 10 again
	1	0	1	~~1~~	~~1~~	~~0~~	
–			1	0	1	1	
	1	0	0	0	1	1	

Check: 46 – 11 = 35 ✓

Now test yourself
TESTED ◯

7 Complete the following binary subtractions:
   a) 11010 – 100
   b) 10010 – 1111
   c) 11001 – 10101

Answers on p. 215

Adding and subtracting using two's complement

Addition
Adding two's complement numbers follows the same process as adding together non-signed integers.

Worked example

0	0	1	1	0	0	1	0
0	0	1	0	0	0	0	1
0	1	0	1	0	0	1	1
	1						

Now check the result

110010 = 32 + 16 + 2 = 50

100001 = 32 + 1 = 33

1010011 = 64 + 16 + 2 + 1 = 83 ✓

Adding two large numbers illustrates a problem with overflow.

Worked example

Using 8-bit, two's complement binary, add 01100010 and 01110001

```
0  1  1  0  0  0  1  0
0  1  1  1  0  0  0  1
1  1  0  1  0  0  1  1
1  1
```

Now check the result:

01100010 = 64 + 32 + 2 = 98

01110001 = 64 + 32 + 16 + 1 = 113

98 + 113 = 211

11010011 is a two's complement number so = –128 + 64 + 16 + 2 + 1 = –45 ✘

The result of the calculation is too large to be stored in an 8-bit two's complement number and it has caused **overflow**.

> **Overflow** When a calculation produces a result that is too large to be represented accurately in the available space.

Subtraction

We can use two's complement to subtract one binary integer from another.
1 Write the number to be subtracted and calculate its two's complement form.
2 Add the two numbers together.

This is similar to saying 56 – 23 is the same as 56 + (–23).

Taking the two's complement of a binary number gives the negative of the original number.

Worked example

In binary, what is 01010111 – 00110001?

Number to be subtracted (49 in denary):	`0 0 1 1 0 0 0 1`
1's complement: Change 1s to 0s and 0s to 1s	`1 1 0 0 1 1 1 0`
Add 1 to create the two's complement form (–49 in denary):	`1 1 0 0 1 1 1 1`
Add the number we were subtracting from (87 in denary)	`+ 0 1 0 1 0 1 1 1`

```
(1) 0 0 1 0 0 1 1 0
 1          1 1 1 1
```

When using this method we ignore the overflow to get the result:

01010111 – 00110001 = 00100110

00100110 is 38 in denary.

Check 87 – 49 = 38 ✓

Note we can ignore the overflow when using this approach to subtracting binary values, but in general overflows should be considered when carrying out a calculation.

> **Least significant bit (LSB)** The smallest value bit in the number, or the right-most bit.

Representing positive integers in hexadecimal and converting to binary and denary

Hexadecimal (hex) is a base 16 number system, commonly used by programmers working with low-level code or with codes for various types of data, for example when coding in HTML the code for the colour orange is FFA500.

Hex We often use the shorter form to describe hexadecimal.

+ Computers do not work in hexadecimal but it provides a shorthand for binary that is simpler to understand and remember.
+ For example, it is hard to remember and easy to make a mistake entering the binary number 1100111000110001101.
+ However the hexadecimal equivalent, CE38D, is much easier to remember and less likely to be entered incorrectly.
+ Hexadecimal is convenient because the base is 16 and $16 = 2^4$. This means one hexadecimal digit can represent a 4-bit binary number, making direct conversion between binary and hexadecimal easy.
+ Hexadecimal is based on 16 and we therefore need 16 symbols to represent the possible values in each column. We use 0–9 for the first ten then A, B, C, D, E and F to represent 10, 11, 12, 13, 14 and 15.

Denary	Binary	Hex	Denary	Binary	Hex
0	0000	0	8	1000	8
1	0001	1	9	1001	9
2	0010	2	10	1010	A
3	0011	3	11	1011	B
4	0100	4	12	1100	C
5	0101	5	13	1101	D
6	0110	6	14	1110	E
7	0111	7	15	1111	F

+ Converting from binary to hexadecimal simply requires each group of 4 bits to be replaced by the equivalent hexadecimal symbol.
+ Converting from hexadecimal to binary, each symbol is replaced by the corresponding group of 4 bits.
+ For example, B7D in hexadecimal is 1011 0111 1101 in binary.

Exam tip

With practice you will recognise the binary equivalent of the hex symbols, but it can be easier to convert the hex to denary then convert to binary.

Converting hexadecimal to denary

To convert a hex number to its denary equivalent, we multiply each hex digit by its column value.

Worked example

Converting B7D in hex into denary:

Column value	$16^2 = 256$	$16^1 = 16$	$16^0 = 1$
	B = 11	7	D = 12

So B7D in denary is

11 * 256 + 7 * 16 + 12 = 2941

TESTED ○

Now test yourself

8 Convert the following denary values to hexadecimal:
   a) 26
   b) 92
   c) 175

9 Convert the following hexadecimal numbers to binary:
   a) ABC
   b) A5D
   c) BBC3

10 Convert the following hexadecimal numbers to denary:
   a) A5
   b) 5F
   c) 2DE

11 Convert the following binary numbers to hexadecimal:
   a) 10000011
   b) 11000111
   c) 11101101

Answers on p. 215

Representation and normalisation of floating-point numbers in binary

REVISED ○

+ Floating point is a similar concept to standard form as used in science and mathematics.
+ In standard form, we represent numbers as a decimal fraction raised to a power of 10. For example, $1.236 * 10^2$ to represent 123.6.
+ The decimal point 'floats' two places to the right in the number to convert from standard form to standard decimal form.
+ In floating point we use a binary fraction multiplied by a power of 2

Worked example

Consider the binary floating-point number $0.101 * 2^{11}$

Converting the exponent to denary, this is the same as $0.101 * 2^3$

To write this without the exponent, we float the binary point three places to the right to get 101.0

Which is 5 in denary.

In floating-point representation we use a mantissa, the fractional representation of the number, and an exponent, the binary power to which the number must be raised.

The mantissa is a binary fraction stored in two's complement form. The MSB is –1 and the remaining bits are positive fractional values starting at ½ and divided by 2 for each column as we move right.

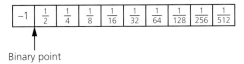

Binary point

> **Mantissa** The part of the floating-point number that represents the significant digits of the number.
>
> **Exponent** The power of two to which the number in the mantissa must be raised; the number of places the binary point should be moved.

The exponent is a two's complement integer. For example, with a 6-bit exponent it would be:

–32	16	8	4	2	1

91

Worked example

Using a 10-bit mantissa and a 6-bit exponent:

The binary floating-point number 0110100000 000010

Is the same as $0.110100000 * 2^2$

The binary point is after the first digit in the mantissa in floating-point form.

Move the binary point 2 places to the right to get

−4	2	1	$\frac{1}{2}$	$\frac{1}{4}$
0	1	1 •	0	1

which is 11.01 in binary or 3.25 in denary.

Worked example

The binary floating-point number 0110000000 111111

Is the same as $0.11 * 2^{-1}$

Move the binary point 1 place to the left to get

0.011 or 0.375 in denary.

If the first bit of the mantissa is 1, then it is a negative number.

To deal with this, we use the technique from earlier in the chapter to switch between a two's complement form and an unsigned magnitude:

1 take a 1s complement
2 add 1 – this gives the magnitude of the original negative number
3 we then adjust the number by floating the binary point the number of places indicated by the exponent.

We then convert the result back to a negative number.

Worked example

Convert this binary number to denary.

The number is a binary floating-point number using a 10-bit mantissa and a 6-bit 2's complement exponent.

1010100000 000011

We consider first the magnitude of the mantissa by:

taking the 1's complement	0101011111
adding 1	0101100000

Now adjust for the exponent, 11 in binary, by moving the binary point three places to the right.

We get the value 0101.100000

This is the magnitude of the negative value 5.5 in denary, so we now know that:

1010100000 000011 is equal to −5.5 in denary.

We can check this by adjusting the original mantissa according to the exponent : 1010.100000

Using the place values, the denary equivalent is −8 + 2 + .5 = −5.5

Exam tip

These examples use 10-bit mantissa and 6-bit exponent, both in two's complement, but check carefully the format used in the question, it may not be the same.

Now test yourself

TESTED ◯

12 Using an 8-bit floating point number with 5-bit mantissa and 3-bit exponent in two's complement form:
   a) Convert 01010 001 to denary
   b) Convert 10110 010 to denary
   c) Convert 01100 111 to denary

13 Using a 16-bit floating point number with 10-bit mantissa and 6-bit exponent in two's complement form:
   a) Convert 0101100000 000011 to denary
   b) Convert 1011000000 111111 to denary
   c) Convert 1100000000 111110 to denary

Answers on p. 215

Normalisation of floating-point numbers

With floating-point numbers there is a balance between accuracy and range.

✚ More bits for the mantissa improves the accuracy of the representation but reduces the range of values that can be represented.

✚ More bits for the exponent improves the range of values but reduces the accuracy of the value represented.

In order to improve the accuracy, the mantissa should not waste bits by having redundant digits at the start of a value.

✚ For a positive mantissa, after the leading 0, the mantissa is floated so that this 0 is followed by a 1.

✚ For a negative mantissa, after the leading 1, the mantissa is floated so that this 1 is followed by a 0.

✚ This is done by adjusting the exponent.

✚ Once the binary point is floated to the right place:
   ✚ positive mantissas are padded with 0s
   ✚ negative mantissas are padded with 1s.

Worked example

Convert the binary fraction 0.0011 into floating-point form using an 8-bit floating point with 5 bits for the mantissa and 3 bits for the exponent.

For the binary fraction 0.0011 we need to float the binary point two places to the right so need an exponent of −2.

In 3-bit two's complement −2 is represented by 110 (−4 + 2)

0.0011 is written as 0.1100 110 in normalised floating-point form.

Exam tip

A normalised floating-point number will always start with either 01 or 10. This means you will be able to recognise immediately if the number is positive or negative before starting the calculation. It also provides an instant check on the sign of the calculated result.

In order to convert a positive denary number into binary floating-point form, we need to convert the denary number to an equivalent binary fraction.

It is important this binary fraction is normalised by floating the binary point to be in front of the leading 1. Remember, a positive floating-point number will start 01.

Worked example

Convert the denary number 5.5 into normalised floating-point form using a 10-bit mantissa and 6-bit exponent.

5.5 in binary is 101.1000000

To normalise, float the binary point to remove the leading 1s in the mantissa.

0.101100000

The binary point has moved three places to the left, so the exponent is 3 or 000011 in 6-bit binary.

The mantissa is 0.1011000000

The exponent is 000011

Converting negative denary numbers to binary floating point is similar to converting positive denary numbers.

+ We convert the magnitude of the denary fraction to a binary fraction and convert to a negative value using 1's complement and adding 1.
+ In the case of a negative number, float the binary point to just before the first 0.
+ In order to normalise a negative value, we need to remove the leading 1s so that the number starts 10.

Worked example

Represent the negative decimal fraction −0.1875 in normalised floating-point form using a 10-bit mantissa and a 6-bit exponent.

0.1875 in binary: 0.001100000 (See the exam tip below for how to do this.)

1's complement: 1.110011111

Add 1 to LSB to get −0.1875:   1.110100000

To normalise, float the binary point to just before the first 0 and remove the leading 1s in the mantissa.

1.010000000

To find the exponent, we count how many places we have moved the binary point, in this case two places to the right so −2.

For the exponent −2

2 in 6-bit binary is 000010

1's complement   111101

Add 1 to LSB   111110

The exponent is 111110

The mantissa is 1.010000000

The exponent is 111110

−0.1875 in floating-point binary is 1010000000 111110

> **Exam tip**
>
> If you cannot immediately see what 0.1875 is in binary there is a simple method.
>
> Repeatedly multiply by 2 until it becomes a whole number.
>
> 0.1875 * 2 = 0.375
>
> 0.375 * 2 = 0.75
>
> 0.75 * 2 = 1.5
>
> 1.5 * 2 = 3
>
> 3 in binary is 11
>
> We have multiplied by 2, 4 times.
>
> Hence, we move the binary point four places to the left:
>
> 0.0011 = 0.1875 in denary.

Now test yourself

 TESTED

14 Using a 16-bit floating-point number with 10 bit mantissa and 6-bit exponent in two's complement form.

Represent the following denary values in normalised floating-point form:

a) 1.625

b) −2.5

c) 0.1875

Answers on p. 215

Floating-point arithmetic

REVISED

When adding and subtracting floating-point numbers we align the decimal point before making the calculation.

Worked example

Using a 16-bit number with a 10-bit mantissa and a 6-bit exponent, add the following two numbers: 0110000000 000010 + 0101000000 000001

For 0110000000 000010 the exponent is 2, so we move the binary point two places to the right:

011.0000000

For 0101000000 000001 the exponent is 1 so we move the binary point one place to the right:

01.01000000

Add

    011.0000000
    +01.0100000
    ‾‾‾‾‾‾‾‾‾‾‾
    100.0100000

To normalise the result, we need to move the binary point three places to the left, so the exponent is 000011

The result is 0100010000 000011

Check 3 + 1.25 = 4.25 ✓

For subtraction, we can use the same approach as for two's complement integers.

Worked example

Subtract the following two numbers:

0111000000 000011 – 0101100000 000010

Number to subtract has exponent 2 so we move the binary point two places.

	010.1100000
1's complement	101.0011111
Add 1 to LSB	101.0100000

Number to subtract from has exponent 3 so we move the binary point three places:

111.000000

Number to subtract	101.0100000
First number	111.0000000
Add and ignore overflow (1)	100.0100000

Normalise: move binary point three places to the left so exponent is 3, or 000011 in binary.

Result:

0111000000 000011 – 0101100000 0000010 = 01000100000 000011

Check your answer:

111.0 = 7

10.11 = 2.75

7 – 2.75 = 4.25

4.25 = 100.01 in binary or 0100010000 000011 in normalised floating-point ✓

Exam tip

Remember, always convert back to denary to check your answer.

Now test yourself

TESTED ◯

15 Using 8-bit floating point with a 5-bit mantissa and 3-bit exponent in two's complement form, complete the following calculations:
   a) 01100 001 + 01000 010
   b) 01000 111 + 01100 001
   c) 01101 010 – 01010 001

16 Using 16-bit floating-point with a 10-bit mantissa and a 6-bit exponent in two's complement form. Complete the following calculations:
   a) 0101000000 000010 + 0100100000 000001
   b) 0110100000 000011 + 0110000000 111111
   c) 0111000000 000010 – 0101000000 000001

Answers on p. 215

Exam tip

Working with long sequences of 0s or 1s, it is easy to miss a digit or add an extra digit. One simple check is to count the number of digits in each step of the process.

Check your understanding and progress at **www.hoddereducation.co.uk/myrevisionnotesdownloads**

Bitwise manipulation and masks: shifts, combining with AND, OR and XOR

Binary shifts

+ Moving the binary digits to the left or right is called a **binary shift**.
+ Moving to the left multiplies the value by 2 for each place the value is shifted.
+ Moving to the right divides the number by 2 for each place the value is shifted.

Shifting the binary point to the left:

> **Worked example**
>
> Starting with the binary number 10110
>
> 10110 has the denary value 22
>
> | 128 | 64 | 32 | 16 | 8 | 4 | 2 | 1 |
> |-----|----|----|----|---|---|---|---|
> | | | 1 | 0 | 1 | 1 | 0 | |
>
> If we shift the number one place to the left we get:
>
> | 128 | 64 | 32 | 16 | 8 | 4 | 2 | 1 |
> |-----|----|----|----|---|---|---|---|
> | | | 1 | 0 | 1 | 1 | 0 | 0 |
>
> The equivalent denary value is now 44, that is, multiplied by 2.
>
> If we shift two places to the left we get:
>
> | 128 | 64 | 32 | 16 | 8 | 4 | 2 | 1 |
> |-----|----|----|----|---|---|---|---|
> | | 1 | 0 | 1 | 1 | 0 | 0 | 0 |
>
> Which has the denary value 88, that is, the original number multiplied by 4 or 2^2.
> + Shifting left n places multiplies the number by 2^n.
> + If we shift too far to the left, we eventually need a ninth bit to store the 1 in the MSB.
> + The number cannot be stored in the available bits, creating an overflow error.

Shifting the binary point to the right:

> **Worked example**
>
> Starting with the same number, 10110
>
> | 128 | 64 | 32 | 16 | 8 | 4 | 2 | 1 |
> |-----|----|----|----|---|---|---|---|
> | | | | 1 | 0 | 1 | 1 | 0 |
>
> Shifting one place to the right we get:
>
> | 128 | 64 | 32 | 16 | 8 | 4 | 2 | 1 |
> |-----|----|----|----|---|---|---|---|
> | | | | | 1 | 0 | 1 | 1 |
>
> The denary value is now 11, that is, 22 divided by 2.
>
> If we shift the number two places to the right, however, we have a problem – we lose a 1.

128	64	32	16	8	4	2	1
					1	0	1

The new value is 5 but 11 / 2 = 5.5

We have lost some information, which has led to a lack of precision.

Shifting the number so that we lose a 1 causes an error.

+ Shifting too far to the left when the MSB is a 1 means that we lose that 1 and we have an overflow error.
+ Shifting too far to the right when the LSB is a 1 means that we lose that 1 and we have a lack of precision.

Logical operators (NOT, OR, AND, XOR) and masks

The ALU can perform bitwise operations using the standard logical operators, NOT, AND, OR and XOR.

NOT is applied to each bit in the binary number to reverse the value of that bit.

> **Bitwise operation** A binary operation that takes two bit patterns of equal length and performs a logical operation on each pair of corresponding bits.

Worked example

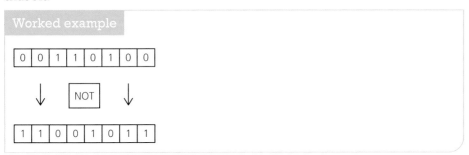

For AND, OR and XOR the operation is applied to matching bits in two binary numbers, the operand and the mask, to determine each bit in the resultant binary value.

> **Operand** The bit pattern being 'operated' on.
>
> **Mask** A bit pattern that is used with the operand. The corresponding bits in the operand and mask are combined using a logical operator to produce a result.

Worked example

Operand	0	0	1	1	0	1	0	0
Mask	1	1	1	1	0	0	0	0
AND	0	0	1	1	0	0	0	0

Operand	0	0	1	1	0	1	0	0
Mask	1	1	1	1	0	0	0	0
OR	1	1	1	1	0	1	0	0

Operand	0	0	1	1	0	1	0	0
Mask	1	1	1	1	0	0	0	0
XOR	1	1	0	0	0	1	0	0

Check your understanding and progress at **www.hoddereducation.co.uk/myrevisionnotesdownloads**

Masking is a very important concept that allows the CPU to manipulate individual bits in the operand, check for values and allow bits through or block them.

✚ AND is useful for checking conditions stored in a binary value:
  ✚ masking with a 1 returns the operand bit value
  ✚ masking with a 0 excludes the operand bit.
✚ OR can reset individual bits in a binary value:
  ✚ masking with 1 will always set the returned bit to 1
  ✚ masking with 0 returns the original operand bit value.
✚ XOR can be used to check whether the corresponding bits in the operand and mask are the same:
  ✚ if both mask and operand are the same, it returns 0
  ✚ if mask and operand are different, it returns 1.

Now test yourself   TESTED ◯

17 Using the operand 00110110, mask this with 10101010 using AND, OR and XOR.

18 Create a mask to reverse the first, fourth and last digits of an operand. State which logical operand is required.

19 Create a mask to check whether the second, fifth and last bits of an operand are set to 1. State which logical operation is required.

Answers on p. 215

How character sets (ASCII and UNICODE) are used to represent text

REVISED ◯

✚ Each character used by a computer has a unique binary code.
✚ This code is used to identify and display a character on screen or for printing.
✚ It is important for systems to agree on these codes and their meanings if the data is to make any sense.
✚ The character set of a computer is all the characters that are available to it.
✚ The number of characters in the character set depends upon how many characters can be represented by the associated codes.
✚ There are agreed international standards that are used to represent the character set for a computer system.

The first agreed standard was based on contextual messages in English with a limited number of extra symbols.

ASCII

The American Standards Association agreed a set of codes to represent the main characters used in English. This is called the American Standard Code for Information Interchange (ASCII). This system was designed to provide codes for the following:

All the main characters, i.e. 26 upper case and 26 lower case	52 characters
All the numeric symbols, 0–9	10 characters
32 punctuation and other symbols plus 'space'	33 characters
32 non-printable control codes	32 characters

In total this is 127 characters, or in binary 1111111 (7 bits). Initially, the ASCII character set used 127 codes for the characters, with 0 meaning 'no character'. This gave a total of 128 characters.

One additional bit was used for error checking purposes. This meant there were 8 bits overall, and that each character required one byte.

Some ASCII codes are:

Binary	Hex	Denary	Character
0100000	20	32	'space'
1000001	41	65	A
1000010	42	66	B
1000011	43	67	C
1100001	61	97	a
1111001	79	121	y
1111010	7A	122	z
1111111	7F	127	'delete'

Wider use of computers, and the need for many more languages and other symbols, has led to the development of more advanced coding standards for character sets.

Extended ASCII

As the need for more characters became necessary, including non-English characters and mathematical symbols, the extended ASCII set used the full 8 bits in the byte to represent another 128 characters, making the available character set 256, rather than the original ASCII limit of 128.

Unicode

+ Unicode was developed to use 16 bits rather than a single byte. This provided the ability to store 2^{16} or 65 536 unique characters.
+ Later developments of Unicode use more bits to represent billions of different characters including graphical symbols and emojis.
+ To ensure compatibility of all of these systems, the original ASCII and extended ASCII character codes are the same in Unicode. ASCII is considered a subset of Unicode.

If the list of animals:
+ Goat, Bear, ape, Zebra, deer

is sorted using ASCII the result will be:
+ Bear, Goat, Zebra, ape, deer

This is because the ASCII codes for the main alphabetic characters are allocated to the upper-case characters in sequence, followed by the lower-case characters in sequence. A is 65 and B is one more at 66 and so on. Lower-case characters start with a as 97, and this means that when text is sorted Z comes before a.

Character set	Number of bits	Number of characters	Examples
ASCII	7	128	Upper and lower case, numbers, punctuation, some control characters
Extended ASCII	8	256	As above plus non-English characters and mathematical symbols
Unicode	16/32 bits	65000 or over 4 billion + are possible but for technical reasons there are just over 1.1 million characters available	As above plus all known language characters and different characters including Wingdings and emojis

Check your understanding and progress at www.hoddereducation.co.uk/myrevisionnotesdownloads

Now test yourself

TESTED ◯

20 Using the table of ASCII values above:
  a) What is the ASCII value for the characters:
    i)   D
    ii) G
    iii) d
  b) What is the character with ASCII value:
    i)   69
    ii) 120
    iii) 100

Answers on p. 215

Data structures

Arrays, records, lists and tuples

REVISED ◯

Arrays

Arrays are structures that store data using indices.

When solving problems with lots of variables describing similar things, rather than create these individually we assign the values to an array.

An array:
+ holds a fixed number of elements; the size is defined as the scope when the array is created
+ can only hold data of the same type
+ uses a single identifier and an index.

> **Scope** When referring to an array, scope is the number of elements allocated to it when it is declared.

Worked example

An array defined under the single identifier Names with a scope of 5 will create five variables:

Names[0], Names[1], Names[2], Names[3],and Names[4]

This array may contain data such as:

Names[0]	Names[1]	Names[2]	Names[3]	Names[4]
Frank	Hameed	Yin	Hannah	Marta

Accessing Names[2] will return 'Yin'

Changing Names[1] to 'Umar' will modify the array to:

Names[0]	Names[1]	Names[2]	Names[3]	Names[4]
Frank	Umar	Yin	Hannah	Marta

We can use a for loop to access the elements of a one-dimensional array:

```
for index = 0 to 4

      print(Names[index])

next index
```

Where there are two categories of information, for example class names and year groups, we can use a two-dimensional array.

A two-dimensional array is accessed using two index numbers similar to (x,y) coordinates in a table.

Worked example

Names	0	1	2	3	4
0	Billy	Johan	Navdeep	Graham	Hua
1	Frank	Hameed	Yin	Hannah	Marta
2	Barry	Wayne	Tracey	Kylie	David
3	Irina	Li	Sundip	Tomasz	Dillip
4	Deborah	James	Michael	Wendy	Charles

Accessing `names[2,3]` returns Kylie

To populate this array with names we could use nested `for` loops:

```
for i = 0 to 4

    for j = 0 to 4

        names[i,j] = input("Enter a name ")

    next j

next i
```

Exam tips

The table is only a representation of a two-dimensional array and there is no 'correct' way to access the data via [row, column] or [column, row]. In exam questions using a table, you will be told how to access the array.

Questions may use arrays with up to three dimensions. A three-dimensional array will allow access to data through three indices similar to coordinates in three-dimensions (x,y,z).

Records

A record is a structure used within a database to store data by categories under key fields.

+ A record is accessed through an attribute (or field).
+ A record is an unordered data structure consisting of different data types.
+ Indices may be programmed to provide the data ordered on a particular attribute.
+ The ability to access data through an attribute makes the record structure more user-friendly.
+ The need to define all the attributes before use makes the record structure more complex to initialise.

In order to create a record, we need to first set up the field names or attributes, for example an address book:
+ `FirstName`
+ `LastName`
+ `Telephone`
+ `Email`

The data for each person is stored under these headings in a table.

A table must have a name to identify it; we shall call it `tblNames`

FirstName	LastName	Telephone	Email	←	Fields
Bill	Wilson	02222347593	bw@somemail.co.uk	←	Records
Graham	Mills	02121398741	graham@othermail.com	←	
Imran	Mahmud	02231974522	imahmud@othermail.com	←	
Sally	Jones	02231987342	sally@somemail.co.uk	←	

Lists

Lists, like arrays, store data using a single identifier and an index, but unlike arrays do not have a fixed size when declared and are not restricted to a single data type.

+ A list is an ordered data structure.
+ A list is accessed through an index that indicates the position of the data in the list.
+ Lists have no predefined scope (number of elements).
+ Not needing to define attributes in advance makes a list easier to initialise than a record.
+ Accessing the data in order by index is straightforward to program.

Worked example

In an address book, organised as a list, data is found by its position in the list.

`address_book [5]` would return the data at position 5 in the list.

Tuples

+ A tuple is a like a list.
+ But unlike a list, a tuple is immutable, which means the data cannot be modified.
+ Tuples are useful for data that must be accessed by index but must not be changed.

Now test yourself   TESTED ◯

21 In the array `names`

names	0	1	2	3	4	5
0	Alan	Kuldeep	Li	Sarah	Harry	Mary
1	Jane	Tomasz	Charles	Thomas	Jane	Irina
2	Wendy	Deborah	Dillip	Umar	Johan	Hua

  a) What is stored in the variable `names[1,4]`?

  b) Show what happens to the array when:

    `names[1,3]` is set to 'Joe'

    `names[1,1]` is set to 'Navdeep'

  c) After these changes have been made, what is output by the program:

```
for x = 1 to 3

    print(names[1,x])

next x
```

Answers on p. 215

Linked list

A linked list is a list of data together with a set of links to sort the data on various factors.

Data is stored in the order it is input and pointers are used to link the data in the desired order.

Worked example

Data item	Fruit
1	Strawberry
2	Banana
3	Apple
4	Damson
5	Cherry

✦ By adding pointers these items can be sorted alphabetically.
✦ We need a start pointer to point to the first item.
✦ We need a pointer from each item to point to the next one in the sorted list.
✦ We need an end pointer to show that we have reached the last item in the sorted list.
✦ We use the data item 0 as an end pointer.

Data item	Fruit	Start (3) Alpha pointers
1	Strawberry	0
2	Banana	5
3	Apple	2
4	Damson	1
5	Cherry	4

This can be shown in a diagram.

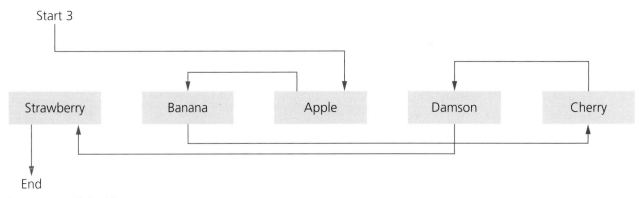

Figure 4.7 A linked list

The data may also be sorted on other factors, for example the weight of the individual item. To do this we simply add another set of pointers.

Data item	Fruit	Start (3) Alpha pointers	Start (5) Weight pointers
1	Strawberry	0	4
2	Banana	5	0
3	Apple	2	2
4	Damson	1	3
5	Cherry	4	1

Check your understanding and progress at **www.hoddereducation.co.uk/myrevisionnotesdownloads**

Now test yourself

TESTED ◯

22 The data Ford, Vauxhall, Alfa, Fiat, Mercedes is stored in a linked list in this order. Draw a table to show the links for accessing the data in alphabetical order.

Answer on p. 215

Adding data to a linked list

✚ Additional data is inserted at the next available free node.
✚ There is a pointer called 'free storage pointer' that points to the first available free location.

Node A position in a data structure that can contain data or links to other nodes.

Worked example

For this linked list:

		Start (3) Free (6)
Data item	Fruit	Alpha pointers
1	Strawberry	0
2	Banana	5
3	Apple	2
4	Damson	1
5	Cherry	4
6		
7		
8		
9		

To add orange to our list

✛ Orange is added to the location indicated by free storage pointer (6).
✛ Once added, the free storage pointer is updated to the next free location (7).
✛ Orange's location in the list is identified (it follows Damson).
✛ The pointer for the preceding location (Damson) is updated to point to the location for the new data item (6).
✛ The pointer for the new item is updated to that previously stored in the item that preceded it (1).

The list becomes:

		Start (3) Free (7)
Data item	Fruit	Alpha pointers
1	Strawberry	0
2	Banana	5
3	Apple	2
4	Damson	6
5	Cherry	4
6	Orange	1
7		
8		
9		

Removing data from a linked list

To remove data from a linked list, the pointers to that data are removed and the data bypassed.

Worked example

Removing 'Cherry' from this data:

| | | Start (3) |
		Free (7)
Data item	Fruit	Alpha pointers
1	Strawberry	0
2	Banana	5
3	Apple	2
4	Damson	6
5	Cherry	4
6	Orange	1
7		
8		
9		

+ The pointer for the item preceding Cherry is updated to the pointer at the node Cherry (so in this example the pointer at node 2, Banana, becomes 4).
+ The node for the deleted item is added to the free storage location list.

When data is removed from a list it leaves spaces within the list available for new data. This information is stored in a list of free pointers that can be reused.

| | | Start (3) |
		Free (7)
Data item	Fruit	Alpha pointers
1	Strawberry	0
2	Banana	4
3	Apple	2
4	Damson	6
5	Cherry	
6	Orange	1
7		
8		
9		

Free pointers	7	8	9	5

Showing the results of all of these changes on a diagram:

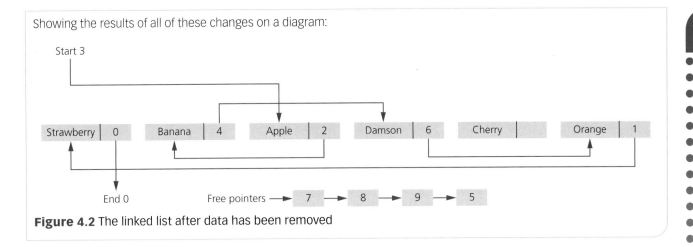

Figure 4.2 The linked list after data has been removed

Exam tip

You may be asked to draw these diagrams. It is a good idea to start with the table of pointers then draw the diagram based on that information. It is much easier to keep track of the data in the table.

Traversing a linked list

To traverse a linked list to output the data in order:

```
set the pointer value to the start value
do
        go to node (pointer value)
        output data at node
        set the pointer to value of next item pointer at the node
until pointer = 0
```

> **Traverse** Travel through the list in the defined order.

Now test yourself   TESTED ◯

23 The data Monkey, Lion, Cheetah, Zebra, Gorilla is stored as a linked list in that order.

The list is sorted alphabetically.

a) Show the data in the original order and the pointers used to sort the list.

b) Show this data with Lion removed.

c) Show this list with Tiger added.

Answers on p. 216

Exam tip

Having a mental image of the structures rather than thinking of them as abstract concepts will help you to work with them.

A linked list is basically a treasure hunt with the directions to each location stored at the previous one.

Stacks and queues

Stacks and queues are implementations of lists that store data in a linear ordered fashion.

These structures have specific methods for inserting and removing data.

Stacks

✚ Data is added to the top of the structure.
✚ Data is removed from the top of the structure.
✚ Stacks are Last In First Out (LIFO) data structures.
✚ PUSH is the command to insert data.
✚ POP is the command to remove data.

Worked example

A stack initially contains:

23	← Top
13	
4	← Bottom

PUSH 7 results in 7 being added to the top of the stack:

7	← Top
23	
13	
4	← Bottom

PUSH 18 results in 18 being added to the top of the stack:

18	← Top
7	
23	
13	
4	← Bottom

POP results in the data at the top of the stack being removed, leaving:

7	← Top
23	
13	
4	← Bottom

✚ We call the top pointer the stack pointer.
✚ If a stack is full, data cannot be pushed on to it.
✚ If a stack becomes empty, data cannot be popped from it.

> **Stack pointer** A register that holds the address of the top location in a stack.

An algorithm to describe a PUSH operation in a stack is:

```
if stack pointer maximum then report stack full
else
        set the stack pointer to stack pointer + 1
        set stack[stack pointer] to data
endif
```

An algorithm to describe a POP operation in a stack is:

```
if stack pointer minimum then report stack empty
else
        set data to stack[stack pointer]
        set stack pointer to stack pointer - 1
endif
```

Exam tips

It is worth learning these algorithms but they do not need to be repeated in this form – it is the process that is important. Try to make sense of what is happening in these algorithms, write them down and remember what you have written down.

A stack is a data structure rather like a plate stack in a canteen: the last plate added to the stack is the first one to be removed.

Now test yourself

TESTED

24 A stack contains 3, 7, 12 with 3 the first value stored and 12 the last. Show how the stack changes when the following sequence of commands is used:

PUSH 9

POP

POP

PUSH 17

POP

POP

Answer on p. 217

Queues

+ Data is added to the end of the structure.
+ Data is removed from the start of the structure.
+ Queues are First In First Out (FIFO) data structures.
+ PUSH is the command to insert data.
+ POP is the command to remove data.

Worked example

A queue initially contains:

23	← Start
13	
4	← End

PUSH 7 results in 7 being added to the end of the queue:

23	← Start
13	
4	
7	← End

PUSH 18 results in 18 being added to the end of the queue:

23	← Start
13	
4	
7	
18	← End

POP results in the data at the start of the queue being removed:

13	← Start
4	
7	
18	← End

Exam tip

In the examples, we refer to start and end pointers. These can also be called front and rear pointers, or sometimes head and tail. You may see examples using this different notation; they are the same.

Queues are often circular: data added at the end of the queue can be stored in locations vacated at the start of the queue.

Worked example

Initially a queue has this data:

| | 12 | 3 | 7 | 8 | 23 | |

Start ↑ (below 12)   End ↑ (below 23)

After the command PUSH 9 this becomes:

| | 12 | 3 | 7 | 8 | 23 | 9 |

Start (below 12)   End (below 9)

POP results in:

| | | 3 | 7 | 8 | 23 | 9 |

Start (below 3)   End (below 9)

PUSH 15 adds the new data in the locations before the start of the queue.

| 15 | | 3 | 7 | 8 | 23 | 9 |

End (below 15)   Start (below 3)

A queue is like a queue to get into a cinema, but a circular queue is much harder to imagine. You can draw a circular queue as a ring of storage locations to represent this structure.

In that format, the last stage of the process above would look like this:

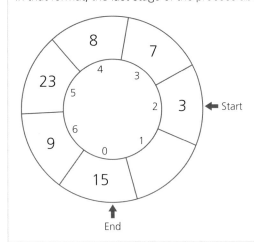

+ If a queue is full, data cannot be pushed to it.
+ If a queue is empty, data cannot be popped from it.

An algorithm to describe a PUSH operation in a queue is:

```
if the start pointer = 0 and the end pointer = maximum then
report that the queue is full

elseif the start pointer = the end pointer + 1 then report
that the queue is full

else

        add data at end pointer + 1

        set end pointer to end pointer + 1

endif
```

An algorithm to describe a POP operation in a queue is:

```
if start pointer = -1 then report queue empty

else

        data = queue[start pointer]

        set start pointer to start pointer + 1

endif
```

Exam tip

Note in this example we are using the convention that when a queue is empty the start pointer and end pointer are reset to –1. In a number of programming languages, for example C++, an empty queue is indicated by setting the start and end pointers to –1. What is important is that before attempting to pop an element from a queue the process checks that it is not empty. When writing an algorithm, the line 'if queue is not empty' should be sufficient unless there is specific guidance provided in the question.

Important points to consider:
+ If the start pointer = the end pointer there is only one item in the queue.
+ If this item is removed, the start pointer should be reset to –1.
+ If the start pointer points to the maximum value for the queue, then it needs to be reset to point at the data item at the start of the structure.

When these situations are accounted for, the algorithm becomes:

```
if start pointer = -1 then report queue empty

else

        data = queue[start pointer]

        if start pointer = end pointer then

                start pointer = -1

                end pointer = -1

        endif

        if start pointer = maximum then

                start pointer = 0

        else start pointer = start pointer + 1

        endif

endif
```

25 A queue contains 5, 3, 7 where 5 is at the start of the queue and 7 at the end. Show how the queue changes when the following sequence of commands is used:

PUSH 12

POP

POP

PUSH 9

POP

PUSH 6

Answer on p. 217

Understanding how these processes work is important. Read the algorithms and write them down in your own words to make sure you appreciate how they work.

Graphs

A graph is a collection of data nodes with connections between them.

+ The data nodes are called vertices.
+ The connections are called edges.
+ Edges may be assigned weightings.
+ A graph may be directional or undirected.
+ In a directed graph, the data connection may flow in one or both directions.
+ In an undirected graph, the edges are all bidirectional.
+ A graph is made up of a set of ordered pairs.

Vertices Nodes in a graph that contain data.

Edges Links or lines between nodes in a graph.

Weightings Values applied to edges in a graph, for example distances.

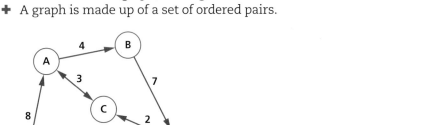

Figure 4.3 A directional graph

This graph might, for example, describe the possible routes between places, with the weightings being the distance via that route.

A graph is a mathematical data structure. Graphs are used in computer science to model real-world systems such as the internet, airline connections or road networks.

The following set of ordered pairs describes the graph shown in Figure 4.3:

{(A,B,4),(A,C,3),(A,D,8),(B,E,7),(C,A,3),(D,A,8),(D,E,9),(E,C,2),(E,D,9)}

The same data can be used to create an adjacency matrix to describe the same graph:

Adjacency matrix A table showing which nodes in a graph are connected and, if the edges are weighted, the weightings associated with those links.

	A	B	C	D	E
A		4	3	8	
B					7
C	3				
D	8				9
E			2	9	

There are two methods for traversing a graph.

Depth-first traversal

In depth-first traversal you:
1 visit the first node attached to the starting node
2 visit all the nodes connected directly or indirectly to this first node
3 visit the second node directly attached to the starting node
4 visit all the nodes connected directly or indirectly to this second node
5 continue until all nodes have been visited.

Depth-first traversal uses a **stack** to store the visited nodes.

```
add the first node onto the stack

mark as visited

do

        visit the next unvisited node to the one on top of
        the stack

        mark as visited

        add this node onto the stack

        if no node to visit remove the node off the stack

until the stack is empty
```

Worked example

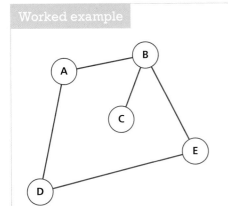

Figure 4.4 Depth-first traversal

Stack							D	
				C		E	E	
			B	B	B	B	B	
		A	A	A	A	A	A	
Visited		A	B	C		E	D	

The nodes are visited in this order.

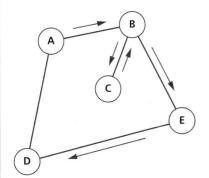

Figure 4.5 Depth-first traversal

Breadth-first traversal

In breadth-first traversal you:

1 visit the first node attached to the starting node
2 visit the second node attached to the starting node
3 continue until all the nodes attached directly to the starting node have been visited
4 move to the first node attached to the starting node and repeat the process, visiting all nodes directly connected to it.

Breadth-first traversal uses a queue to store the visited nodes.

```
add the first node into the queue

mark as visited

do

        visit unvisited nodes connected to first node

        add nodes onto queue

until all nodes visited

do

        remove next node from queue and set as current node

        do

                visit unvisited nodes connected to current node

                add nodes onto queue

        until all nodes visited

until queue empty
```

> **Queue** A data structure that works the same way as, for example, a cinema queue. The first item into the queue is the first item out of the queue.

Worked example

Using the same graph above:

Queue		B	B	D	D	D	C	E	
			D		C	C	E		
					E				
Visited	A	B	D		C	E			
Current	A	A	A	B	B	B	D	C	E

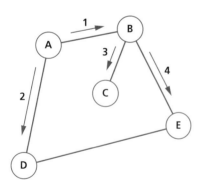

Figure 4.6 Breadth-first traversal

The nodes are visited in this order.

TESTED ◯

Now test yourself

26 Draw the graph represented by this adjacency matrix.

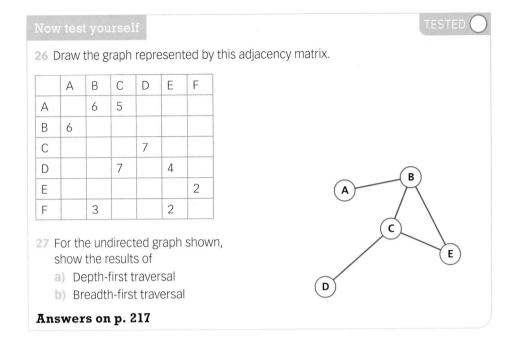

	A	B	C	D	E	F
A		6	5			
B	6					
C				7		
D		7			4	
E						2
F		3		2		

27 For the undirected graph shown, show the results of
a) Depth-first traversal
b) Breadth-first traversal

Answers on p. 217

Trees

For data that does not fit into a list, for example the directory structure on a computer hard drive, we need data structures such as trees.

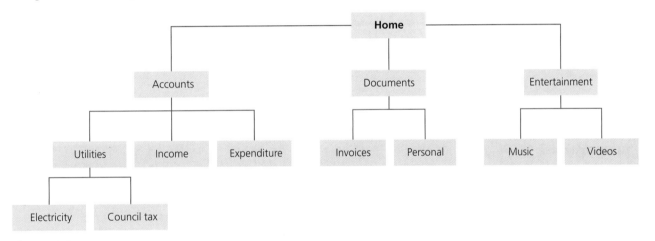

Figure 4.7

A tree is a hierarchical structure with data at a node related to the data in the nodes above it.
+ The node at the start of the structure is called the root node.
+ The nodes immediately down from another node are called children.
+ The nodes with children are called parents.
+ The lines that join the notes are called branches.

Binary search tree

One specific kind of tree is the binary tree where each node is only allowed to have two children. Each node contains:
+ a left pointer
+ data
+ a right pointer.

Worked example

Using the data Cherry, Apple, Damson, Banana we can create a binary tree to store the data alphabetically. To do this:

+ use a left pointer to data that precedes the data in the current node
+ use a right pointer to data that comes after the data in the current node
+ start at the root node and decide where to add each piece of data.

Putting Cherry as the root node, Apple precedes it so goes to the left.

The next item is Damson, which comes after Cherry so it goes to the right.

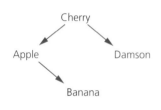

Starting at the root node, Banana precedes Cherry so we go left to reach Apple.

Banana comes after Apple so we insert it to the right of Apple.

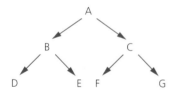

Retrieving data from a tree

There are various ways to retrieve data from a binary tree. Using the following tree as an example:

Preorder

1 Visit the node.
2 Traverse the left sub-tree.
3 Traverse the right sub-tree.

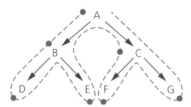

+ Start at the root and visit the node returning the value A.
+ Now start to traverse the left sub-tree and visit the node B.
+ Continue on the left sub-tree to node D.
+ Return to the previously visited node and then traverse the right sub-tree from this node visiting E.
+ Return via previously visited nodes to the root and traverse the right sub-tree C.
+ Then on to F, then G.

This gives the output for this tree: **ABDECFG**

Inorder

1 Traverse the left sub-tree.
2 Visit the node.
3 Traverse the right sub-tree.

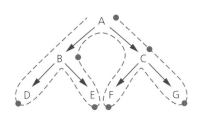

+ The difference here is that we traverse the left sub-tree without visiting intermediate nodes.
+ Go as far as possible along the left sub-tree to node D.
+ Return from that point visiting nodes B E A in that order.
+ Now traverse as far as possible on the right sub-tree to node F.
+ Return to the root visiting nodes C and G.

This gives the output for this tree: **DBEAFCG**

Postorder

1 Traverse the left sub-tree.
2 Traverse the right sub-tree.
3 Visit the node.

+ The difference here is that intermediate nodes are not visited until both left and right sub-trees have been traversed.
+ Go as far as possible along the left sub-tree to node D.
+ Go as far as possible on the right sub-tree at this node (B) to visit E.
+ Return to the root visiting node B.
+ Now traverse the right sub-tree in the same way visiting F G C.
+ Return to the root vising the root node, A.

This gives the output for this tree: **DEBFGCA**

> **Exam tip**
>
> These are left-hand trees: they use left for 'preceding' and right for 'following'. Make sure you read the question carefully to check that it does not ask specifically for a right-hand tree.

Binary trees can be used to represent arithmetic calculations.

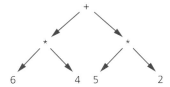

+ Preorder traversal gives + * 6 4 * 5 2
  In mathematics this is known as prefix notation.
+ Inorder traversal gives 6 * 4 + 5 * 2
  In mathematics this is known as infix notation.
+ Postorder traversal gives 6 4 * 5 2 * +
  In mathematics this is known as postfix notation.

Prefix notation is also known as Polish notation and postfix as reverse Polish notation.

My Revision Notes OCR A-level Computer Science Second Edition

Now test yourself

TESTED ◯

28 The data Monkey, Lion, Cheetah, Zebra, Gorilla, Tiger is stored in a binary tree with the left branch preceding the node alphabetically and the right branch following alphabetically.

   a) Put this data into a tree structure.

   b) Show the data retrieved using preorder traversal.

   c) Show the data retrieved using postorder traversal.

29 For the arithmetic calculation (3 + 12) / (7 − 2)

   a) Draw the inorder binary tree to describe this operation.

   b) Use preorder traversal to return the Polish notation for the calculation.

   c) Use postorder traversal to return the reverse Polish notation for the calculation.

Answers on p. 217

Revision activity

Coding simple examples of the structures will also help you to understand them. For most structures and most programming languages, examples and tutorials can be found on the internet.

Hash tables

Hash tables are used to access data that is stored in a random manner.

+ Each item maps to an address in a table containing data about that item.
+ Hash functions are used to calculate a value from a unique number.
+ This value is used as an index in a table containing data associated with that unique number.

> **Hash table** Data structure where each item has its own unique index value.
>
> **Hash function** Maps data, numeric or string, onto an integer value that can be used as an index in a hash table.

For example, mail order customers:

+ Customer accounts are accessed randomly as customers contact the company.
+ The account number can be used to calculate index values for a hash table.

Simple hash functions, for example `account_number MOD 50`, will generate the same value for a number of account numbers, which will cause clashes.

More complex functions are able to avoid this but duplicates may still occur.

Duplicate values can be stored at the same address in an overflow table as either:

+ an unordered list to be searched linearly for the correct data or
+ stored as a linked list with the address as a start pointer.

Making links

Uses of hash tables and hashing for data encryption is covered in Chapter 3.

Worked example

In a club with fewer than 50 members using 3-digit membership numbers, three people have the following membership numbers: 123, 124, 226, 373.

The hash function k MOD m, where k is the key and m the number of locations (or buckets) generates the following values:

123 MOD 50 = 23

124 MOD 50 = 24

226 MOD 50 = 26

373 MOD 50 = 23

Address	...	21	22	23	24	25	26	27	28	...
Data for				123	124		226			
				↓						
				373						

Here, member number 373 is stored at the same location as member number 123, as either a simple linear list requiring a linear search to locate a specific value or as a linked list.

In this case, there is a clash between customer accounts 123 and 373 so they will both be stored using the same index value. A linked list will be created at that index value to point to each item in the list.

The efficiency of the function is improved if m is chosen to be a prime number close to a power of 2. For 50 locations we could choose a prime close to 64 (2^6), for example 61.

Worked example

For our club with membership numbers 123, 124, 226 and 373

123 MOD 61 = 1

124 MOD 61 = 2

226 MOD 61 = 43

373 MOD 61 = 7

There are no longer any clashes using this improved function.

To avoid too many clashes, hash functions can be quite complex but some simple examples are:

address = $(k * k)$ MOD m

or

address = $k(k - 3)$ MOD m

Worked example

Using address = $(k * k)$ MOD m

For 100 accounts

The closest power of 2 is 128

The closest prime to 128 is 127 so $m = 127$

For account number 100

100 * 100 MOD 127

= 10000 MOD 127

= 94

Now test yourself TESTED ◯

30 Using the hashing function $k(k + 3)$ MOD m

Where k is the key field and m is the bucket size.

If m is 251 calculate the addresses for the key fields

a) 101

b) 52

Answers on p. 217

Revision activity

As with the previous section, designing your own questions and answers will focus on the important concepts.

Boolean algebra

+ George Boole was an English mathematician who identified that all logical solutions could be represented using just the values true or false.
+ True and false comprise the Boolean data type.
+ Since computers use switches that can be on or off, represented by 1 or 0, these values can be used to represent the true or false values of Boolean logic.

Logic gates and truth tables

REVISED ◯

By wiring electronic components together, we can create circuits that make simple logical calculations.

We use truth tables to show all the possible input combinations and the resulting output. Inputs are usually labelled with letters from the start of the alphabet, A, B, C and so on, and outputs with letters from later in the alphabet, P, Q, R and so on.

NOT gate

The NOT gate simply reverses the input. If we input 1 it outputs 0; if we input 0 it outputs 1.

The NOT gate, symbol is: ¬

A	P
0	1
1	0

Figure 4.8 NOT gate

AND gate

The AND gate outputs 1 only if both of the inputs are 1, otherwise it outputs 0.

The AND gate symbol is: ∧

Check your understanding and progress at **www.hoddereducation.co.uk/myrevisionnotesdownloads**

A	B	P
0	0	0
0	1	0
1	0	0
1	1	1

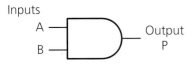

Figure 4.9 AND gate

OR gate

The OR gate outputs 1 if either or both of the inputs are 1. If both inputs are 0 it outputs 0.

The OR gate symbol is: ∨

A	B	P
0	0	0
0	1	1
1	0	1
1	1	1

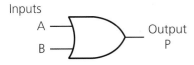

Figure 4.10 OR gate

XOR gate

The XOR gate (Exclusive OR) outputs 1 if just one of the inputs is 1. If both inputs are 0 or both inputs are 1 it outputs 0.

The XOR gate symbol is: ⊻

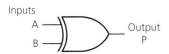

Figure 4.11 XOR gate

A	B	P
0	0	0
0	1	1
1	0	1
1	1	0

> **Exam tip**
>
> In the examples, we have used the notation identified in the OCR specification, but OCR will accept all equivalent notation and it may be easier to use the words, NOT, AND, OR and XOR, rather than the symbols.

Define problems using Boolean logic

Logic gates can be combined into more complex functions.

If we are given the Boolean expression to describe a circuit we can create the truth table for the expression.

Worked example

$R \equiv \neg (A \lor B) \land C$

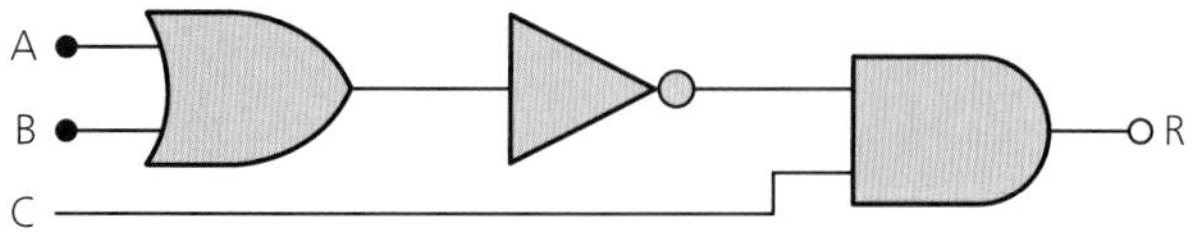

Figure 4.12 Logic circuit

By listing all the possible input combinations and identifying the outputs at each stage, we can use a truth table to calculate the output from these functions.

$R = \neg (A \lor B) \land C$					
A	B	C	$A \lor B$	$\neg(A \lor B)$	R
0	0	0	0	1	0
0	0	1	0	1	1
0	1	0	1	0	0
0	1	1	1	0	0
1	0	0	1	0	0
1	0	1	1	0	0
1	1	0	1	0	0
1	1	1	1	0	0

Boolean logic can be used to express written problems mathematically to identify solutions.

Worked example

A family wish to buy a new car. They have £20000 available for a car with removable rear seats or an estate car. If they can get a hybrid car with removable seats or an estate they are willing to pay more than £20000.

Using the following

A = cost less than or equal to £20000

B = Removable rear seats

C = Estate car

D = Hybrid

the Boolean expression to describe their requirements, P, is

P = (A AND (B OR C)) OR (D AND (B OR C))

which simplifies to

P = (A OR D) AND (B OR C)

A	B	C	D	P = (A OR D) AND (B OR C)			
				(A OR D)	(B OR C)	P	
0	0	0	0	0	0	0	
0	0	0	1	1	0	0	
0	0	1	0	0	1	0	
0	0	1	1	1	1	1	a)
0	1	0	0	0	1	0	
0	1	0	1	1	1	1	
0	1	1	0	0	1	0	
0	1	1	1	1	1	1	
1	0	0	0	1	0	0	b)
1	0	0	1	1	0	0	
1	0	1	0	1	1	1	
1	0	1	1	1	1	1	
1	1	0	0	1	1	1	
1	1	0	1	1	1	1	
1	1	1	0	1	1	1	
1	1	1	1	1	1	1	

The truth table can be used to identify suitable options.

The highlighted rows describe:

a) an acceptable choice: hybrid estate car costing more than £20,000

b) an unacceptable choice: costs less than £20,00 but without removable seats, not an estate and not a hybrid

Now test yourself

TESTED ◯

31 Complete the truth tables for the expressions:

a) (A ∧ B) ∨ ¬C

b) ¬(A ∧ B) ∨ C

32 Draw the logic circuits for these expressions.

Answers on p. 217

Simplify statements in Boolean algebra

REVISED ◯

There are rules about how to manipulate Boolean expressions.

As with arithmetic operators, logical or Boolean operations are carried out in order of precedence:

1 NOT
2 AND
3 OR.

We also define everything and nothing:

+ Everything is 1.
+ Nothing is 0.

For the NOT operator we have the following rules:

+ ¬(¬A) = A   (double negative law)
+ A ∧ ¬A = 0   (complement law)
+ A ∨ ¬A = 1   (complement law).

There are also rules similar to standard mathematical operations that are very similar to * and +.

123

Associative $(A \wedge B) \wedge C \equiv A \wedge (B \wedge C)$

$(A \vee B) \vee C \equiv A \vee (B \vee C)$

Commutative $A \wedge B \equiv B \wedge A$

$A \vee B \equiv B \vee A$

Distributive $A \wedge (B \vee C) \equiv (A \wedge B) \vee (A \wedge C)$

There are also some simplification rules for Boolean algebra.

> **Making links**
>
> See Chapter 6. Pattern recognition is a critical element in computational thinking.

De Morgan's rules

De Morgan's rules are:

$\neg(A \vee B) \equiv \neg A \wedge \neg B$

$\neg(A \wedge B) \equiv \neg A \vee \neg B$

These rules can be used to simplify expressions.

> **Example**
>
> | | |
> |---|---|
> | $C \vee \neg(B \wedge C)$ | original expression |
> | $C \vee \neg B \vee \neg C$ | De Morgan |
> | $(C \vee \neg C) \vee \neg B$ | Commutative and associative laws |
> | $1 \vee \neg B$ | Complement law |
> | 1 | Identity |

> **Now test yourself**   TESTED ◯
>
> 33 Simplify the expressions.
>   a) $(A \vee B) \wedge (A \vee C)$
>   b) $(A \wedge B) \vee A \vee (B \vee C)$
>   c) $\neg A \vee C \vee (A \wedge B)$
>
> **Answers on p. 217**

Manipulate Boolean expressions, and the use of Karnaugh maps

REVISED ◯

+ Karnaugh maps are tables of possible inputs mapped against outputs.
+ Karnaugh maps use a slightly different order of inputs from a truth table to make it easier to spot patterns more effective: `00 01 11 10`.
+ Karnaugh maps use pattern recognition to simplify Boolean expressions.

The rules for Karnaugh maps are:
+ list the inputs in column and row headings
+ ensure only one digit is different between adjacent column and row headings, for example `00 01 11 10`
+ list the outputs for each set of inputs
+ groups of 1s are grouped together as a block
+ each block must contain 1, 2, 4, 8 and so on 1s
+ no zeros are allowed in the blocks
+ no diagonal blocks are allowed
+ overlapping blocks are allowed
+ wrap-around blocks are allowed
+ blocks should be as large as possible while following these rules
+ aim for the smallest possible number of groups.

Worked example

Simplify this three-input Karnaugh map:

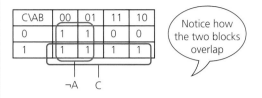

C\AB	00	01	11	10
0	1	1	0	0
1	1	1	1	1

¬A   C

Notice how the two blocks overlap

The simplified Boolean expression represented by this Karnaugh map is therefore $¬A ∨ C$

When working with more inputs, we need to consider more possibilities. It is important to note that the order of the binary values in the heading and side columns is 00, 01, 11, 00.

Worked example

Simplify this four-input Karnaugh map:

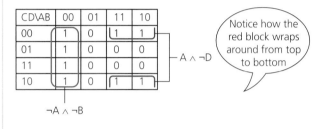

CD\AB	00	01	11	10
00	1	0	1	1
01	1	0	0	0
11	1	0	0	0
10	1	0	1	1

$A ∧ ¬D$

¬A ∧ ¬B

Notice how the red block wraps around from top to bottom

The expression is $(¬A ∧ ¬B) ∨ (A ∧ ¬D)$

We can use Karnaugh maps to simplify complex expressions.

Worked example

Simplify:

$A ∧ B ∧ C ∨ A ∧ ¬B ∧ C ∨ A ∧ B ∧ ¬C$

We identify the values of the inputs that result in an output of 1 for each element of the expression separated by ∨, in turn:

For $A ∧ B ∧ C$ the output is 1 only when A, B and C are all 1:

C\AB	00	01	11	10
0				
1			1	

Now add $A ∧ ¬B ∧ C$

C\AB	00	01	11	10
0				
1			1	1

Finally add $A ∧ B ∧ ¬C$

C\AB	00	01	11	10
0			1	
1			1	1

We can see two overlapping blocks that will include all the 1s:

$A ∧ B$

$A ∧ C$

The expression simplifies to: $A ∧ B ∨ A ∧ C$

34 Simplify the expression shown in these Karnaugh maps:

a)

CD\AB	00	01	11	10
00	1	1	1	1
01	1	1	0	0
11	0	0	0	0
10	0	0	0	0

b)

CD\AB	00	01	11	10
00	0	0	0	0
01	0	1	1	0
11	1	1	1	1
10	1	0	0	1

35 By completing a Karnaugh map, simplify the expression:

$(\neg A \wedge B) \vee (B \wedge \neg C) \vee (B \wedge C) \vee (A \wedge \neg B \wedge \neg C)$

Answers on p. 217–18

Exam tip

When simplifying an expression, if the question says use a particular method then do so. Otherwise, use whichever method you are most comfortable with. You can always check your answers using your preferred method if time allows.

The logic associated with half and full adders, and D type flip-flops

REVISED ○

Half-adder

A half-adder is a logic circuit with two inputs that can output the sum and carry for the two input digits.

That is, 1 + 1 would output 0 and the carry 1.

The two outputs are labelled here as S and C for the sum and carry.

The truth table for a half-adder is:

A	B	S	C
0	0	0	0
0	1	1	0
1	0	1	0
1	1	0	1

From this table we can see that

S is $A \veebar B$

(This can also be written as S = A XOR B.)

C is $A \wedge B$

(This can also be written as C = A AND B.)

This circuit is a half-adder:

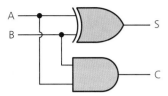

Figure 4.13 A half-adder

Full adder

A full adder allows the carry from a previous calculation to be carried forward in the calculation.

To deal with carries from previous calculations, there need to be three inputs:
+ A, B and C_{in} (the input from the carry in the half-adder)
+ it needs to produce two outputs, S and C_{out}.

The truth table is:

A	B	C_{in}	S	C_{out}
0	0	0	0	0
0	0	1	1	0
0	1	0	1	0
0	1	1	0	1
1	0	0	1	0
1	0	1	0	1
1	1	0	0	1
1	1	1	1	1

Using two half-adders (labelled 'HA' in the diagram) and an OR gate, we can construct the circuit for a full adder:

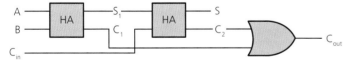

Figure 4.14 A full adder

If we combine a series of full adders, we can build a circuit for a computer that will add two binary numbers.

NAND (NOT AND)

There is another commonly used logic gate, NAND, (NOT AND).

The circuit:

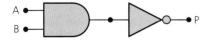

Can be represented by the NAND gate:

127

Flip-flop circuits

+ There are some important circuits that differ from the gate circuits we have considered so far.
+ These circuits are capable of storing information and can be used in, for example, RAM memory.

Consider this basic circuit:

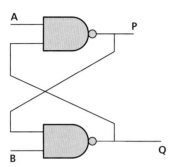

Figure 4.15 A flip-flop circuit

The truth table for this differs from the others we have seen because when A is 1 and B is 1 there are two possibilities:

A	B	P	Q
0	0	1	1
0	1	1	0
1	0	0	1
1	1	0	1
		1	0

This circuit can exist in either state, storing 1 or 0.

Which state depends upon the previous values stored. For instance:
+ if the input was A = 1 and B = 0 …
+ … then the input was changed so that A = 1 and B = 1 …
+ … the outputs would remain as P = 0 and Q = 1.

Alternatively, if the previous inputs were A = 0 and B = 1 …
+ … then when A = 1 and B = 1 the outputs would be P = 1 and Q = 0.

This means the previous values of P and Q would be stored.

This circuit is called a flip-flop and it can store one bit of information.

(It is called a flip-flop because it can flip the data from 0 to 1 or 1 to 0.)

By combining flip-flops, we can create a number of circuits.

Two flip-flops combine to make a D-type flip-flop.

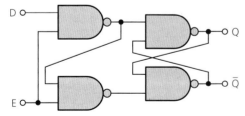

Figure 4.16 D-type flip-flop

The D stands for delay and the D-type flip-flop:
+ uses a clock pulse to delay the output
+ has two inputs
    + data
    + clock
+ and has two outputs
    + the data (1 or 0)
    + the inverse of the data (0 or 1).

Check your understanding and progress at **www.hoddereducation.co.uk/myrevisionnotesdownloads**

Clock	Input	Q	¬Q	Comment
0 (low)	Has no effect	Current state	Inverse of current state	Does not change state
1 (high)	0	0	1	Sets the values of the output to 0
1 (high)	1	1	0	Sets the value of the output to 1

If the clock is high (= 1), the output will be the same as the input.

If the clock is low, the circuit will not change state and will store whatever data was present in the output before the clock changed.

Now test yourself

TESTED ◯

36 Draw the truth table and logic diagram for a half-adder.

37 Complete the table showing the output, Q, from a D-type flip-flop

Clock pulse	0	1	0	1	0	1	0	1
Input	0	0	0	1	1	1	1	0
Output Q	0							

Answers on p. 218

Summary

Data types

+ All data in a computer is stored in binary.
+ Non-binary formats such as denary or hexadecimal can be represented in binary.
+ When adding binary numbers we use the fact that 1 + 1 = 10 and 1 + 1 + 1 = 11
+ Negative binary numbers can be represented using sign and magnitude or two's complement formats.
+ Sign and magnitude requires one bit to represent a + (0) or a – sign (1).
+ Two's complement works by making the most significant bit (MSB) negative.
+ To subtract in two's complement, we add a negative version of the number we are subtracting.
+ To convert from hex to binary, we convert the hex digit to denary then the denary value to a binary nibble.
+ Floating-point numbers are similar to standard scientific notation with a mantissa and exponent.
+ The binary point in the mantissa is immediately after the MSB.
+ To convert a floating-point number:
  + convert the exponent to decimal
  + move the binary point in the mantissa according to the exponent.
+ Normalisation maximises the precision for a given number of bits.
+ For a binary number, the mantissa is adjusted so that it starts with
  + 01 for a positive number
  + 10 for a negative number.
+ To add or subtract floating-point numbers, adjust the exponents for the numbers so that they are the same.
+ To subtract floating-point numbers, convert to two's complement and add.
+ Shifting the bits in a binary number:
  + to the left multiplies the number by 2 for each place
  + to the right divides the number by 2 for each place.

+ Masks can be applied to a binary number using a logic gate, that is, AND, OR and XOR.
+ Masks are used to check the state of individual bits in a binary number.
+ The computer's character set is represented using Unicode, allocating a numeric value to all characters that can be represented.
+ ASCII is a subset of Unicode using the same numeric codes.

Data structures

+ Arrays define a set of variables under a single descriptor with an index.
  + Two-dimensional arrays have two indices similar to coordinates.
  + Three-dimensional arrays use three indices.
+ A record is an unordered data structure accessed by an attribute.
  + The attribute must be defined before the structure is used.
  + Using attributes makes the structure more user-friendly.
+ Lists are ordered data structures accessed by an index representing the position of the data in the list.
  + Lists have no predefined scope (size).
+ Tuples are immutable lists: the data cannot be modified.
+ Linked lists use pointers to sort data by pointing from one data item to the next item.
  + Linked lists use a start pointer and an end pointer.
  + The end pointer usually points to null.
  + Linked lists can have multiple sets of pointers to sort the data by different attributes.
+ Stacks are Last In First Out (LIFO) data structures.
  + Data is added and removed from the top of the stack.
+ Queues are First In First Out (FIFO) data structures. →

129

+ Data is added at the end of the queue and removed from the front of the queue.
+ Queues can be circular, so data added at the end of the queue can be added in the locations vacated at the front of the queue.
+ Graphs are a mathematical data structure consisting of:
  + vertices (data nodes)
  + edges (links between nodes) that can be weighted with a numerical value that relates to the linked nodes
+ Graphs can be unidirectional or bidirectional.
+ Trees are hierarchical data structures.
  + The start node is called the root.
  + Nodes branch from the start node, then from subsequent nodes to form a tree-like structure.
  + Binary search trees allow only two branches from each node.
  + Binary trees can be traversed using inorder, preorder or postorder methods.
+ Hash tables are used to locate data stored in a random order.
  + An attribute associated with the data is processed using a hash algorithm to identify a location for that data.
  + If calculated locations clash with other stored data then a linked list, or possibly just a list, is used to store multiple data items at that location.

Boolean algebra

+ Four logic gates are:
  + AND: both inputs must be true for the output to be true
  + OR: one or both inputs must be true for the output to be true
  + XOR: just one of the inputs must be true for the output to be true
  + NOT: inverts the input from true to false or false to true.

+ A Boolean expression consists of inputs combined with logic gates to form a logic circuit.
+ There are standard rules for manipulating Boolean expressions, similar to those used in algebra:
  + Double negation:
    + NOT(NOT A) = A
  + Association:
    + A AND (B AND C) = (A AND B) AND C
    + A OR (B OR C) = (A OR B) OR C
  + Commutation:
    + A AND B = B AND A
    + A OR B = B OR A
  + Distribution:
    + A AND (B OR C) = (A AND B) OR (A AND C)
  + De Morgan:
    + NOT(A AND B) = NOT A OR NOT B
    + NOT(A OR B) = NOT A AND NOT B
+ Karnaugh maps use pattern recognition to simplify Boolean expressions.
  + They use tables of all possible inputs mapped against the required outputs.
  + By identifying blocks of 1s and the equivalent Boolean expression, the original expression may be simplified.
  + Blocks must be groups of 2, 4, 8 and so on 1s with no 0s in the block.
+ Adder circuits are the basic building blocks of the processor.
  + A half-adder takes two inputs and outputs the sum and carry.
  + A full adder combines two half-adders using an OR gate to output the sum and carry for three inputs.
+ Flip-flops can store one item of data (0 or 1).
  + A D-type flip-flop can delay a signal by one clock pulse.
  + A D-type flip-flop has two inputs, data and clock.
  + A D-type flip-flop has two outputs: the data and the inverse of the data.

Exam practice

1 a) Convert the denary number 206 into:
    i)   binary   [1]
    ii) hexadecimal   [1]
  b) Explain why programmers use hexadecimal. [2]

2 Convert the denary value −112 into:
  a) an 8-bit binary value in sign and magnitude form [1]
  b) an 8-bit binary value in two's complement form [1]

3 Subtract the binary integer 11011 from 100000 [3]

4 a) The following 8-bit floating-point numbers use a 5-bit mantissa in two's complement and 3-bit exponent in two's complement.
    Convert each number to denary:
    i)   01110 001   [1]
    ii) 01100 111   [1]
  b) Using a normalised 8-bit floating-point number with a 5-bit mantissa and 3-bit exponent calculate:
    01110 001 − 01100 111   [6]

Check your understanding and progress at **www.hoddereducation.co.uk/myrevisionnotesdownloads**

5 a) Show the byte below after having an OR applied with the masking byte.

Byte	1	0	1	1	0	1	1	0
OR	1	1	1	1	0	0	0	0
Result								

[2]

  b) Explain what effect this has on the operand. [2]

6 The items 5, 7, 2, 8, 4 are stored in a linked list.
  a) Draw a table showing these items sorted numerically using pointers. [3]
  b) Draw a diagram showing the data stored in a linked list sorted numerically. [3]
  c) Modify the diagram to show the item 8 removed from this linked list. [3]

7 In dictionaries of words, the words are stored in sequence of first letter, second letter and so on. A tree created to represent this process with the four words:

CHAIR

CHASE

CARD

CASE

would look like this:

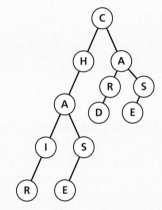

  a) Annotate the diagram, by crossing out nodes, to show how the word CHASE would be removed from the tree. [2]
  b) Annotate the diagram, by adding in nodes, to show how the word CASTLE could be added to the tree. [2]

8 The items 8, 12, 19, 6, 14, 5, 7 are stored in a binary tree.
Draw the left-hand tree for this data. [3]

9 Draw the graph represented by the order pairs:
{(A,B,5),(B,A,5),(B,D,4),(C,B,3),(C.E,2),(D,B,4),(D.E,6),(E,D,6)} [3]

10 Show the traversal of the following graph using depth-first and breadth-first traversal methods. [8]

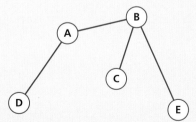

11 Where k is the key value and m is 113, find the locations used to store the data with key field 57 using the hashing algorithm $k * k$ MOD m. [2]

12 Simplify the expressions:
  a) $\neg(\neg A \lor \neg B)$ [1]
  b) $(A \lor B) \land (A \lor C)$ [2]
  c) $(A \land B) \lor (B \land C) \land (B \lor C)$ [2]
  d) $(A \lor C) \land (B \lor C)$ [2]

13 An online retailer provides free delivery for a customer if:

they are an existing customer with a voucher code

they are a new customer and open an account.

A existing customer

B voucher code

C new customer

D open an account

P free delivery

Write an expression for P. [3]

14 a) Complete the truth table for the expression $(A \wedge B) \vee (C \wedge D)$ [4]

    b) Draw the logic circuit for this expression. [3]

15 Simplify the expression shown by the Karnaugh map:

CD\AB	00	01	11	10
00	1	1	0	0
01	1	1	1	1
11	0	0	1	1
10	0	0	0	0

[3]

16 a) State the purpose of a flip-flop. [1]

    b) State what the inputs to a D-type flip-flop must be for the output, Q, to be changed from 0 to 1. [2]

    c) Describe the output from a half-adder. [2]

Answers available online

5 Legal, moral, cultural and ethical issues

Computing-related legislation

There are a number of Acts of Parliament that apply to the use of computer technology in the UK.

The Data Protection Act 1998

REVISED

Computers hold vast amounts of data and it is important this data is collected, stored and processed by organisations in ways that protect the individual.

Every organisation in the UK holding personal data, apart from those with specific exemptions (see below), must register with a body called the Information Commissioner's Office and disclose what data they are holding, why they are collecting it and how it will be used.

The Data Protection Act (1998) sets out the requirements about the collection, processing and storage of data about individuals.

There are eight principles covered in the Data Protection Act 1998:

1 Data should be processed fairly and lawfully (that is, the data must not be obtained by deception and the purpose of the data being collected should be revealed to the data subject).
2 Data should only be used for the purpose specified to the Data Protection Agency and should not be disclosed to other parties without the necessary permission.
3 Data should be relevant and not excessive.
4 Data should be accurate and up to date.
5 Data should only be kept for as long as necessary.
6 Individuals have the right to access data kept about them and should be able to check and get the data updated if necessary.
7 Security must be in place to prevent unauthorised access to the data.
8 Data may not be transferred outside the European Union (EU) unless the country has adequate data protection legislation. (Note: this is still the case even though the United Kingdom (UK) has left the EU.)

> **Data subject** The individual whose data is being stored.
>
> **Data controller** The person who is responsible for implementing the provisions of the Data Protection Act within an organisation.

The data controller in an organisation is responsible for the accuracy and security of data kept about the data subjects.

There are some exemptions to the principles of the Data Protection Act 1998:

+ National security and crime: any data processed in relation to national security or to prevent crime is exempt from the Act (e.g. some police databases).
+ Taxation: any data used to assist with the collection of taxes is exempt from the Act.
+ Domestic purposes: any data used solely for individual, family or household use is exempt from the Act.

GDPR updates to the DPA, 2018

REVISED

In 2018, the Data Protection Act was updated to comply with European General Data Protection Regulation (GDPR).

The Data Protection Act 2018 sets out seven key principles that should be central to processing personal data.

133

Lawfulness, fairness and transparency

+ There must be valid reasons for collecting and using personal data.
+ Nothing must be done with the data that would break any other laws.
+ Personal data can only be used in a way that is fair. This means data must not be processed in a way that is damaging, unexpected or misleading.
+ The person or organisation collecting the data must be open and honest with people from the start about how they will use their personal data.

Purpose limitation

+ The purpose for processing the data must be clear from the start.
+ The purpose must be documented and specified in privacy information that is communicated to individuals.
+ Data must not be used for a new purpose unless this is compatible with the original purpose. If it is not, then additional consent must be obtained unless there is a clear obligation or function set out in law. For instance, if you signed up to a website's email newsletter, they cannot send you separate marketing emails unless that was stated in the sign-up process.

Data minimisation

Data being processed must be:
+ adequate
+ relevant
+ limited to what is necessary.

For instance, imagine you signed up to a free online revision class service that asked for your email address, telephone number and your GCSE results. The data being processed would not be:
+ Adequate: they did not ask you which subjects you are studying. This is a problem because they might not offer revision for your subject, and in fact simply want to collect your data for other purposes.
+ Relevant: your telephone number is irrelevant for an online class.
+ Limited: your GCSE results might seem relevant but they do not appear to be necessary to actually provide a revision class, therefore should not be collected.

Accuracy

+ All reasonable steps must be taken to ensure the personal data held is not incorrect or misleading.
+ Data must be kept up to date.
+ If any data is incorrect or misleading it must be corrected or erased as soon as possible.
+ Challenges to the accuracy of personal data must be considered.

Storage limitation

+ Data must not be kept for longer than necessary.
+ How long data is kept for must be justified and specified in a policy statement.
+ There must be a periodic review of the data held, and data no longer required should be erased or anonymised.
+ Individuals have a right to have data erased if it is no longer required.
+ Data can be kept for longer if it is only kept for public interest archiving, scientific or historical research, or statistical purposes.

Security

+ There must be adequate security measures in place to protect the data held.

> **Making links**
>
> Security measures include encrypting data. See Chapter 3 for more on encryption.

Accountability

The data controller, and all staff within the organisation, must take responsibility for how the data is used and for compliance with the other principles.

Now test yourself   TESTED ◯

1 Describe two instances where inaccurate data held by a credit checking company might cause problems for an individual.
2 Explain why it is important that data is held for only as long as necessary.
3 List four provisions of the Data Protection Act 1998.

Answers on p. 218

Exam tip

The specification requires knowledge of the 1998 Data Protection Act and you must be able to provide detailed discussion of the principles. If you are answering a question about data protection in general, however, it is perfectly acceptable to refer to the provisions in the 2018 Act.

The Computer Misuse Act 1990   REVISED ◯

The Computer Misuse Act 1990 makes unauthorised access to computer systems illegal.

Under the provisions of the Act the following are criminal offences:
+ unauthorised access to computer materials
+ unauthorised access with intent to commit or facilitate further offences
+ unauthorised access with intent to harm or break a computer system.

The first provision refers to unauthorised access (commonly called hacking).

The second provision refers to hacking with the intent of committing further crimes, such as stealing money.

The third provision refers to anything that impairs the performance of a computer system including the distribution of viruses

Hacking Unauthorised access to computer systems.

Hackers

There are various reasons for hacking, not all of which are with criminal intent. There are three categories of hacker, often called black, white and grey hat hackers.
+ Black hat hackers are intent on causing damage or making a financial gain. This is criminal activity and illegal.
+ White hat hackers are ethical hackers often employed by the service owner to seek out vulnerabilities so that they can be fixed. Because they have advance permission from the system owners, white hat hackers are not gaining *unauthorised* access and as such their actions are perfectly legal.
+ Grey hat hackers will seek out vulnerabilities in a system in order to report them to the system owner for a fee. Non-payment of the fee may lead the grey hat hacker to exploit the vulnerability. Ultimately, since it is unauthorised access, this is illegal.

Making links

See Chapter 3 for more on how hackers target networks and how to prevent them.

The hats refer to old cowboy films where the villain always wore a black hat and the hero a white one.

Features used to minimise the threat of hackers include:
+ Digital signatures or certificates that use encrypted messages to confirm the identity of the sender.
+ Secure Sockets Layer (SSL), a protocol that enables encrypted links between computers to ensure the security of a transaction.

Digital signature A digital code (generated and authenticated by public key encryption) that is attached to an electronically transmitted document to verify its contents and the sender's identity.

Secure Sockets Layer (SSL) A security technology for establishing an encrypted link between a server and a client.

135

- User IDs, passwords and access rights, used for basic identification of users and their legitimate rights to access specific data.
- Anti-malware software such as antivirus and anti-spyware applications used to identify and remove suspicious software on a computer system.
- Firewalls, which can be software applications or hardware, that sit between the system and external networks to prevent certain types of data and users accessing the system; firewalls can also be set to simply deny access to all external users.

Firewalls are the principal defence against Denial of Service (DoS) attacks, where a user or group of users saturate the service with requests in order to make the service unavailable to other users.

> **Making links**
>
> See Chapter 3 for more on public and private key encryption.

> **Now test yourself**   TESTED ◯
>
> 4 Describe what is meant by hacking.
> 5 Under what circumstances might hacking be legal?
> 6 Describe two features that can be used to minimise the threat from hackers.
> 7 What is the purpose of the Computer Misuse Act 1990?
>
> **Answers on p. 218**

> **Firewall** A network security device that monitors incoming and outgoing network traffic and permits or blocks data packets based on a set of security rules.
>
> **Denial of Service (DoS)** An attack meant to shut down a machine or network by overwhelming it with requests, making it inaccessible to its intended users.

The Copyright, Design and Patents Act 1988   REVISED ◯

The Copyright, Design and Patents Act 1988 protects the intellectual property of an individual or organisation.
- Copyright refers to the automatic protection given to written work, music, photography, web content, software and films.
- Under the Act it is illegal to copy, modify or distribute any copyright material, including software, without the relevant permission.
- The Act also covers patents, which is the intellectual property associated with new inventions and products, for example a new computer chip.
- Unlike copyright, patents have to be applied for and are not automatic.

Using the internet to download free copies of copyright material (e.g. software, films, books, music) is illegal since no money or credit will have been passed on to the original creator.

While peer-to-peer streaming is perfectly legal, the technology has been used to illegally share video and audio, which has had a significant impact on the income of the copyright owners.

The Copyright, Design and Patents Act is enacted through a number of licensing approaches.

Most commercial software will come with a licence agreement specifying how the purchaser may use the product. In most cases, a licence key will be required to access the software to prevent unauthorised copying and distribution.

Proprietary software versus open source software

Much of the software we buy is written by organisations trying to make a profit. This is called proprietary software. The source code of such software is kept secret and is protected by copyright law.

Open source software is developed under open standards, which means its source code is freely available to view or modify. It is often free or very low cost.

> **Making links**
>
> Peer-to-peer streaming makes use of peer-to-peer networks, covered in Chapter 3.

> **Peer-to peer streaming** Allows data to be shared directly between lots of different users/clients rather than downloading from a central server.
>
> **Proprietary software** The owner of the copyright material retains intellectual property rights.
>
> **Open source software** The original source code is made freely available and may be redistributed and modified.

136

Open source software	Proprietary software
Access to the source code	No access to source code
May be free of charge or very cheap	Almost always some cost involved
Users can modify the software	Copyright law means users cannot modify the software
Can be installed on as many computers as necessary	Extra licences must normally be obtained before installing on additional computers
No one is responsible for any problems with the software	Full support from the software developer – fully tested before release, regular updates to fix bugs and improve features, faulty software replaced
Usually only community support	Commercial and community support available
Often of very high quality because of the community of highly skilled developers	High-quality software because a lot of money is spent developing it
Updates are often provided by a community of highly skilled developers, to fix bugs and improve features	Updates provided by the developer, sometimes with extra costs involved

+ There are no 'typical' users for open source or proprietary software – many large organisations such as Amazon rely on open source software because they have the in-house expertise to manage it effectively.
+ The choice will be based on the level of expertise within the organisation balanced against the need for commercial support.
+ Typical users of proprietary software need to have readily available support to solve problems but are likely to have limited access to in-house support. These users might include individuals who rely on a piece of software but have limited expertise in finding and understanding the community support available for open source software.

Making links

See Chapter 2 for more on open source versus closed source applications.

Creative Commons licences

Creative Commons is an organisation that issues licences that are less restrictive than proprietary licences. The licenses include:
+ public domain: which has no restrictions on use for any purpose
+ attribution: where the work can be freely reproduced but the original creator must be credited
+ attribution non-commercial: where the work can only be used for non-commercial purposes.

The Creative Commons form of licence is often referred to as 'some rights reserved' as opposed to the CPDA's 'all rights reserved'.

Now test yourself   TESTED ◯

8 What is the difference between proprietary and open source software?

9 Explain two benefits of using proprietary software rather than open source software.

10 Describe when peer-to-peer streaming to share software may be illegal.

11 Describe what is meant by 'creative commons'.

Answers on p. 218–19

The Regulation of Investigatory Powers Act 2000   REVISED ◯

The Regulation of Investigatory Powers Act provides certain public bodies, such as the police and other government departments, with the right to monitor communications and internet activity. For example, to:
+ demand internet service providers (ISPs) provide access to a customer's communications
+ allow mass surveillance of communications

> **Internet service provider (ISP)** A company that provides access to the internet, for example BT, Virgin Media, Sky, Talk Talk, Hyperoptic and so on.

+ demand ISPs fit equipment to facilitate surveillance
+ demand access be granted to protected information
+ allow monitoring of an individual's internet activities
+ prevent the existence of such interception activities being revealed in court.

The Act is intended to allow suitable authorities (e.g. GCHQ, MI6) access to communications to prevent criminal or terrorist activities.

It was designed specifically to take account of the growing importance and use of the internet and the use of strong encryption in electronic communications, which criminals can use to hide their activities.

There was some concern about the range of public bodies with powers under this Act when it was first introduced. There are examples of this Act being used for reasons other than monitoring criminal or terrorist activities, for example to monitor the activities of journalists.

The Investigatory Powers Act 2016 is a further piece of legislation, and some modified regulations from it came into effect between May and August 2018. These changes take account of advances in communication technology and respond to the criticism of law enforcement use of data to identify journalists' sources.

> **Now test yourself**   TESTED ◯
>
> 12 Describe the purpose of the Regulation of Investigatory Powers Act 2000.
>
> **Answer on p. 219**

Moral and ethical issues

There are moral, social, ethical and cultural opportunities and risks associated with digital technology.
+ Moral relates to behaviour that is right or wrong.
+ Social relates to society and its organisation.
+ Ethical relates to moral principles that govern an individual's behaviour.
+ Cultural relates to the ideas, customs and social behaviour of a society.

Computers in the workplace   REVISED ◯

Computer technology in various forms plays a major part in the workplace.
+ Computer technology has changed the skill set required from the modern workforce. Instead of a human welder making cars, factories now require a technician to maintain welding robots instead.
+ The way we access shops and services has changed the job market significantly, with fewer traditional high street shops and 'in-person' roles.
+ Online shopping: instead of a shop assistant we now use automated warehouses with workers collecting and packing objects.
+ Online banking: we now use banking apps and no longer need as many high street banks and the associated workforce.
+ The workforce is subject to monitoring by computer technology to assess their productivity, the way they work and their effectiveness. It can be used to monitor any online activity, phone calls, work patterns, work quality, social media activity and so on.

> **Revision activity**
>
> Research how the introduction of computer technology has changed the workplace since the year 1990. Consider which roles have gone and which ones have been created. Consider how this impacts on education and training.

Automated decision-making   REVISED ◯

Computers are used for automated decision-making.
+ They do this by analysing data to reach a conclusion about what action to take.
+ It is often used in situations where decisions have to be made frequently and rapidly.

Check your understanding and progress at **www.hoddereducation.co.uk/myrevisionnotesdownloads**

+ Automated decision-making systems use complex algorithms to reach a decision.
+ It is important to get these algorithms right in order to avoid incorrect decisions that in some circumstances would have serious consequences.
+ Automated decision-making can make some processes very impersonal.

Automated decision-making has many applications including:
+ Electrical power distribution, which means getting electricity to each and every home and office in the country. This requires rapid responses to changing demand.
+ Emergency services, who use algorithms when responding to major incidents in order to deploy resources quickly and effectively.
+ Stock market trading, also known as algorithmic or automated trading, which can react to markets and make trades in fractions of a second.
+ Industrial plant automation, for example chemical plants or distribution centres.
+ Airborne collision avoidance systems in planes.
+ Driverless cars.
+ Finance, when banks use algorithms to decide whether someone can have a bank account or credit card based on their financial history. In the past, a person would make this decision.

Artificial intelligence

Artificial intelligence (AI) is an area within computer science that devises software that behaves as if it were intelligent. Examples of AI have been around for some time and early examples include chess playing programs that are able to analyse millions of possible alternative scenarios in order to make a move.
+ AI is a catch-all term for any system that displays any degree of human intelligence.
+ Machine learning is a subset of AI.

An artificial intelligence system will use pattern recognition to determine the nature of objects or situations and compare this with stored information about similar objects and situations.

AI is particularly useful for, for example:
+ spotting fraudulent activity
+ game playing (e.g. the computer program AlphaGo)
+ medical diagnosis
+ handwriting recognition
+ face recognition.

In all these applications, AI can match or better a human's ability to spot patterns while processing far more data than a human can. For these reasons, AI is a very important technology that will have a profound effect on our lives in the future

As an example, an AI company called DeepMind uses AI to predict how 3D proteins 'fold'. This could contribute to a new understanding of a range of diseases and complement existing research methods, because malfunctions of protein folding are responsible for many diseases. By predicting the most promising avenues for research, we can enable precise development of effective drugs.

General AI

Examples of general AI are expert systems or intelligent knowledge-based systems. They can perform at a level similar to human experts in certain areas.

There are numerous examples where these systems are used on a daily basis including:

+ speech recognition systems that identify key words and patterns in the spoken word to interpret the meaning
+ medical diagnosis systems used to self-diagnose illness from the symptoms and to support medical staff in making diagnoses
+ control systems that monitor, interpret and predict events to provide real-time process control, for example chemical plants.

All of these systems have a similar structure:
+ a knowledge base that holds the collected expert knowledge, usually as 'if then' rules
+ an inference engine that searches the knowledge base to find potential responses to questions
+ an interface to connect with the user or to a system it is controlling.

> **Knowledge base** A collection of information in a specific field of study.
>
> **Inference engine** Interprets and evaluates the facts in the knowledge base in order to provide a potential solution.

Machine learning

Machine learning uses algorithms and statistical models to analyse and draw inferences from patterns in data to develop computer systems that are able to learn and adapt without following explicit instructions.

There are a number of different machine learning algorithms that have been developed to solve problems such as:
+ credit card checking that looks for unusual patterns in credit card use to identify potential fraudulent use
+ creating automatic filters to catch spam email
+ to predict what you might be looking for as you type into a search engine or online store
+ detecting computer viruses.

> **Making links**
>
> The concept of algorithms is covered in Chapter 8.

Many tasks humans find straightforward are hard for computers and require significant computer processing power. For example, relatively simple things like:
+ recognising objects
+ deciding whether a station platform is full or not.

These kinds of problems require complex algorithms for a computer program to complete. Much of the work in this area is based on artificial neural networks, which emulate structures within the human brain.

> **Artificial neural network** A series of algorithms that tries to recognise underlying patterns and relationships within a set of data, through a process that mimics the way the human brain operates.

Artificial neural networks learn from data sets with known inputs and outputs (i.e. results) by generating mathematical weightings for particular patterns.
+ When new similar but unknown data is provided to the network, it uses these weightings to predict the result.
+ If there is any difference between the actual and predicted result, the network applies this new knowledge to adjust the weightings it gives to the rule it has applied.

Artificial neural networks are used for the most complex machine learning problems, such as, for instance, driverless cars.

Intelligence is more than just pattern recognition however; there are other aspects that define what we know as intelligence, including:
+ creativity
+ social intelligence – our ability to interact with other humans.

The Turing test is a test for intelligence in a computer. The test requires that a human being should be unable to distinguish a machine from another human being, based on the replies to questions. One interpretation of the Turing test is: 'Can a computer fool an interrogator into thinking it is a human being?'

Check your understanding and progress at **www.hoddereducation.co.uk/myrevisionnotesdownloads**

It is worth mentioning the philosophical debate about the development of effective AI. If such an intelligence were strong enough to have a consciousness:

+ Would the program have rights?
+ Would it be right to terminate such a program?
+ Should the programmer be accountable for the actions of such a program?

We can apply the last questions to the AI systems that are used on driverless cars: who is responsible for any accident involving a driverless car?

Now test yourself   TESTED ◯

13 Explain how computer use has contributed to the decline of the high street shop.

14 Describe one way in which machines can learn how to solve problems.

15 Describe two benefits that result from the use of driverless cars.

16 Describe two uses for artificial intelligence.

Answers on p. 219

Revision activity

These topics are vast and constantly changing. It is worth reading around to provide insights and information that can be used to inform responses to questions on these topics. Typically, questions on these topics allow you to discuss any relevant areas you may have researched.

Environmental effects

REVISED ◯

There is an environmental impact from the manufacturing, running and disposing of computer systems and hardware. There is further impact associated with infrastructure on which networks, and the internet in general, is built on.

While there are ongoing attempts to change, there is still a 'throw away' culture when it comes to technology:

+ People sometimes want frequent updates and access to the latest device despite the previous version working perfectly well.
+ Manufacturers have often made devices that cannot be repaired economically, in order to reduce the price in an increasingly competitive environment.
+ Computers are considered hazardous waste, but are often shipped to countries with lower environmental standards to be disposed of, in order to save money.
+ In some cases, children pick over the waste to extract metals that can be recycled and sold, thus exposing them to significant danger.

Common toxic materials within a computer include:

+ PVC
+ bromine compounds
+ polychlorinated biphenyls (PCBs)
+ chromium
+ mercury.

Environmental movements have highlighted the effects of this approach on the world we live in, and the environmental credentials of technology businesses is now much more in focus. This has led to:

+ recycling devices to recover precious materials
+ refurbishing devices so they can be used by others.
+ devices being designed to last longer and be easily repaired when faults occur.

Computer technology is also a major consumer of energy:

+ While most modern computers consume low levels of electricity, they are often left running permanently and it is estimated that cloud data centres use more energy than the aviation industry.
+ There are large energy costs associated with extraction of the raw materials, manufacture of the technology and the air conditioning associated with large installations.
+ The increasing array of computer-based devices in the modern home also contributes to this use of energy, much of which is still generated from fossil fuels and contributing to global warming.

On the positive side:
+ Devices have become significantly more efficient and many will automatically go into stand-by mode to save electricity.
+ A great deal of office work can now be done remotely using computer networks, reducing the need for travel and therefore lowering carbon consumption.

Computer technology also contributes to the battle against global warming through, for example:
+ smart home devices that provide more effective control of central heating
+ computer-controlled car engine management that improves fuel efficiency
+ more efficient logistics to ensure goods are moved more effectively using computerised route planning.

> **Revision activity**
>
> Research the Internet of Things (IoT) and consider its potential for positive and negative environmental impacts.

Censorship and the internet

REVISED ●

Internet censorship is the deliberate suppression of what can be accessed or published on the internet.

Governments or organisations may impose these restrictions for various reasons:
+ to limit access to socially unacceptable material
+ to limit access to politically unacceptable material
+ to limit access to what they regard as dangerous information.

The extent to which the internet is censored varies from country to country, depending on the political and social situations in those countries. In some parts of the world, access to any information other than officially sanctioned versions of the facts is strictly controlled for political reasons.

The main categories of website content being blocked by ISPs in the UK include:
+ extremist politics
+ extreme pornography
+ sites that infringe copyright.

In the UK, ISPs have blocked access to various categories of site by default, for example drugs, self-harm, violence and so on. The customer has to request to opt out of this filtering to gain access to this blocked content.

There are arguments about the extent of the blocking in certain areas, for example legitimate websites may be blocked because they cover sensitive topics.

Censorship is usually carried out centrally or by ISPs at the request of, or under instruction from, governments. However:
+ Total control of information through censorship is very difficult to apply unless there is a single central censor.
+ Despite censorship, many will still share information through underlying data transfer networks including file-sharing networks, for example the 'deep web' – a part of the World Wide Web that cannot be found by search engines.
+ Access to websites is filtered by reference to blacklists that are set up with unacceptable sites and through dynamic examination of the website for unacceptable content.

> **Revision activity**
>
> Research areas of the world where what we consider 'normal' internet access is blocked for political or social reasons.

Monitor behaviour

REVISED ●

People are increasingly monitored by computer technology. There are a number of reasons why authorities or organisations might want to monitor communications:
+ employers, to monitor the activities of the workforce while at work
+ law enforcement, to monitor criminal activity
+ transport authorities, to monitor the flow of people within a transport terminal.

Check your understanding and progress at **www.hoddereducation.co.uk/myrevisionnotesdownloads**

Some examples of monitoring include:

+ Performance in a workplace role: some employers track how long people take to complete tasks, how many tasks are completed in a set time, and how many and how long people take for breaks.
+ Internet activity while at work or school.
+ Monitoring known criminals with tagging devices to ensure they remain within a prescribed area or away from areas they are banned from.
+ Internet use to ensure individuals are not accessing sites or content they are not allowed to.
+ The use of facial recognition to identify individuals in public areas.
+ Young drivers reducing insurance costs through devices that monitor how they drive, where they drive and when they drive.
+ Social media posts and activities: these can be monitored by various people including the press and employers. Once data is on the internet, it is difficult to remove and may be available for many years after the event; it may be accessed by employers, potential employers, the authorities or the press in the future.

Many message services use end-to-end encryption, meaning only the sender and receiver have the key to access the message. This makes it very difficult for the authorities to monitor such communication.

> **Exam tip**
>
> It is common for questions to ask about these issues from a specific viewpoint – the employer, the authorities or the individual. Make sure you are aware of both sides of the argument. If you are asked to discuss the issue, then you should provide points from all relevant viewpoints.

> **Revision activity**
>
> Consider the following statement: 'Your school/college will be implementing monitoring software on all school computers, and all computers that connect to the school network, in order to stamp out plagiarism.' Discuss with your classmates the moral, legal, cultural and ethical issues that would be raised by implementing such a system.

Analyse personal information

REVISED ⬤

Data about individuals is collected by many organisations. While the data collected may be harmless in isolation, when combined with data collected elsewhere it could create issues for the individual.

+ Data is a valuable commodity and is used to analyse shopping and leisure activities to focus advertising more effectively.
+ Analysing data can provide significant insights into an individual's likes, dislikes, political views or even physical health.

The Data Protection Act provides suitable legislation about sharing data between organisations, but any problems may not be identified until data is shared in contravention of the Act.

+ Organisations are obliged to identify what information they are collecting and why, but this is often hidden away and not obvious to the data subject.
+ The newer GDPR legislation obliges organisations to be clearer about this when asking for data from an individual.

Data mining is an automated process that searches for patterns in large data sets to predict events.

+ Data mining is a valuable tool in the fight against organised crime; data about individual activities including social media, financial transactions, travel, internet histories and shared contact details have provided valuable information in the fight against crime and terrorism.
+ In business, it is used to identify patterns to inform strategic business decisions. The data can be used to predict future sales and hence stock requirements and effective and targeted marketing strategies to improve business profitability.
+ In science and engineering, analysis of human DNA sequences and matching this to medical information has led to the development of effective treatments for various conditions.
+ In retail, loyalty cards are used so that businesses can track consumer buying behaviour, allowing retailers to predict future behaviour and tailor their marketing messages to individuals.

> **Revision activity**
>
> It is useful to read around these topics and keep track of recent events in the news. These can be used to illustrate your discussion in any question on these topics.

Now test yourself
TESTED ○

17 Describe two environmental benefits of widespread computer use.

18 Explain why censorship of the internet by a government might be problematic for the citizens of that country.

19 Describe what is meant by data mining.

20 Identify three ways computers may be used to monitor the workforce in a distribution warehouse.

21 Describe three environmental problems related to the use of computer technology.

22 Explain why access to some websites on the internet may be censored in the UK.

Answers on p. 219–220

Piracy and offensive communications

REVISED ○

Piracy

Piracy is the unauthorised reproduction of copyright material. The Copyright, Designs and Patents Act makes it illegal to copy content without authorisation from the owner of the material.

There are sources on the internet that provide access to copyright material without the required authorisation. Accessing and copying this material:
+ deprives the author of some income for their work
+ deprives the rightful author of the work being identified – this is known as their attribution
+ risks criminal charges for breach of copyright laws.

Users of pirated software often find that:
+ the software does not work correctly
+ they have no access to software support
+ they may have introduced malware onto their system.

There are a number of methods used to try and reduce piracy:
+ digital rights management uses product keys to ensure that only one user with the decryption key can access the material
+ watermarks that are visible on the product to show that it is not a legitimately obtained copy
+ attempts are made to shut down websites that are offering pirated material.

Offensive communications

We often hear that individuals are affected very badly by unsolicited and offensive communications. Social media provides cover for those who wish to be offensive to others, especially celebrities and vulnerable individuals most susceptible to this type of abuse:
+ cyberbullying
+ trolling
+ stalking.

Under the Communications Act 2003 it is a criminal offence to send indecent or offensive communications and if traced the offender may end up with a criminal record.

The Act is in place to deal with communications that contain credible threats of violence, such as trolling or stalking, or communications that contain material grossly offensive to identified individuals and intended to cause harm.

The Communications Act has several provisions that impact on the use of computer technology.

> **Cyberbullying** Any form of bullying that takes place online.
>
> **Trolling** Deliberately upsetting people with social media posts in order to start an argument or offend someone.
>
> **Stalking** The use of the internet, or other electronic means, to harass and intimidate someone.

Among the provisions in the Act are that it is illegal to:

+ access an internet connection with no intention to pay for the service, making it a crime to piggyback onto other people's Wi-Fi without their permission
+ send offensive communications using any communications system, including social media.

Those who repeat the messages are also subject to the provisions of this Act, and re-sharing or re-posting an offensive message may be illegal.

+ Governments have pressed social media providers to put into place systems to deal with offensive communications.
+ There is evidence that filtering of offensive messages by social media providers has improved significantly, but there may be scope for more action on the matter.

> **Exam tip**
>
> This is an area where the news provides many examples of offensive communications and how they have affected individuals. Many refer to celebrities but there are many more cases where vulnerable individuals are subject to bullying with terrible consequences. It is worth researching websites that provide support for these individuals, to be aware of ways to mitigate the effects of such activities and bring the perpetrators to justice.

Layout, character sets and colour paradigms

REVISED ●

Layout

The layout of a document has a significant impact on how effective it is.

For example, when visiting a website on a computer the viewer will scan the page for key information. For text-based sites, people who read left to right will scan in an 'E' pattern:

+ scan down the left-hand side first
+ then scan the first few words of the first two or three paragraphs.

This means the important information or 'hook' needs to be in the left-hand vertical column or in the first few words of the first two paragraphs.

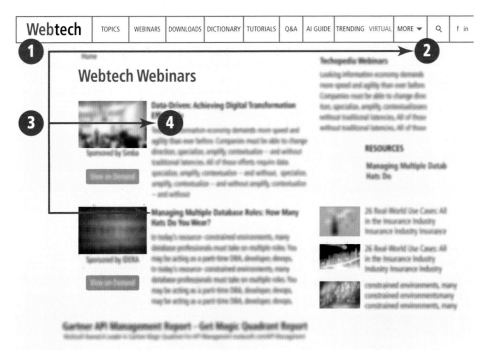

Figure 5.1 Reading pattern for text-based website accessed from a computer

With graphics-based sites the viewer scans in a 'Z' pattern:

+ scans across the top row, for example looking at the menu options
+ scans diagonally from the top right to the bottom left-hand corner
+ scans across the bottom row looking for important links.

This means for a graphics-heavy site, key information should be horizontally along the top or bottom row.

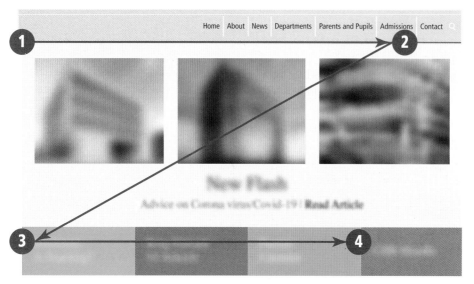

Figure 5.2 Reading pattern for graphics-based website accessed from a computer

For different cultures this needs to be varied. For readers who read right to left, for example Arabic, this pattern is generally mirrored from right to left. So in Figure 5.1 an Ǝ shape and in Figure 5.2 a ꙅ.

+ Knowing who is visiting the site – for instance, knowing which country they are in, from their IP address – will help to determine the most effective layout for a website and the most effective design.
+ Knowing which device is accessing the website is also very important because the screen sizes are so different. Website developers will adapt the layout according to whether the website is accessed from a smartphone, tablet or laptop/desktop.

Character sets and colour paradigms

Initially electronic communication used ASCII, which was based on a basic set of English characters used for telegraph systems. ASCII provided just 128 characters.

The need to be able to communicate in languages other than English, use scientific notation or include graphical symbols was addressed through the creation of the Unicode character set. Unicode can represent over 1.1 million characters.

The large number of different languages, and graphical and scientific symbols provided by the Unicode character set makes it possible to produce material that is accessible to a wide audience and can meet the demands of most disciplines.

Colour paradigms refer to established ideas about the messages that different colours send, and how colours can work together within a design. Exactly the same information may be communicated quite differently simply by using different colours. However, it is important to note that some of these ideas are deeply informed by culture:

> **Paradigm** A common set of ideas or ways of thinking.

+ in some cultures the colour red is considered a lucky colour
+ in other cultures red signifies danger.

A designer must also take account of the Equality Act 2010 and Disability Discrimination Act 1995 as it is illegal to discriminate against a group of people when providing a service. This makes it important for it to be easy to navigate between pages for all users. For example:

+ For the partially sighted, a website should provide:
    + alternative text for images
    + screen magnification
    + the ability to adjust the contrast
    + good contrast between the text and the background
    + clear character sets that can be read easily.
+ For people with hearing impairments, the site should provide a transcript or closed captions for any video footage, and any sound notifications should also have a visual signal.
+ For people with physical disabilities, there could be the ability to navigate using voice commands.

Now test yourself

TESTED ⃝

23 Describe two methods to reduce piracy.
24 Define the term 'colour paradigm'.
25 Discuss how legislation in the UK protects individuals from offensive communications.

Answers on p. 220

Revision activity

Computer technology has the ability to improve the lives of those living with disabilities. Research how developments in computer technology have impacted on the lives of people with learning disabilities in education.

Making links

See Chapter 3 for information on CSSs, which is used to define the presentation of information on a website. The same HTML content can be made to look radically different with a different CSS applied.

Summary

Computing-related legislation

+ The Data Protection Act 1998 sets out the rights of individuals and the responsibilities of organisations regarding the storage of personal data.
+ The Computer Misuse Act 1990 makes unauthorised access illegal. It is this Act that makes hacking and the distribution of malware an offence.
+ The Copyright, Design and Patents Act 1988 protects the intellectual property rights of individuals and organisations.
+ The Regulation of Investigatory Powers Act 2000 gives public bodies the right to monitor communications and internet activity.

Moral and ethical issues

Computers in the workforce:
+ increase efficiency and productivity
+ reduce cost and provide more online services
+ replace repetitive roles with more technical support roles
+ replace many jobs with low-level service roles.

Automated decision-making:
+ is used when it is impossible for a human to react quickly enough
+ uses algorithms that make decisions that affect people's lives
+ for example whether to protect the driver or the pedestrian in a potential collision.

Artificial intelligence:
+ is used in expert systems to make the experience of an expert in the subject available more widely, for example in diagnosing illness
+ uses a knowledge base and an inference engine to make decisions/suggestions

+ is commonplace in voice recognition technology, for example smart home devices
+ is used in neural networks for pattern detection.

Environmental effects:
+ 'throw-away' attitude to technology a concern for the environment
+ many components in computers are toxic
+ discarded computer equipment is often sent to countries with lower environmental standards
+ energy and valuable resources are used to manufacture computer equipment
+ energy use for computers and large data centres is considerable and contributes to global warming
+ computer technology is behind the development of environmentally friendly technology
+ the use of computers for remote working and remote meetings cuts down on carbon consumption caused by travelling.

Censorship and the internet:
+ Censorship is the deliberate act of suppressing content deemed unsuitable.
+ Censorship can be used to protect individuals.
+ Censorship can be used to repress individuals by restricting their freedom to communicate or view different points of view and promote an ideology.

Monitor behaviour:
+ used to monitor criminal and terrorist activity in order to protect society
+ used to monitor people and productivity in the workplace
+ closed-circuit television(CCTV) and facial recognition can monitor people's activities
+ phone locations can track individuals.

147

Analyse personal information:

+ Data can reveal insights into behaviour and preferences, for example commerce and social media sites will promote products that are likely to be of interest.
+ Data mining can identify societal trends or research patterns associated with a medical condition in order to find a treatment or cause.

Piracy and offensive communications

+ Piracy is theft and deprives individuals and organisations payment for their intellectual property
+ Offensive communications are illegal through the Malicious Communications Act
+ Offensive communications include cyber bullying, trolling, stalking and the distribution of offensive materials

Layout, character sets and colour paradigms

+ the layout of a document or website affects who can access it

+ the Equality Act 2010 makes it illegal to discriminate against providing a service to a group of people
+ websites must be accessible and easy to navigate for all groups of people.

Typically, in order to meet legal requirements, websites will include:

+ readability features such a large text, magnifier options, alternative text and transcripts.

Colour paradigms should consider:

+ interpretation of colours by groups, for example by ethnic origin
+ the effect of the colours used on readability for all groups of people.

When choosing a character set, its readability should be taken into account, for example san-serif fonts are easier to read on screen.

Exam skills

Questions for these topics are likely to be longer discussion questions requiring extended writing.

They are marked on the quality of the communication as well as the quality of the argument. Simply listing facts is not enough. Before answering the question, write a plan by listing any facts or points from all sides of the discussion. Try to match these points against each other and in order of importance. Use this template to structure your response. Try to justify any opinions with facts and use the balance of the argument to support any conclusions.

You will normally be expected to:

+ Demonstrate your knowledge and understanding of the topic.

+ Apply this knowledge by making arguments, both for and against, backed up with evidence and sound reasoning.
+ Evaluate all the arguments and come to a well-reasoned conclusion, taking into account all of the points you have made. There is not a 'right' or 'wrong' answer, so it doesn't matter which conclusion you come to – as long as it takes into account all of your points and is based on reasonable arguments.

A typical mark scheme for these questions will identify the points that might have been made and how these points were used to discuss the topic in a balanced way, and how this discussion was used to support a conclusion.

Exam skills

A sample mark scheme for a question on the confidentiality of data held on a computer might look something like this.

Mark band 6–8. High-level response

+ Discussion of the effects on the confidentiality of data held on computers.
+ Positive and negative points have been made.
+ A number of measures to protect the confidentiality of the data have been described. These points have been linked to negative or positive points affecting the confidentiality of the data.
+ The candidate has used appropriate technical terminology throughout.
+ There are no spelling errors or errors of grammar.

Mark band 3–5. Medium-level response

+ The discussion of points is from one viewpoint, either positive or negative.
+ A number of measures related to protect the confidentiality have been identified.
+ The candidate has used some technical terminology in the response.
+ There may be spelling errors or grammatical errors, but they are not obtrusive.

Mark band 0–2. Low-level response

+ There are a limited number of points about confidentiality of data.
+ The candidate has failed to use technical terminology in the response.
+ Spelling errors and grammatical errors are obtrusive.

Points may include (use a bulleted list like this to plan your response):

+ Positive:
  + access to the data is required to view it
  + access to data can be monitored
  + security measures can be put in place.
+ Negative:
  + files can be copied
  + data can be shared
  + the system may be hacked without triggering any alarms
  + harder to ensure all copies of data removed.
+ Measure that can be used:
  + passwords
  + encryption
  + physical security
  + firewall.

Check your understanding and progress at **www.hoddereducation.co.uk/myrevisionnotesdownloads**

Exam practice

1   Discuss the implications under the Data Protection Act 1998 for a mail order company who keeps detailed records of customers and wishes to share these with a sister company selling a different range of products.   [8]

2   Discuss the potential consequences for an individual posting images and thoughts on social media.   [8]

3   Discuss the measures a website developer should put into place to ensure they do not disadvantage people with disabilities.   [8]

4   'Computers should be used to monitor workplace communications and work progress in the office of a large bank.'

   Discuss to what extent you agree with this statement.   [8]

5   Discuss the way computers have changed how people spend their leisure time and the impact this has had on their well-being.   [8]

Answers available online

6 Elements of computational thinking

Computer professionals have developed techniques to solve real-world problems and turn them into computer solutions. Collectively these techniques are known as computational thinking. Computational thinking does not require a computer but can be implemented on one.

Computational thinking is important because some of the biggest problems facing people are difficult to understand.

At its heart, computational thinking is used to change a messy problem into something that can be:
+ understood
+ formally represented and solved.

Computational thinking involves algorithmic thinking. Algorithmic thinking requires the following stages:

1 **Understand the problem**: this can be a serious stumbling block. How do we know that we understand a problem sufficiently? This does not mean understand the solution but what it is we are trying to solve.
2 **Formulate the problem**: in this stage we need to produce a concise representation of the problem. This will normally involve abstraction and some form of mathematical notation.
3 **Design an algorithm**: once a clear representation of the problem is obtained, we can set about designing algorithms that apply to, and solve, the representation of the problem.
4 **Implement the algorithm**: in this stage we write computer code that implements the algorithm.
5 **Run the code and solve the original problem**: in this stage we actually try out the solution. After this, it is necessary to evaluate the results to see if they have solved the problem.

There are well-defined thinking approaches that can be deployed when solving problems.

> **Computational thinking**
> A set of problem-solving methods that express problems and solutions in ways that a computer could execute.

Thinking abstractly

The nature of abstraction

REVISED

Abstraction is a representation of reality. It is the process of hiding non-essential detail, leaving just the key elements of the problem. This process requires us to recognise what is important in a problem, and then formulate it in a way that can be passed to an algorithm. The algorithm can then be used to design a coded solution.

Examples of abstraction include:
+ variables
+ objects
+ layers
+ data models
+ data structures
+ entity-relationship diagrams.

> **Abstraction** Hiding details or attributes when studying objects or systems to focus attention on the essential elements of the problem
>
> **Object** An object is an abstract data type used by a programmer – see later in this chapter.

Data abstraction is using a data structure without being concerned about how it is implemented. Programmers might well use a subprogram to manage a stack, queue or linked list without needing to know how those data structures are being implemented. Large projects programmed by teams often use routines developed by others without needing to know how they work, just that they do.

Generalisation is part of the process of abstraction. By grouping together items with similar features that are relevant to the problem (i.e. ignoring different features that are irrelevant to the problem), a common approach may already exist or can be created. From experience of using approaches to solutions, these can be reused to solve similar problems.

> **Making links**
>
> The major data structures are covered in Chapter 4.
>
> The relationship between high-level and low-level code is described in Chapter 2.

All high-level coding is an abstraction because one high-level command may well require several machine code instructions to complete. The programmer does not need to know how the high-level command is implemented by the computer at a machine code level.

> **Example**
>
> When designing a game where characters move around a virtual landscape, the programmer will remove unnecessary details when planning the layout of the landscape.
>
> The characters will be replaced by simplified versions. Objects such as plants and trees can be represented by blocks of colour or simple shapes. None of this detail is significant to the layout of the game. Therefore, it is removed so that the programmer can simply focus on how the character moves around the environment.
>
> Including such complex detail is unnecessary, would be time-consuming to program and would significantly impair the performance of the game.

Layers Organising programs into separate functional components that interact in a hierarchical way. Each layer usually only has an interface to the layer above it and the layer below it.

Data model An abstract model that organises elements of data and how they relate to one another and to real-world entities.

Entity-relationship diagram A graphical model to represent the relationships between different entities. See Chapter 3.

Generalisation Solving new problems based on previous problems for which we have an existing solution. This involves using an algorithm that solves a problem and adapting it so that it solves similar problems.

The need for abstraction

REVISED

Abstraction enables the programmer to focus on the important aspects of a problem rather than getting bogged down with messy and unnecessary detail. This:

+ enables teams of programmers to work on different aspects of a problem and
+ enables programmers to use pre-built and built-in functions without concerning themselves with how they work.

Layering is an example of abstraction. How one layer is implemented is of no concern to another layer. For the programmer developing one layer of a system, all that is necessary is to know what the input requirements are for the next layer and what outputs to expect from the previous layer.

> **Making links**
>
> The TCP/IP layers are an example of abstraction. Each layer does not need to know how the others work. The layers are developed and modified independently of each other, but it is important they remain compatible with each other. See Chapter 3 for details.

The differences between an abstraction and reality

REVISED

Abstraction is just a simplification of reality. Entities in the real world are represented by containers such as variables or data structures. The real-world data is the values stored in these containers.

In object-oriented programming, the objects are abstractions of real-world entities and the attributes and methods represent the real-world characteristics and actions.

> **Making links**
>
> See Chapter 2 for more detail about object-oriented programming techniques.

Devise an abstract model for a variety of situations

REVISED

A computer program is effectively an abstract model of a real-world situation. When developing such a model we first need to consider:
+ Can the problem be solved using a computer program?

If yes, then we need to consider:
+ What are the key features of the problem?
+ How will it be used?
+ Who will be using it?
+ What is the skill set of the target user group?
+ What features are required by the target audience for the program?

By considering all of these factors, only the relevant features need be included, and unnecessary detail, not required by the target user group, can be omitted.

Example

When fitting a new room such as a kitchen, interior design programs are often used. These programs will start with some basic objects that can be resized or modified:
+ basic room shapes
+ standard graphics for door and window positions
+ blocks to represent fixtures and fittings, like cupboards and fridges
+ a range of textures and colours that can be applied to the objects.

The detail of these objects is not required when designing the basic layout. For instance, the model does not need to show how the hinges on the cupboards will operate. Using this simplified model, it is possible to construct a working layout to examine how the room will function and what fixtures and fittings can be incorporated.

Note, too, that by using sets of objects that can be selected and placed in the design, it simplifies the use of the program, making it accessible to a wide range of potential users.

Now test yourself

TESTED

1 Describe what is meant by the term abstraction.
2 Describe what is meant by the term generalisation.
3 Describe what is meant by the term data abstraction.

Answers on p. 220

Thinking ahead

In computing, thinking ahead involves planning inputs and outputs. This is a useful technique to apply to a range of problems. For example, asking:
+ What answers do we need?
+ What do we need to know or have before we can get what we need?
+ How can we turn the inputs into the required outputs?

Identify the inputs and outputs for a given situation

REVISED

Thinking ahead about how the software needs to function, and how it will be used, provides the programmer with insights that will inform the design.

The output from any software is the key element for the design. When the functions of a program are described, they are essentially a description of what outputs it will produce. These may be:
+ on-screen information
+ printed data
+ data to be stored
+ actions for the computer to complete.

In order to produce the necessary outputs, the program must have the necessary inputs. At this stage, the source of those inputs and the order and format in which they are supplied is an important consideration.

The designer must decide upon the data types and data structures required for the proposed solution to the problem.

Example

Some of the outputs and inputs for a simple maze game might include:

Outputs	Inputs
Image moves on screen	Key presses for direction
Sound to indicate collision with wall	Key press for movement
Sound when reward objects intercepted	Player name
Points score displayed	
Timer	

Determine the preconditions for devising a solution to a problem

REVISED

Preconditions are the requirements that must be met before the program can run.

Some of these preconditions can be specified within documentation and can include:
+ requirements for the device specification to be able to run the program
+ the operating system required to run the program
+ any necessary additional software or hardware.

When planning the development of a program or routine:
+ subprograms will need the correct data passed to them
+ input data should be validated to ensure it meets essential criteria
+ actions need to be validated to ensure they will not crash the program if erroneous results are returned.

Preconditions need to be established to ensure the routine or program will execute successfully. For example, when creating an algorithm to traverse a tree we need to know:
+ what type of tree it is, for example binary
+ if it is ordered
+ the traversal order.

> **Preconditions**
> Requirements that must be met before a program can run.

> **Making links**
> In Chapter 4 the algorithms for popping data from a stack or a queue include checking that the stack or queue are not empty before trying to remove an item. This is an example of a precondition that was required when these algorithms were written.

The nature, benefits and drawbacks of caching

REVISED

A cache is a temporary store where instructions or data that are likely to be needed are anticipated and stored, ready for fast access. This is an illustration of 'thinking ahead'.

Cached data can replace the need for recalculations, or the need to transfer data from slow-to-access storage online or on disk.

> **Cache** A temporary store where instructions or data an algorithm anticipates will be needed are stored, ready for fast access.

153

Caching is used extensively for web access, where frequently used pages are stored for future use. This means:
+ content can be loaded with minimal delay
+ any images and text do not need to be downloaded every time the page is visited.

This frees up bandwidth for other tasks.

The size of the cache determines how effective it is:
+ too small and it may not be able to store sufficient data to be effective
+ too large and the longer it will take to search it.

Prefetching is where an algorithm predicts which instructions or data are likely to be required by a program. The data likely to be needed next is fetched and stored in a cache ready to be used by the program, minimising delays waiting for data or instructions to be fetched from storage.

Prefetching can significantly improve the performance of a program or subprogram, but is limited by the accuracy of the algorithm: it is only predicting what will be required and may not get it right.

> **Prefetching** Loading a resource before it is needed. This can refer to commonly used web pages being requested before they are used. In this section, we are talking about instruction prefetching where the CPU caches instructions and data blocks before they are executed.

Making links

The description of how cache is used in a computer system is explained in Chapter 1.

The need for reusable program components

REVISED

When developing programs, there are certain functions that are commonly used, for example print, random number generation and sort routines. These commonly used functions are often pre-written and provided as libraries within the programming language, for reuse by the programmer.

The advantage of reusing pre-written components are:
+ they are reliable and bug free, having been tested and used many times
+ they save time for the programmer
+ they save on development costs for a project
+ in some cases, for example mathematical techniques, they will be optimised by experts for computational efficiency.

To provide the necessary features of a coded solution, it will often make sense to modify a similar pre-written code segment or function to fulfil the requirements. This can reduce the time taken for development since it may only be the new elements that will require detailed testing. However, there may be compatibility issues, which mean this is not possible. In this case, it is more reliable and effective to start from scratch.

Example

In our game there will be pre-written code for:
+ movement control
+ timer routines
+ high-score tables
+ rendering of images

that can all be reused in different games.

Now test yourself

TESTED

4   Identify the inputs and outputs for an automatic teller machine (ATM – cashpoint).
5   Describe what is meant by preconditions.
6   State two advantages of using pre-written program components.
7   Describe how prefetching might help to improve computer performance.

Answers on p. 220

Thinking procedurally

When writing programs, thinking about all aspects of the problem simultaneously can be impossible. Most problems are multifaceted and need to be broken down into smaller, more manageable tasks that are easier to understand and resolve.

Identify the components of a problem

REVISED

The first stage of thinking procedurally is decomposition. Decomposition is the process of breaking down a problem into smaller and smaller parts until each aspect of the problem can be dealt with effectively.

Top-down design is used to make complex problems easier to understand and solve. Each branch is repeatedly subdivided until the problem is broken down into tasks at the lowest level that are able to be solved.

> **Decomposition** Breaking down a complex problem into smaller parts that are easier to understand. The smaller parts are simpler to work with in order to find or develop solutions.

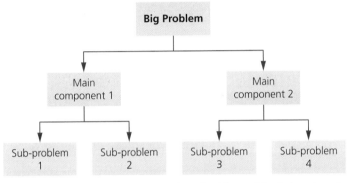

Figure 6.1 A tree diagram showing the hierarchical structure for top-down design

This example assumes that a hierarchical structure is able to represent the problem. Event-driven programs do not fit easily into this model since there are parallel strands for linked objects. However, the top-down design approach can instead be used for the processes within the linked objects.

Identify the components of a solution to a problem

REVISED

Once the problem has been broken down into its component parts, solutions can be created for each of them. Each solution could be:
+ a pre-written function or subprogram
+ an existing solution that can be modified
+ an individual task that can be allocated to a programmer.

Ideally, each of the sub-problems represents a single, self-contained solution module that can be developed and tested independently. Each component of a solution will eventually need to be integrated into the main solution.

Determine the order of the steps needed to solve a problem

REVISED

Having identified the individual modules required to solve a problem, the order in which they are developed and tested is important.

Data passes from one component of a solution to the next (just like with layers of network protocols, as seen in Chapter 3):
+ If the data required for one module comes from another, then the order in which these modules are developed becomes crucial.
+ Data from one module must be checked for validity before being passed on to another.

Similarly, when a program is being used, it is important for processes to be executed in the correct order – for instance, it would be pointless to make the payment module for an online store available before any purchases are made.

For a large program with several programmers working together, a plan showing the order in which modules are needed, and those which can be produced simultaneously, is required.

Worked example

This project plan shows how three programmers, represented by different colours, might be allocated to complete a project over nine weeks.

The plan indicates which sub-problems depend on others. For example:

✚ Sub-problems 1, 4 and 8 are not directly connected so can be started simultaneously by three different programmers (red, green and purple).

✚ Sub-problem 2 depends on sub-problem 1 and sub-problem 3 on sub-problem 2 so they cannot be started until the previous sub-problem has been completed.

✚ In week 4, the green programmer splits their time between sub-problem 4 and sub-problem 7.

By careful planning, the three programmers have completed a task that would take one programmer three times as long.

Task	Week 1	Week 2	Week 3	Week 4	Week 5	Week 6	Week 7	Week 8	Week 9
Sub-problem 1	██	██							
Sub-problem 2			██	██					
Sub-problem 3					██	██	██		
Sub-problem 4	▓▓	▓▓	▓▓	▓▓					
Sub-problem 5					██	██	██	██	
Sub-problem 6							▓▓	▓▓	▓▓
Sub-problem 7				▓▓					
Sub-problem 8	██	██	██	██					
Sub-problem 9								██	██
Sub-problem 10									██

Making links

The concept of multiple programmers working simultaneously on a problem relates to section later in this chapter, 'Thinking concurrently'.

Identify sub-procedures necessary to solve a problem

REVISED

A sub-procedure, or procedure, is a named part of a larger process that may be used several times, like a function, but unlike a function, it will not return any values to the calling code.

Sub-procedures are used to solve sub-problems within the program and it is important to identify the sub-problems that form part of the main task. The order in which these problems are dealt with can be important.

Example

With our game example, we might identify several sub-problems that need to be solved in order, for example:

✚ We will need a scoring system before we can set up a high-score table.

✚ We need to set up movements before we deal with interactions with other objects.

Check your understanding and progress at **www.hoddereducation.co.uk/myrevisionnotesdownloads**

Now test yourself — TESTED

8 Describe what is meant by decomposition.

9 Explain why it is beneficial to identify the components of a problem.

10 Explain why it is important to consider the order of the steps needed to solve a problem.

Answers on p. 220

Thinking logically

Thinking logically requires inferring things from what is known. In programming, it requires understanding where decisions need to be made and their consequences.

There are basically two approaches.

+ Induction proposes a hypothesis (or idea) based on observations. When developing a solution for a stakeholder, the programmer or analyst will observe and collect evidence of existing systems in order to propose a solution. This approach is particularly useful when modelling real-world systems.

+ Deduction uses underlying rules to determine how a system should work. When developing a simulation or model for a scientific or mathematical problem, the known rules will be applied to produce the required output.

Identify the points in a solution where a decision has to be taken

REVISED

When developing a computer solution to a problem, choices have to be made including the:

+ choice of programming paradigm or approach (e.g. procedural or object-oriented language)
+ programming language that provides the most appropriate features to solve the problem
+ peripheral devices required.

Once these initial decisions are made, planning where decision points in the program occur is essential. It is necessary to understand where decisions need to be made and the consequences of these decisions.

To think logically when solving a problem, it is necessary to:

+ identify when decision-making is required
+ identify what decisions need to be made
+ identify the conditions to enable a decision to be made
+ understand the interactions between decisions
+ apply decision-making to the real-world problem.

Identifying these decision points can be achieved in several ways, but often a flowchart or a pseudocode plan for the solution are used. In flowcharts, the decisions are usually shown as a diamond shape with two paths, one for true and one for false.

> **Paradigm** A programming paradigm is an approach to programming, not a particular type of language. Programming languages can be classified by their features, but many will fit more than one paradigm.

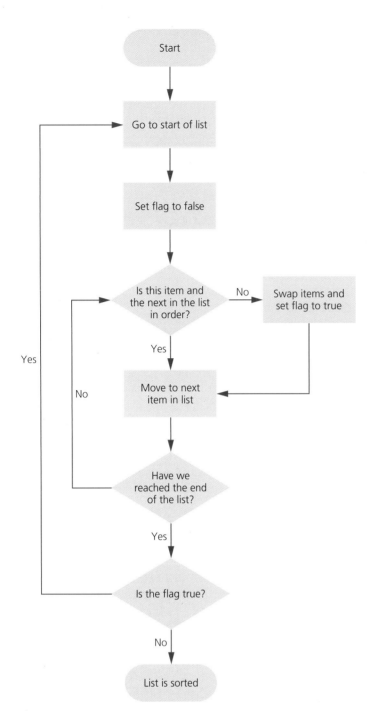

Figure 6.2 Flowchart for a bubble sort

Determine the logical conditions that affect the outcome of a decision

REVISED

When developing a solution to a problem, decisions need to be made.

The choice of programming language will determine what is possible. Alternatively, what is required will determine the choice of programming language. When developing a program for a small embedded system, an assembler is a more likely choice than a high-level language.

The format of a decision may affect the structure of the program being developed. A simple change, for example from 'greater than or equal to' to 'less than' in a condition, could make a significant change to the code structure that follows.

For example, the choice of `repeat` or `while` iterations can affect the outcome. A `repeat` loop will always execute at least once so is unsuitable when there is a possibility the loop may never need to execute.

Check your understanding and progress at **www.hoddereducation.co.uk/myrevisionnotesdownloads**

Determine how decisions affect flow through a program

As well as decisions made in the program to determine how to proceed, there will be decisions made by the user that affect the flow through the program.

When developing software, it is necessary to:
+ identify where the user needs to make decisions
+ identify and provide for all the possible outcomes from those decisions
+ prepare routes through the program for all the possible outcomes from decisions.

Good decision-making and planning for the outcomes of all possible decisions are key to an effective program.

Where a decision point occurs within the program can also have an impact on the code.

For example, if we are checking a password for length, use of upper case, lower case and numbers, the decision about when to check the length of the password is important:
+ Check the length and set a flag. Then check for upper case, lower case and numbers. This means each password is checked for all attributes each time.
+ Check and reject passwords that are too short. This means that only passwords that are long enough are checked for other attributes.

The second approach is potentially much more efficient.

> **Now test yourself**   TESTED
>
> 11 State two things that must be considered before starting to develop a program.
>
> **Answer on p. 220**

Thinking concurrently

Concurrently means 'at the same time'. Sometimes it can be more efficient to consider how to solve more than one problem at the same time. This can often result in more efficient algorithms that are quicker or use less computing resource.

If we have more resources, such as parallel processors, we can divide up jobs to be performed at the same time.

> **Making links**
>
> See Chapter 1 for details about parallel processors.
>
> See below for details of how multiple programmers can work as a team on a program.

A large, modular program will often be developed by a team of programmers working on modules simultaneously.

Determine the parts of a problem that can be tackled at the same time

In a concurrent approach to a problem, the designer looks for tasks that can be completed at the same time. In many cases, this will be a choice between going through all of the tasks in list A followed by all the tasks in list B or task 1 in lists A and B simultaneously, then task 2 in lists A and B and so on.

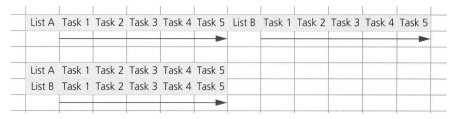

Figure 6.3 Concurrent tasks

Determining which tasks can be completed simultaneously, for example within the same loop, can then be dealt with concurrently.

Outline the benefits and trade-offs that might result from concurrent processing in a particular situation

REVISED

Concurrent processing is about using a computer to implement concurrent thinking.

The benefits of concurrent processing include:
+ more tasks can be completed in the same time frame, which is particularly useful for graphics processing
+ processor time is used more effectively: the program can get on with other tasks while it waits for a process to complete, for example user input or data retrieval.

> **Concurrent processing**
> Where several computations are carried out simultaneously.

The trade-offs include:
+ in more complex programs there may be delays while other parts of the program complete
+ organisation of the separate tasks and switching between processes can cause delays in processes starting and slow the program
+ some problems just cannot be broken down into tasks that can be completed simultaneously
+ problems with large sections that need to be completed sequentially will not benefit from other parts being processed simultaneously.

Genuinely processing more than one thing at a time requires multi-core processors and is called parallel processing. Parallel processing may have significant benefits if the problem is suited to being broken down into modules that can be processed simultaneously.

Because processors work so quickly it often appears that tasks are being completed simultaneously, when in fact they are being completed sequentially.

> **Making links**
>
> Parallel processors are covered in Chapter 1.

> **Now test yourself**
> TESTED
>
> 12 Explain why parallel processing may not be the best approach to solving a problem.
> 13 Describe two trade-offs related to concurrent processing.
>
> **Answers on p. 221**

Summary

Thinking abstractly

+ Abstraction is the removal of details to identify the key elements of a problem.
+ Abstraction allows programmers and non-specialists to use systems without needing to know the detail about how they work.
+ High-level languages use abstraction to hide away the details of the low-level code needed to implement each high-level command.
+ Abstraction is a simplification of reality.
+ When devising an abstract model, we need to consider the nature of the problem, who will use the solution, how the solution will be used, and the relevant detail required by the user.

Thinking ahead

+ By thinking ahead, it is possible identify the inputs and outputs for a given situation.
+ The required outputs will determine the necessary inputs; this in turn will determine the processing required.
+ Any data structures must be identified and how to capture the input data should be considered.
+ Preconditions for a solution to a problem that must be considered include:
  + any software or hardware requirements
  + identification of any subprograms and the data that will need to be passed to them
  + validation of input data to ensure it meets essential criteria
  + validation of actions to ensure they will not crash the program or return erroneous results.
+ Caching is the temporary storage of instructions or data the program anticipates will be needed, in locations that can be accessed quickly.
+ Caching saves time by speeding up access to data.
+ Algorithms are used to prefetch data that they predict will be required.
+ Different sizes of cache have limitations:
  + a small cache is quick to access but cannot store much data
  + a large cache can store more data but it takes more time to locate data within it.
+ Reusable program components such as frequently used routines are stored in program libraries for the user to access.
+ Reusable components have been thoroughly tested and require no further testing, saving time and resources.

+ Reusable components that do not quite match the requirements can be modified as required.

Thinking procedurally

+ Thinking procedurally enables the developer to identify the components of a problem.
+ Decomposition is the process of breaking a problem down step by step until each sub-problem can be solved.
+ The solution to a problem can be built from the low-level sub-problems by solving them and combining them into a complete solution.
+ The order of the steps needed to solve a problem is important.
+ Data from one module needs to be available and validated before it can be passed to another one.

Thinking logically

+ It is important to identify the points in a solution where a decision has to be taken.
+ The outcome of a decision will determine the process.
+ It is important to identify and consider the consequences of any decisions.
+ Decisions will affect the flow through a program.
+ Different decisions produce different paths through a program.
+ Decisions made by the user should be anticipated and appropriate measures built in to deal with all possible choices.

Thinking concurrently

+ Thinking concurrently will determine which parts of a problem can be tackled at the same time.
+ Multiple programmers may be able to work on different modules simultaneously if the modules are not interdependent.
+ There are benefits and trade-offs that might result from concurrent processing:
  + more tasks can be completed in the same time frame
  + the program can get on with other tasks while it waits for a slower process
  + there may be delays while other parts of the program complete
  + some problems, however, just cannot be broken down into tasks that can be completed simultaneously.

Exam practice

1 **a)** A group of programmers are working on a multi-player role-playing game. In the game, players move around a virtual environment based on a small city. The developers study a small city to design their environment.

    i) Identify two features of the real-world environment that will be included in the model. [2]

    ii) Identify two features of the real-world environment that will not be included in the model. [2]

  b) The players will have to move through the environment using the keyboard.

    Describe two ways the input should be validated to ensure the players can move around the virtual environment as realistically as possible. [4]

  c) The game has a number of players and other characters interacting throughout the game and when they encounter each other.

    Identify a suitable programming paradigm and explain why it is the most appropriate choice. [4]

  d) The game has high-resolution graphics and fast-response action. The organisation developing the program requires the programmers to use the cache when the program is running.

    Explain what is meant by cache and how it can be used within this type of program. [4]

  e) The developer has suggested the program be written using concurrent processing.

    i) Explain two benefits of using concurrent processing. [4]

    ii) Explain two trade-offs when using concurrent processing. [4]

2 **a)** A regional transport authority is planning to develop an app showing the local rail and metro networks.

    Explain what is meant by abstraction and why the developers will need to use abstraction before designing the virtual network diagram. [3]

  b) In the abstraction of the network, there will be similarities and differences.

    i) Identify two similarities and explain why they are included in the virtual network diagram. [4]

    ii) Identify two differences and explain why they are included in the virtual network diagram. [4]

  c) The finished app will be able to locate the user and identify the closest stops or stations and the services that run through that location.

    i) Identify two outputs from the system. [2]

    ii) Identify two inputs required for the system. [2]

    iii) Identify two preconditions for the real-world network to make this data available. [2]

  d) The app is designed using decomposition.

    i) Explain what is meant by decomposition. [2]

    ii) Explain what is meant by generalisation and how this can help the programmers when developing the program. [3]

    Once the problem has been decomposed, the tasks with a pre-written solution are identified.

    iii) Explain two reasons why it is beneficial to use pre-written components. [4]

  e) The remaining tasks are allocated to the team of programmers to work on concurrently.

    Describe how the order in which these tasks are completed is important. [4]

  f) The programmers are instructed to write subprograms using standard rules.

    Explain why enforcing standard rules for the subprogram is important. [4]

Answers available online

Programming techniques

Programming constructs: sequence, branching and iteration

REVISED

There are three fundamental constructs from which all programs can be built. These are:

+ sequence
+ branching
+ iteration.

Sequence

A sequence is the order in which statements are executed.

+ Computers will execute statements one after another, in the order they are presented.
+ This means that the order of instructions is very important as the same instructions in a different order will not produce the same result.

```
a = 5
b = a * 2
a = a + 1
c = a * 4
print b, c
```

This program will display: 10, 24

```
a = 5
a = a + 1
b = a * 2
c = a * 4
print b, c
```

This program will display: 12, 24

Do this

↓

Then this

↓

Then this

Figure 7.1 A sequence

Branching

Branching (often referred to as selection) is where a decision as to which part of a program is to be run is made, based on the state of a Boolean expression. Program control continues or is diverted to another part of the program according to whether the expression evaluates to 'true' or 'false'.

Selection Another term for branching.

Boolean expression An expression to which the answer is either true or false. Examples include:

```
x == 1
y < 9
password == "foo"
and attempts <= 3
```

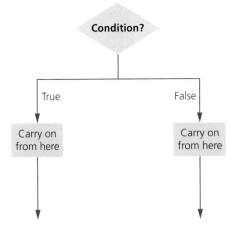

Figure 7.2 A decision with a Boolean expression

163

There are two main ways of branching in high-level programming languages: if/else and switch/case.

If/else statements
+ present a Boolean condition and a block of code that is run if the condition is true.
+ can have further conditions (using else if) that are run if they are true and the previous conditions are false
+ can optionally end with an else that runs a block of code if all previous conditions are false.

Example

```
if number > 100 then
   print("Too high")
else if number < 50 then
   print("Too low")
else
   print("Accepted")
end if
```

Exam tip

It is common for students to refer to 'if statements' as 'if loops'. This terminology is incorrect as 'if statements' do not repeat. Ensure you use the term 'if statements' and not 'if loops' in the exam to avoid dropping marks.

Switch/case statements
+ do not use explicit Boolean conditions, but instead a variable is given after the keyword switch
+ have case statements that are considered true (and therefore execute) if the variable after switch matches their value
+ can also have a default statement, run if none of the cases is true.

Example

```
switch day:
   case "Mon":
     print("Monday")
  case "Tue":
     print("Tuesday")
  case "We":
     print("Wednesday")
  case "Thu":
     print("Thursday")
  case "Fri":
     print("Friday")
  default:
     print("Not a weekday")
endswitch
```

Assembly language performs selection using branch instructions such as:
+ BRA (branch always)
+ BRP (branch if the value in the accumulator is positive).

Making links

You can find out more about branch instruction in assembly code in the section on Little Man Computer in Chapter 2.

Exam tips

The Python programming language doesn't contain an equivalent to switch/case. If you are a Python programmer, you should spend some time getting familiar with switch/case prior to the exam.

Note the OCR pseudocode doesn't have an equivalent of break, which is used in switch/case statements in some languages. You should assume the switch statement terminates after a successful case.

Check your understanding and progress at **www.hoddereducation.co.uk/myrevisionnotesdownloads**

Iteration

Iteration means repetition. It is used to make a section of code repeat itself. The repeated section is called a 'loop'.

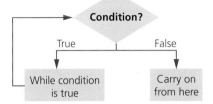

Figure 7.3 Iteration using a while loop

Loops can be:
+ count controlled; they run a certain number of times
+ condition controlled; they run as long as a Boolean expression is true.

Count-controlled loops

For loops are count-controlled loops.

> **Example**
>
> ```
> for i = 1 to 10
>     print(i)
> next i
> ```

> **Exam tip**
>
> For loops in OCR pseudocode are inclusive of their starting and ending number. That means that the OCR pseudocode:
>
> ```
> for i = 1 to 10
>     print(i)
> next i
> ```
>
> will print the numbers: 1, 2, 3, 4, 5, 6, 7, 8, 9, 10.
>
> This is equivalent to the Python code:
>
> ```
> for i range(1,11):
>     print(i)
> ```
>
> and the C style code:
>
> ```
> for(int i=1; i<11; i++)
> {
>     print(i);
> }
> ```
>
> or
>
> ```
> for(int i=1; i<=10; i++)
> {
>     print(i);
> }
> ```

Condition-controlled loops

While loops are condition-controlled loops with the condition at the start.

Example

```
while x * x < 1024
    x = x + 1
endwhile
```

Do ... Until loops have their condition at the end.

Example

```
do
    answer = input("What word beginning with 'i' means
    repetition?")
until answer == "iteration"
```

+ While loops may never run if the initial condition is not met.
+ Do ... until loops will always run at least once.

Exam tip

The Python programming language doesn't contain do ... until loops. However, you should spend some time getting familiar with them prior to the exam, as there may be questions on them.

Some languages (such as C-style languages C, C++, C#, Java etc.) use do ... while (the loop continues as long as a condition is true) instead of do ... until (the loop continues as long as the condition is false.

The OCR pseudocode

```
do
    answer = input("What word beginning with 'i' means
    repetition?")
until answer == "iteration"
```

would be the C-style equivalent of:

```
do
{
    answer = input("What word beginning with 'i' means
    repetition?")
}while(answer!="iteration")
```

Now test yourself

TESTED

1 Look at the bubble sort algorithm on page 76. Identify one example of:
   a) Sequence   b) Branching   c) Iteration
2 Look at the binary search algorithm on page 192. Identify one example of:
   a) Sequence   b) Branching   c) Iteration
3 Where you have identified iteration in questions 1 and 2, state whether it is count controlled or condition controlled.

Answers on p. 221

Recursion

REVISED

Recursion is where a procedure or function calls itself. This can be used as an alternative to iteration.

Worked example

The program below uses recursion to count upwards.

```
procedure counting(n)
    print(n)
    counting(n + 1)
endprocedure
//Main program
counting(1)
```

When the procedure `counting` is called it prints out `n` then calls counting again on `n + 1`

So:
+ calling `counting(1)` will print 1 and then call `counting(2)`
+ `counting(2)` prints 2 and calls `counting(3)`
+ `counting(3)` prints 3 and calls `counting(4)` and so on.

The line `counting(n + 1)` is where recursion takes place – it is said to be a recursive call.

+ Every time a subroutine is called, the state of the program (including values of all local variables) is put on a stack.
+ This means each time a new version of counting is called, all information related to the current version of counting is stored on this stack.
+ This causes a problem, however. The stack has a finite amount of space and eventually will be able to hold no more.

While the program in the previous worked example starts counting, as we'd expect at some point it will run out of space on the stack, causing a stack overflow error.

In order to avoid this, we need a base case; a situation in which we stop the recursion. For example:

```
procedure counting(n)
        if n == 100 then
                print("Done")
        else
                print(n)
                counting(n + 1)
        endif
endprocedure
```

The program now terminates after printing 99:

95

96

97

98

99

Done

Once the base case is true, the subroutine returns control to the subroutine that called it rather than running another recursive instance. This means values start getting returned back to each instance of the function that has made a recursive call (known as 'unwinding' the stack).

You might think the program finishes at the line `print("Done")` but after running that line it still has to take each instance of the procedure `counting` from the stack.

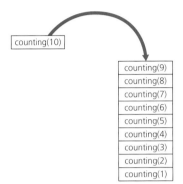

Figure 7.4 Calling `counting(11)` would result in `counting(10)` being put on the stack

Recursive call An instance of a subroutine calling itself (i.e. causing recursion).

Stack overflow When a stack runs out of space to store data.

Base case A condition in a recursive subroutine that, when true, returns control to the subroutine that called it rather than running another recursive instance.

If there were more lines after `counting(n + 1)`, it would then go on to run them, first for `count(99)` then `count(98)` and so on. This can be seen if we change the order of `print(n)` and `counting(n + 1)` in the subroutine:

```
procedure counting(n)
        if n == 100 then
                print("Done")
        else
                counting(n + 1)
                print(n)
        endif
endprocedure
```

Now the program starts by printing Done then counts down from 99:

```
Done
99
98
97
96
95
```

and so on.

Worked example

The factorial function is often used to demonstrate recursion. The factorial function, written as !, denotes a number being multiplied by every integer from 1 up to and including itself. For example:

$4! = 4 * 3 * 2 * 1$

We can write a program to calculate the factorial for any given integer, n. To write this recursively, we should first consider the base case. We want our function to return 1 when given the value 1 (as $1! = 1$)

```
function factorial(n)
   if n == 1 then
     return 1
   endif
endfunction
```

Next consider the following. When n is not 1, $n! = n * (n - 1)!$

So 4! is the same as 4 * 3! …

… and 3! is the same as 3 * 2! …

… and 2! is the same as 2 * 1! …

We have already established 1! is 1.

We can write this out as:

```
function factorial(n)
   if n == 1 then
     return 1
   else
     return n * factorial(n - 1)
   endif
endfunction
```

Check your understanding and progress at **www.hoddereducation.co.uk/myrevisionnotesdownloads**

Anything that can be achieved through recursion can be achieved through iteration and vice versa. There are some programming languages that do not have iteration and rely solely on recursion.

The advantages of recursion:
+ Some problems are easier to think of recursively.
+ Recursive solutions can be more elegant and easier to follow than their iterative counterparts.

The disadvantages of recursion compared to iteration are:
+ It requires more memory in order to maintain the stack of calls.
+ If the space on the stack runs out the program will crash.
+ The overheads of maintaining the stack means a recursive solution can perform more slowly than an iterative equivalent.

Exam tip

If you are asked to write a recursive algorithm in the exam, make sure you have a base case (or base cases) so you know your program will eventually stop and not crash.

Making links

You can find out more about stacks in Chapter 4. Note that a stack is used to store recursion calls because it is a 'last in first out' data structure. This means that when the base case is reached, the stack can be 'unwound' each time, going back to the previous step.

You can use recursion with object-oriented programming to make data structures. For more about object-oriented programming, see later in this chapter and Chapter 2, and for more about data structures, see Chapter 4. A node class that contains an attribute that is itself an instance of node can build a linked list. A node class that contains two instances of a node can build a binary tree.

Now test yourself   TESTED ◯

4   The function foo is recursive.

```
function foo(n)
    if n == 0 then
        return true
    else if n == 1 then
        return false
    else
        return foo(n - 2)
    endif
endfunction
```
a) State the result of foo(5).
b) State the result of foo(6).
c) State the purpose of the function foo.
d) Explain what would happen if the statement foo(-1) were run.

Answers on p. 221

Global and local variables   REVISED ◯

All non-trivial programs use variables.

Variables:
+ are named locations that store data
+ have contents that can be changed during program execution
+ have data types
+ have scope (whether a variable is global or local).

Scope A variable's scope is the extent to which it can be seen within different parts of a program. Scope can be said to be global or local. A variable is said to be *in scope* at any particular part of the program if it can be used.

In most languages, variables need to be declared before they can be used. This is known as variable declaration and normally defines what data type is associated with each variable. When a variable is assigned its first value, it is said to be initialised.

Global variables can be 'seen' throughout a program. They are declared outside any functions or subprograms and then can be accessed from any part of the program.

Local variables are set or declared inside a function or other subprogram. They can only be accessed from within that subprogram. (In some languages, such as C# and Java, variables can be local to the structure in which they are declared, for example an `if` statement or a `while` loop.) Once a program leaves the structure the local variable is scoped for, that local variable ceases to exist.

> **Variable declaration** The point at which a variable is created.

> **Exam tip**
>
> OCR's pseudocode does not require variables to be declared separately before use; they are declared at the point they are initialised, hence the worked examples in this chapter do not show this. If you have learned the Python programming language you will be familiar with this approach. However, this is contrast to many other languages, so ensure you are familiar with the concepts of declaration.

Worked example

```
max = biggest(3,8)

print(max)

print(a)


function biggest(a,b)

  if a > b then

    return a

  else

    return b

  endif

endfunction
```

The local variables a and b do not exist until the function `biggest` is called. Once the line `return b` has been run, both a and b are destroyed. Therefore, the line `print(a)` would cause an error, because a does not exist in the main program.

It is considered best practice to avoid global variables whenever possible. Having a variable that can be changed in any part of a program, affecting completely different parts of the program, can make for some very hard to solve bugs.

Because global variables are never destroyed, having more global variables also increases a program's memory requirements.

It is possible for a local variable to have the same name as a global variable. On these occasions, the local version is used whenever it is in scope.

> **Bug** An error or mistake within program code that causes a program to behave in ways other than intended.

Worked example

```
num = 5

print(num)

foo()

print(num)

procedure foo()

  num = 10

  print(num)

endprocedure
```

The program above outputs

```
5

10

5
```

Check your understanding and progress at **www.hoddereducation.co.uk/myrevisionnotesdownloads**

TESTED ◯

Now test yourself

5 Describe the difference between a global and a local variable.

6 In the program below:
   a) State whether the variable n is local or global.
   b) Explain why running the program generates an error.

```
foo()
print(n)
procedure foo()
  print("Hello")
  n = 10
endprocedure
```

Answers on p. 221

Modularity: functions and procedures

REVISED ◯

Programs are often written in separate sections called **subroutines**. The property of a program being split into subprograms is called **modularity**. Modularity has the advantages that:

+ The program is easier to test. Each subroutine can be tested individually to confirm that it works wherever it is called – regardless of whether the rest of the program or other subroutines are working properly.
+ The program is easier to read. If the subroutines are well named, the reader can understand what is being done by looking at the subroutine's name, rather than needing to look at the code in the subroutine itself.
+ Subroutines can be reused within the program (and other programs) saving time.
+ It is easier to share work among a team, with different members working on different subroutines.

There are two types of subroutines, functions and procedures:
+ **Functions** are subprograms that return a value.
+ **Procedures** perform some operation but do not return a value.

> **Making links**
>
> Note that in object-oriented programming, subroutines within classes are referred to as methods. For more about object-oriented programming, see Chapter 2.

Parameter passing

Subroutines can have data, known as **arguments**, passed to their **parameters**.

When the code below is run, the values 7 and 9 are passed to the parameters a and b respectively.

```
print(biggest(7,9))

function biggest(a,b)
    if a > b then
        return a
    else
        return b
    endif
endfunction
```

> **Exam tip**
>
> Students sometimes get confused between arguments and parameters.
>
> Parameters are the variables whose values are taken in by a subroutine and the arguments are the values passed to them.
>
> In the example shown, a and b are the parameters and 7 and 9 are the arguments.

Passing by value

In most languages, values are passed to subroutines by value. This means a copy of the value is passed to the subroutine.

In the exam board pseudocode, unless specifically stated otherwise, you should assume arguments are passed by value.

If it is relevant to the question, it will be flagged in the code with the :byVal postfix.

Example

```
num = 5

print(num)

print(triple(num))

print(num)

function triple(n:byVal)

        n = n * 3

        return n

endfunction
```

In the code above:
+ The variable `num` is assigned the value 5 and printed.
+ A copy of 5 gets passed to the function `triple` and assigned to `n`.
+ `n` gets multiplied by 3 to become 15.
+ 15 gets sent back to the main program and printed (and `n` ceases to exist when the function `triple` finishes).
+ Throughout this process, `num` remains unchanged from its starting value of 5 meaning `print(num)` outputs 5.

So the program outputs:

```
5

15

5
```

Passing by reference

Passing by reference means that the parameter is set to point to the same memory location as the variable. In the exam board's pseudocode, this is denoted by `:byRef` after the parameter.

Example

```
    num = 5

    print(num)

    print(triple(num))

    print(num)

    function triple(n:byRef)

      n = n * 3

      return n

    end function
```

In the code above:
+ The variable `num` is set to 5 and printed.
+ In the line `print(triple(num))`, instead of a copy of 5 being passed to n, its reference is, meaning n now points to the same memory location as `num`.
+ n (which is the same memory location as `num`) is multiplied by 3, and 15 is sent back to the main program (again n ceases to exist when `triple` finishes).

Because n and num are both stored in the same location, when n became 15 so did num. This means, this program will output:

```
    5

    15

    15
```

As previously stated, global variables are to be avoided where possible. Passing by reference is one way of avoiding the need for a global variable in a subroutine.

In the example below, function popA requires the variable top to be global. However, function popB can have top passed to it by reference, allowing the variable top to be local.

```
top = 5
function popA()
        if top >= 0 then
                topValue = stack[top]
                top = top - 1
                return topValue
        else
                print("Stack empty")
                return null
        end if
endfunction
function popB(top:byRef)
        if top >= 0 then
                topValue = stack[top]
                top = top - 1
                return topValue
        else
                print("Stack empty")
                return null
        end if
endfunction
```

Passing by reference instead of using global variables is still not ideal, as it is good programming practice for subroutines to have no side effects on the wider program.

Now test yourself   TESTED ◯

7   Describe an advantage of making a program modular.

8   State what the following program would output:

```
a = 10
b = 10
foo(a,b)
print(a)
print(b)
procedure foo(x:byValue, y:byRef)
    x = x + 5
    y = y + 5
endprocedure
```

Answers on p. 221

Use of an IDE to develop/debug a program

In the past, programs were written in text editors, which can create and change text files but little else. Once written, the files created would then be run through a compiler or interpreter. If any errors were identified, the file would be amended in the text editor before being run through the translator program again.

Over time, the number of tools programmers use has increased. Examples include Linters, version control software and unit testing programs:

+ Linters: check code for any syntax errors or stylistic approaches that can be improved.
+ Version control software: keeps track of changes made to code allowing programmers to work together on code, combine their contributions and roll code back to a previous state if there are any errors.
+ Unit testing programs: allows programmers to design tests to check aspects of a program's functionality. This means they can be sure no part of the program has been inadvertently broken when changes are made.

Rather than having to move back and forth between multiple software tools to perform these functions, integrated development environments (IDEs) started to be used.

An IDE combines the functionality of an advanced text editor and compiler/interpreter along with tools like linters, version control software and unit testing programs into one application.

> **Integrated development environment (IDE)** A coding environment that incorporates numerous software tools to aid the writing, executing and debugging of code.

Making links

Refactoring is a key part of extreme programming (covered in Chapter 2). In extreme programming, programmers are encouraged to continually refactor code.

In addition, IDEs offer other functionality to help the programmer with the coding process. This includes:

+ Refactoring tools: refactoring is the process of improving code without changing its functionality. This may be to improve code's readability or to improve its efficiency. IDEs often include tools to help with this. For example, they may allow the programmer to rename a variable, and automatically rename every instance of it. It may also allow them to select code that is repeated throughout the program and automatically place it in a subroutine.
+ Code completion: this is when the IDE detects what the user is typing and suggests how to complete the part they are typing. This can speed up the programmer's work and saves them having to remember the exact names of every routine they are calling.
+ Code generation: there are common pieces of code that programmers have to regularly create (for example getters and setters in classes). With code generation, IDEs automatically create these pieces of code for the programmer.
+ Syntax error, inline highlighting: the IDE can draw the programmer's attention to syntax errors in a similar way a spellchecker would do in a word processor. This saves the programmer having to go through the process of compiling and only then being faced with a list of errors. In some cases, the IDE may be able to suggest corrections to the errors.
+ Syntax highlighting: an IDE can work out which part of the program each word is as it is typed (e.g. a variable, a comment, a reserved word etc.) and then colour it accordingly. This not only makes the code easier to read but may also help the programmer detect typos. If, for example, they mistype the reserved word `while` as `whole` it will appear in the same colour as a variable rather than the reserved word used to make a loop.

> **Syntax error** An error in a program that breaks the rules of the language's structure. For example, `2 + 3 = a`

> **Reserved word** A word put aside by the language as having a special purpose and so cannot be used as a variable name. Examples vary from language to language but may include: `if`, `else`, `for`, `while`, `return`.

IDEs also have tools specifically able to help with debugging:

+ Breakpoints: these allow points to be set within the program where it will be paused when run to allow the programmer to try and detect where and why errors are occurring.

> **Debugging** The process of finding and removing bugs (or errors in the behaviour) of a program.

Check your understanding and progress at **www.hoddereducation.co.uk/myrevisionnotesdownloads**

+ Stepping: this allows the programmer to run the program line by line, stepping through the code.
+ Variable inspection, watches and watchpoints: often an IDE will allow you to inspect the values of variables while you are debugging. If there are variables you want to keep a particular eye on, you can also set a variable watch that will keep the programmer updated as to their values. Programmers can also set watchpoints that pause the program's execution when a variable or expression reaches a given value.
+ Stack inspection: every time a subroutine is called the computer places the current state of the program into a stack. Stack inspection allows the programmer to see the chain of subroutines that have been called in order to lead the program to its current state.

Making links

You can find out more about stacks being used with subroutines in the section on recursion earlier in this chapter.

Revision activity

Investigate at least two IDEs that can be used with your usual programming language.

1 For each one, find out the facilities that it offers the programmer.

2 Try some of these out on a program that you have written.

These debugging tools are often used in conjunction with each other. For example, a programmer may set a breakpoint, and when the program reaches it, step through each line, examining the variables.

Now test yourself   TESTED ◯

9 State three features an IDE has to help programmers debug their code.

10 Explain why, for very small programs, programmers may prefer a text editor over an IDE.

Answers on p. 221

Use of object-oriented techniques   REVISED ◯

Object-oriented programming is discussed in detail in Chapter 2.

In paper two you should be able to:
+ use classes to make objects with attributes to define their state and methods to define their behaviour
+ use encapsulation to ensure attributes can only be manipulated in the intended way for a class
+ use inheritance to create subclasses with the attributes and methods of their parent class as well as their own
+ use polymorphism to allow classes of the same parent class to be treated in the same way and allow for overloading and overriding of methods.

Computational methods

Features that make a problem solvable by computational methods   REVISED ◯

For a problem to be solvable using computational methods, it must be able to be represented in a structured, algorithmic form.

For example, many problems based on mathematics or known physical laws lend themselves to computational solutions, such as:
+ plotting a course to the moon
+ predicting eclipses
+ estimating the amount of steel necessary to build a new model of car to a given specification.

Computational methods
Any method that can be used to solve a problem by computational means. For example, searching, sorting, modelling and mathematical methods.

In all the cases in these examples, it is feasible to acquire enough data in order to apply calculations and expect a reasonably accurate solution.

A problem is said to be computable if it can be:
+ represented by an algorithm
+ solved within a finite timescale
+ solved at a reasonable cost.

However, while a problem may be computable it may be impractical to apply computational methods if the problem:
+ cannot be solved within a realistic time frame
+ requires resources that are not available.

This means when deciding if a problem is solvable the available resources must be taken into consideration:
+ processing power
+ memory limitations
+ financial resources
+ time available
+ available peripheral devices.

Problem recognition

REVISED ●

Having decided that a problem is computable, and can be potentially solved within a realistic time frame, at a reasonable cost and using the available resources, the exact nature of the problem needs to be identified.

To define a problem we need to:
+ identify what the problem actually is – this might not always be immediately apparent
+ identify the stakeholders' requirements for the solution
+ analyse existing solutions to similar problems and identify the strengths and weaknesses of these solutions
+ decide what features in existing solutions can be incorporated into the proposed solution
+ decide whether a partial solution can solve a significant part of the initial problem and have value, if the problem is becoming too large to solve as one task
+ consider the data requirements, including the necessary inputs and storage requirements.

> **Making links**
>
> For the analysis of the problem in the non-examined assessment programming project, you should apply these methods to identify and research the problem. The results of the process can then be used to specify the proposed solution.

Problem decomposition

REVISED ●

Decomposition is the process of breaking down a problem into sub-problems until the lowest level of sub-problem is recognisably solvable. Usually this will mean decomposing the solution until it becomes a set of self-contained subprograms.

This process will to help identify:
+ whether any solutions already exist for particular sub-problems
+ whether any subprograms can be reused in other parts of the solution
+ the overall structure of the solution
+ the order in which sub-problems need to be dealt with.

For large projects, each sub-problem can be allocated to different teams of programmers based on:
+ their specialisms
+ tasks that can be completed concurrently by different programmers.

Check your understanding and progress at **www.hoddereducation.co.uk/myrevisionnotesdownloads**

Teams of programmers working concurrently can speed up the time to create an overall solution.

Once a sub-problem has been solved by a subprogram, each subprogram can be reused in other solutions to different problems in the future.

Making links

Problem decomposition is linked to procedural thinking, covered in Chapter 6.

Now test yourself   TESTED ◯

11 List three features that make a problem solvable by computer methods.

12 Describe two features of problem recognition that help to define a problem.

Answers on p. 221

Use of divide and conquer   REVISED ◯

Divide and conquer is an approach to solving a problem. It does this by repeatedly dividing the problem into two or more similar, but simpler, sub-problems, which themselves are divided until they become simple enough to solve.

Once the individual sub-problems can be solved, the solution is built recursively by merging the solutions at each stage. This process is often referred to as 'divide – conquer – merge'.

Making links

Recursively refers to a function or process that calls itself repeatedly in order to solve a problem. Recursion is discussed above. Merge sort and quick sort are examples of recursive algorithms – see Chapter 8.

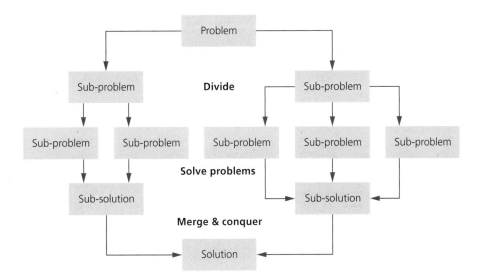

Figure 7.5 Divide – conquer – merge

Examples of the use of divide and conquer algorithms include the binary search tree technique in Chapter 4 and the binary search and merge sort in Chapter 8.

The advantage of divide and conquer is that the problem is simplified at each iteration and reduces to a set of solvable sub-problems quite quickly.

However, there are disadvantages when using recursive solutions:
+ they can generate a lot of data to be stored in the stack, potentially causing stack overflow
+ the code for these sub-problems can be quite complex, making it difficult to trace data flows when debugging a solution.

Use of abstraction

REVISED

Abstraction is a representation of reality that removes unnecessary detail. It:
+ allows the programmer to identify the important aspects of the problem
+ helps to identify elements of the program that are similar and can be solved using a similar approach
+ identifies reusable components that can be incorporated into the solution.

Examples of abstractions used to represent real-world entities in a program include:
+ variables
+ objects
+ layers
+ data models
+ data structures
+ entities.

> **Making links**
>
> Abstraction is discussed in Chapter 6.

> **Making links**
>
> For the programming project, these methods are used when designing a solution to the problem.

> **Now test yourself**
> TESTED
>
> 13 Describe what is meant by the term divide and conquer.
>
> 14 Explain why abstraction helps to define the elements of a problem that are suited to a computational solution.
>
> **Answers on p. 221**

Problem-solving techniques

REVISED

There are a number of well-defined computational techniques that can be deployed to solve problems.

Backtracking

Backtracking is essentially a trial-and-error approach. The problem is solved by following a sequence of actions until it no longer works. At this point, we return to the last known working stage and try a new path.
+ When writing a program, we develop the code section by section, testing at each stage. Once that section is tested and working we save it as a version of the program. If at the next stage we introduce an error, we can backtrack to the saved version that we know to work and try another approach.
+ Playing chess uses backtracking. When planning a chess move the consequences of that move are considered. If the consequences are not good, we backtrack and consider alternative moves until we find one that is likely to be successful.

> **Making links**
>
> Depth-first traversal is an example of backtracking. Look at algorithms for depth-first traversal in Chapter 8. There is also an example of depth-first traversal for graphs in Chapter 4.

> **Exam tip**
>
> You will be expected to apply your knowledge of these topics to scenarios developed as part of longer questions in the examination paper.

> **Backtracking** An approach to finding a solution that explores a possibility until it is no longer deemed feasible. At that point we backtrack to the last point at which it worked and follow a new path.
>
> **Data mining** Looking for patterns in large data sets.

Data mining

Data mining examines large data sets looking for patterns and relationships in order to find new insights.

Databases are defined to store and process data in predefined ways but, when they become large enough, unexpected patterns and relationships can emerge, especially if combined with other large databases.

Check your understanding and progress at **www.hoddereducation.co.uk/myrevisionnotesdownloads**

Data mining is used extensively for medical research. AI is used to look at large data sets in order to identify previously unknown patterns and relationships. This can be used to predict the onset of a disease, in order to prevent or intervene earlier and more effectively, or to look for potential cures for diseases.

> **Making links**
>
> In Chapter 5 we look at the analysis of personal data. Data supplied for specified purposes may not present a problem, but if two or more data sets are combined and processed in a way that was not identified, information about the individual that may cause concern could be revealed.

Data mining incorporates:
+ cluster analysis: grouping objects that have similarities together
+ pattern matching: finding and checking specific patterns of data, for example a compiler parsing source code to check if it is syntactically correct
+ anomaly detection: identifying outliers – data that does not fit the pattern for a data set
+ regression analysis: a modelling technique that looks at the relationship between variables where one variable affects the other.

> **Parsing** The process of analysing a string of symbols in a computer language to determine whether there are any syntax errors.
>
> **Heuristic solutions** An approximate, non-optimal, but sufficient solution – used when finding an exact solution is impractical.

Heuristics

Heuristic solutions are approximate solutions used when finding an exact solution is not feasible, for example because of complexity or cost or time.

Instead of supplying a perfect solution, we provide one that is good enough and solves the major elements of a problem. These are often called 'rule of thumb' solutions.

Heuristics are used to provide estimates for intractable problems and are typically used in machine learning or voice recognition.

Performance modelling

It is not always possible to test the full performance of a system. It may not be feasible to test all possibilities for reasons of:
+ safety
+ time
+ expense.

For example, in avionics or traffic management, we might want to test that software responds correctly in an emergency but do not want test this out on a real-life emergency. Instead, we use a mathematical model to simulate the potential outcomes.

The performance of software solutions should also be tested when the system is under maximum stress, for instance with:
+ the maximum number of users
+ extreme data
+ unusual activity.

Performance modelling is an important tool in computational thinking but is only useful if the model and the data used are accurate.

Various mathematical tools will form part of such a model:
+ statistics: relevant existing data will be used to formulate the model
+ randomisation: where we cannot predict real-life events, for example when simulating the performance of a transport system, randomised data (such as the random arrival of passengers at a station) can be provided to simulate a range of potential situations.

Pipelining

Pipelining is where the output from one process provides the input for another.

Complex tasks can often be split into multiple streams using separate pipelines so that processes can be completed in parallel.

The RISC processor is an example of a processor where the fetch, decode and execute stages can be queued, speeding up the process.

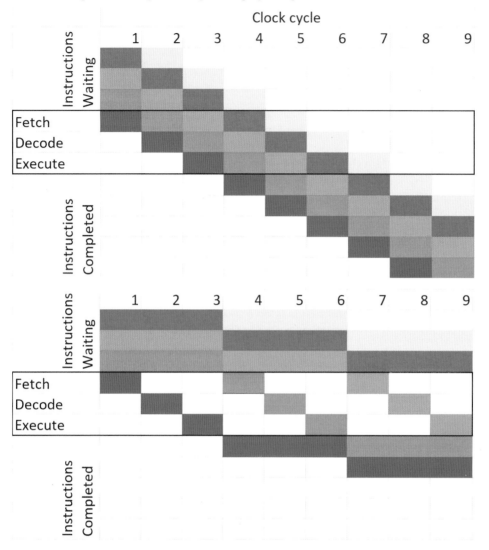

Figure 7.6 In both images, instructions are queued by the CPU before being fetched, decoded and executed. In the first image, the next instruction is fetched while the previous one is decoded and so on. This is pipelining. In the second image, pipelining is not used, and each instruction waits until the previous one has been fetched, decoded and executed. This means that parts of the CPU are idle at certain times and instructions wait in the queue for longer

> **Making links**
>
> Pipelining in relation to CPUs, and RISC processors are discussed in Chapter 1.

Check your understanding and progress at **www.hoddereducation.co.uk/myrevisionnotesdownloads**

Visualisation to solve problems

Problems can often be better understood if presented as a visual model. A visual model will often identify key features and trends in a complex situation.

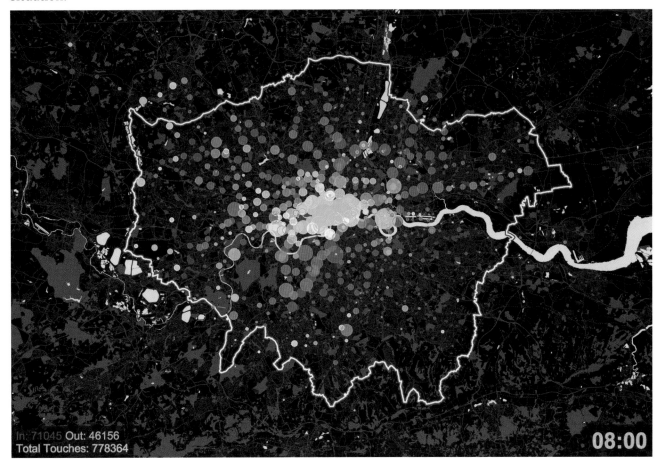

In: 71045 Out: 46156
Total Touches: 778364

08:00

Figure 7.7 A visualisation of Oyster card use on the London underground

In hotspot visualisation, circles are used to indicate events; the relative size of the circles indicates the numbers involved.

For instance, circles could be superimposed on a map of central London to show where people begin and end their tube journeys. The relative size of the circles would indicate the number of people beginning or ending a journey at each tube station.

Using such models can show interesting and unexpected trends that could not be produced by traditional methods.

Making links

Graphs and trees, in Chapter 4, are an example of a visual representations of a real-life situation.

Now test yourself TESTED ○

15 Describe what is meant by the term heuristic solution.

16 Explain when you would use performance modelling to test a solution

17 Explain why visualisation is used to examine problems.

Answers on p. 221–22

181

Summary

Programming techniques

+ Programs are based on three fundamental constructs: sequence, branching and iteration.
+ Sequence means that lines of code are run consecutively in the order they are written.
+ Branching is when a program uses a condition to determine which code is executed next.
    + In the case of an `if`/`else` statement, this is based on a Boolean expression.
    + `Case`/`switch` statements choose the code to execute, based on whether it matches a stated variable.
+ Iteration means the repetition of code and takes place using loops. There are three types of loops:
    + count controlled, for example `for` loops
    + condition controlled with the condition at the start, for example while loops
    + condition controlled with the condition at the end, for example `do ... until` loops.
+ Recursion is where a subroutine calls itself and can be used as an alternative to iteration.
+ Recursive subroutines should have a base case to avoid stack overflow errors.
+ Recursive solutions can be easier to follow than some iterative solutions but require more memory.
+ Variables have scope, which specifies where in the program they exist.
+ Local variables only exist in the part of the program in which they are created, usually a subroutine.
+ Global variables exist through the entire program.
+ Local variables should be used in preference to global variables where possible as this reduces the risk of introducing bugs.
+ Modularity is the breaking down of a program into subroutines. This helps with the readability and maintainability of the code.
+ Subroutines can be functions (which carry out code and return a value) or procedures (which carry out code but do not return a value).
+ Parameters are the variables whose values are taken in by a subroutine and arguments are the values passed to the parameters.
+ Arguments can be passed to parameters by reference or by value.
+ Passing by value sends a copy of the value to the subroutine.
+ Passing by reference send the location of the argument to the subroutine meaning the parameter points to that location.
+ Integrated development environments (IDEs) combine a number of programming tools (including text editors and compilers) into a single application.

+ IDEs have features that assist the programmer with writing their code (including syntax highlighting, refactoring tools and code completion).
+ IDEs also have features to help the programmer debug their code (including breakpoints, stepping and variable watches).
+ You are expected to be able to use the object-oriented programming techniques you studied for paper one in Chapter 2, in paper two, too. This includes using classes, objects, encapsulation, inheritance and polymorphism.

Computational methods

+ Identifying whether a problem can be solved using computational methods. Can it be:
    + represented by an algorithm
    + solved within a finite timescale
    + solved at a reasonable cost?
+ Problem recognition by defining the stakeholder and system requirements: strengths and weaknesses, input, output and data requirements.
+ Problem decomposition means breaking down problems into smaller problems until each sub-problem can be solved.
+ Divide and conquer simplifies complex problems very quickly:
    + divide the problem into sub-problems
    + conquer each sub-problem recursively
    + merge the solutions.
+ Abstraction is used to remove excessive detail and simplify the problem:
    + real-world entities are represented by computational elements
    + problems that already have a solution are identified
    + similar problems are grouped together
    + which makes the project more manageable.
+ Problem-solving techniques:
    + backtracking: trying a sequence of actions until it no longer provides a solution, then backtracking to the last known working stage and following a different path
    + data mining: examining large data sets to identify new patterns and relationships in the data
    + heuristics: rule of thumb, approximate solutions that produce solutions described as 'good enough'
    + performance modelling: using models to test complex solutions where it would be unfeasible to test in real life because of issues such as safety, cost or time
    + pipelining: computer technique where the output from one module provides the input for another
    + visualisation to solve problems: using visual models of a situation to highlight unexpected patterns and relationships.

Check your understanding and progress at **www.hoddereducation.co.uk/myrevisionnotesdownloads**

Exam practice

1   The function `head` returns the first item in a list.

   The function `tail` returns a list with everything but the first item.

   `numbers = [1,2,3,4,5]`

   `head(numbers)` returns 1

   `tail(numbers)` returns `[2,3,4,5]`

   Using `head` and `tail`, write a recursive version of the linear search algorithm. (You may wish to refer to page 191 to reacquaint yourself with linear search.)   [5]

2   Discuss how an IDE can save a programmer time.   [9]

3   Describe how a Boolean expression can control the operation of a loop.   [4]

4   Describe the difference between a `while` loop and a `for` loop.   [2]

5   Explain the disadvantages of using global variables.   [2]

6   In terms of a function, explain what a parameter is.   [1]

7   Explain the differences between passing parameters by reference and by value. [4]

8   Explain the difference between a class and an object.   [2]

9   Explain how we use visualisation to represent arrays.   [2]

10 A programmer applies decomposition to a complex problem.

   a) Explain what is meant by decomposition.   [2]

   b) Identify two features that decomposition will reveal to the programmer and explain how each of these features will help the programmer solve the problem.   [4]

11 A government department has several large databases of citizens. One stores employment income and tax records, another stores home ownership records, another stores vehicle registrations details and another stores details of foreign travel.

   The department uses this data to identify unexplained income to track down criminal activity.

   Evaluate how this government department could use data mining with this data to identify criminal activity.   [6]

12 When buying stocks and shares, an investor wants to write a program that attempts to identify which shares to buy and which to sell. The program should look for patterns in the data in order to identify trends in the market based on past events.

   Explain how such a program might be designed using a range of computational methods.   [6]

Answers available online

Algorithms

Analysis and design of algorithms for a given situation

An algorithm is a set of instructions to carry out a given task. There are a number of ways to express algorithms such as using flowcharts and pseudocode.

When we want a computer to carry out an algorithm, we write it as a program.

The aim of writing algorithms is to produce a process that will work on a generalised representation of a problem, that is, it can be reused for similar problems.

It is not straightforward to produce algorithms. We need to ensure that an algorithm is both correct and as efficient as it can be.

Proving that an algorithm is incorrect can be trivial; we just need to show that, in one case, it fails.

Proving that an algorithm is correct is much more difficult and often requires mathematical induction (which is beyond the scope of this course). Sometimes a problem is 'too hard'. We then need to decide if there is a 'good enough' solution that is acceptable.

In the next few sections, we will look at evaluating an algorithm's efficiency.

> **Algorithm** A set of instructions explaining how to carry out a given task.

Making links

When designing algorithms, you may wish to consider the computational methods discussed in Chapter 7. These help with the process of breaking down a problem and constructing an algorithm to solve it.

Now test yourself
TESTED ◯

1 Describe the difference between an algorithm and a program.
2 State two ways algorithms could be represented.

Answers on p. 222

The suitability of different algorithms for a given task and data set

REVISED ◯

There may often exist more than one algorithm to perform a given task. For example, as you will see later in this chapter, there are a number of algorithms that can be used to sort data. We need to determine which algorithm is best for any given situation. Algorithms can vary in terms of:
+ execution time (how long they take to run)
+ execution space (the amount of working memory they need).

This is known as an algorithm's efficiency.

It is often the case that there is a trade-off to be made between these two factors. A number of algorithms can be made to run more quickly (reducing

> **Efficiency** A reflection of the amount of CPU time or memory an algorithm requires to execute.

the execution time) by using more memory (increasing the execution space). One example of this is implementing a cache.

The choice of algorithm will also depend on the data that is being used. Binary search has a far quicker execution time than linear search but is only able to operate on sorted data.

Answer on p. 222

> **Making links**
>
> As an example of the effect of a data set, compare the RLE and dictionary coding compression algorithms in Chapter 3. RLE performs well on text with repeated consecutive characters, whereas dictionary coding performs well where large chunks of text repeat in a document. For example, RLE would perform well on:
>
> XXXXXXXYYYYYXXYYYYYYYYXXXYXXXXXXXYYYYYYYYYY
>
> Whereas dictionary coding would perform well on:
>
> How much wood would a woodchuck chuck if a woodchuck could chuck wood?

> **Now test yourself**
>
> 3 State the ways algorithms can differ in terms of their performance.
>
> **Answer on p. 222**
>
> TESTED

Measures and methods to determine the efficiency of different algorithms

REVISED

One way to compare how efficiently algorithms will perform is by looking at their complexity.

Complexity doesn't show us how quickly an algorithm executes (that would depend on the CPU running it) or exactly how much space it requires, but rather how well it scales when given larger data sets to act upon. In other words, complexity looks at how much longer an algorithm will take to run, or how much more space it needs, as the amount of data that the algorithm acts upon gets bigger.

We can use Big-O notation to denote an algorithm's worst-case complexity. If we know the expression for the number of steps, n, an algorithm takes to execute, we can get the Big-O expression by:
+ removing all terms except the one with the largest exponent (remembering that n is treated bigger than any constant)
+ removing any constant factors.

> **Complexity** How well an algorithm scales in terms of time to execute or space needed as the size of the data upon which it operates increases.
>
> **Big-O notation** A notation used to represent an algorithm's worst-case complexity.

> **Worked example**
>
> An algorithm takes $3n^3 + 5n^2 + 4n - 4$ steps.
>
> Remove all terms except the one with the highest exponent:
>
> $3n^3$
>
> Remove any constant factors:
>
> n^3
>
> This gives a complexity of $O(n^3)$.

There are different classes of complexity:

Constant	$O(1)$	Slowest growing
Logarithmic	$O(\log n)$	
Linear	$O(n)$	
Polynomial	$O(n^k)$ Where k is a constant $>= 0$	
Exponential	$O(k^n)$ Where k is constant > 1	Fastest growing

If there is a mixture of different terms in the expression, then we discard all but the fastest growing term listed in the table above.

Worked example

An algorithm takes $8a^n + n^2 + \log n$ steps to complete, where a is a constant > 1.

In this case, we discard all terms except the exponential one because we know that the exponential term is the fastest growing:

$8a^n$

And then discard the constant, leaving a complexity of $O(a^n)$.

Although it is most common to use Big-O notation to look at algorithms' time complexity, as we have in this section, it can also be used to look at their space complexity. Whereas time complexity looks at the how long an algorithm takes to run, space complexity looks at the amount of extra space, in addition to the data itself, an algorithm needs in order to run.

In practical terms, time complexity relates to CPU time used and space complexity relates to the amount of RAM required.

Now test yourself

4 An algorithm takes $3n^2 + 2n - 1$ steps to run on an array of size n. State the complexity of the algorithm in Big-O notation.

Answer on p. 222

TESTED ⃝

Comparison of the complexity of algorithms

REVISED ⃝

You need to be aware of five different types of complexity: constant, linear, logarithmic, polynomial and exponential.

Constant complexity O(1)

Algorithms that show a constant complexity take the same time to run regardless of the size of a data set.

An example of this is pushing an item onto, or popping an item off, a stack; no matter how big the stack, the time to push or pop remains constant.

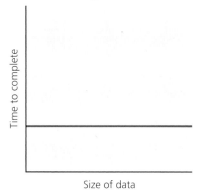

Figure 8.1 Constant complexity

Linear complexity O(n)

Algorithms with linear complexity increase at the same rate as the input size increases. If the input size doubles, the time taken for the algorithm to complete doubles.

An example of this is the average time to find an element using linear search.

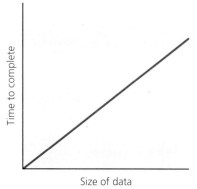

Figure 8.2 Linear complexity

Check your understanding and progress at **www.hoddereducation.co.uk/myrevisionnotesdownloads**

Logarithmic complexity O(log *n*)

If you are studying A level mathematics, you may well have encountered logarithms (and if you haven't you certainly will do). A full discussion of what logarithms are is outside the bounds of this course. However, a simple description is that a logarithm is the inverse of exponentiation (raising to the power of). This means that:

If $y = x^z$ then $z = \log_x y$

> **Worked example**
>
> We know that:
>
> $2^3 = 8$
>
> Using the identity above we can say:
>
> $\log_2 8 = 3$ (said as 'log to the base 2 of 8 equals 3').

Algorithms with logarithmic complexity scale up extremely well. The rate of increase in execution time decreases with more data. In other words, the difference in execution time between $n = 100$ and $n = 150$ will be less than the difference in execution time between $n = 50$ and $n = 100$. This means that logarithmic algorithms become more time efficient with more data.

A good example is binary search. As the size of the data set doubles, the number of items to be checked only increases by one.

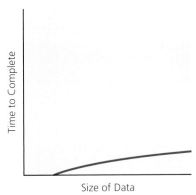

Figure 8.3 Logarithmic complexity

Polynomial complexity O(n^k) (where k >= 0)

Polynomial complexity is expressed as n^k where k is a constant value. There are two special cases:

+ when k = 0, $n^0 = 1$, which corresponds to constant complexity
+ when k = 1, $n^1 = n$, which corresponds to linear complexity.

However, as k gets larger, complexity grows faster. Other polynomial complexities include quadratic O(n^2) and cubic O(n^3).

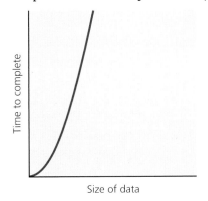

Figure 8.4 Polynomial complexity with k = 2, that is, showing O(n^2)

Exponential complexity $O(k^n)$ (where k > 1)

Algorithms with exponential complexity do not scale well at all. Exponential complexity means that, as the input n gets larger the time taken increases at a rate of k^n where k is a constant value.

To put this into context, if a computer takes 0.0001 seconds to run an algorithm with complexity $O(2^n)$ on a data set with 1 item, it will take over 1785 years to run the same algorithm on a data set with 50 items.

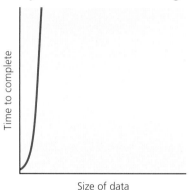

Figure 8.5 Exponential complexity

Summary of complexity algorithms

Table 8.1 Examples of growth under the different complexities

n	Growth type				
	Constant	Logarithmic	Linear	Polynomial	Exponential
	1	$\log_{10}n$	n	n^2	2^n
10	1	1	10	100	1024
20	1	1.30	20	400	1048576
30	1	1.48	30	900	$1.07 * 10^{09}$
40	1	1.60	40	1600	$1.1 * 10^{12}$
50	1	1.70	50	2500	$1.13 * 10^{15}$
60	1	1.78	60	3600	$1.15 * 10^{18}$
70	1	1.85	70	4900	$1.18 * 10^{21}$
80	1	1.90	80	6400	$1.21 * 10^{24}$
90	1	1.95	90	8100	$1.24 * 10^{27}$
100	1	2	100	10000	$1.27 * 10^{30}$

In the table above, notice how large an exponential algorithm becomes when $n = 100$, that is, there are only 100 data items to process. Algorithms with exponential complexity take an impractically long period of time with large data sets.

The following rules of thumb will give you a good idea as to the complexity of an algorithm, though further investigation of the algorithm may be needed.

+ An algorithm with no loops (or recursion) is likely to have constant time complexity as the same number of instructions are always run.
+ Algorithms with non-nested loops, where the number of times they run are determined by the size of the data set, are likely to have at least linear complexity.

```
for i = 0 to names.length - 1

        print(names[i])

next i
```

In the code above, the execution time is proportional to the size of the array.

Check your understanding and progress at **www.hoddereducation.co.uk/myrevisionnotesdownloads**

Note, even if there are multiple for loops, the complexity is still linear.

```
for i = 0 to names.length - 1

        print("Hello " + names[i])

next i

for i = 0 to names.length - 1

        print("Bye " + names[i])

next i
```

✚ A program with nested loops, where the number of times they run is determined by the size of the data set, will likely have at least polynomial complexity.

```
for i = 0 to numbers.length - 1

        for j = 0 to numbers.length - 1

                print(str(numbers[i]) + " times " + str(numbers[j])
                + " is " + str(numbers[i]*numbers[j]))

        next j

next i
```

The number of loops nested determines the type of polynomial complexity. Two nested loops would indicate quadratic complexity $O(n^2)$, whereas three nested loops would indicate cubic $O(n^3)$ complexity.

✚ `While` loops could mean anything from logarithmic to exponential complexity, depending on their conditions.

As previously mentioned, these are just guidelines. The key is to determine how the data set affects the number of times the loops run.

For example, the loop below would only have linear complexity, despite having two nested loops. (This is because the inner loop does not depend on the size of the data set.)

```
for i = 0 to numbers.length - 1

        for j = 0 to 10

                print(str(numbers[i]) + " times " + str(j) +
                " is " + str(i*j))

        next j

next i
```

Conversely, this singular loop has polynomial complexity. (This is because the length of the loop depends on the square of the number of data items.)

```
for i = 0 to numbers.length - 1 * numbers.length - 1

        print(i)

next i
```

> **Exam tip**
>
> One algorithm can be more complex than another but still perform better with small enough values. Imagine an algorithm has a constant complexity and on a given CPU takes 100 seconds to execute on any given piece of data. Another algorithm with exponential complexity might take a thousandth of a second to execute on piece of data. So, for one piece of data the exponential algorithm would actually be quicker. However, the time taken by the exponential algorithm will rapidly increase with more data, quickly overtaking the constant complexity algorithm.
>
> In an exam question, always keep in mind complexity is about how the time or memory requirements of an algorithm grow with the size of the data on which it operates, not about the precise time or memory required.

> **Making links**
>
> For details of the time and space complexities of a range of standard algorithms that you need to know about, see the very end of this chapter.

189

Now test yourself TESTED ◯

5 An algorithm takes five steps to run on an array of size *n*. State the complexity of the algorithm in Big-O notation.

6 State the complexity of the algorithm below, justifying your choice.

```
max = -1
for i = 0 to numbers.length - 1
    if numbers[i] > max then
            max = numbers[i]
    endif
next i
print(max)
```

7 State the complexity of the algorithm below, justifying your choice.

```
n = input("Enter a number")
while(n > 0)
    print(n)
    if n MOD 2 == 1 then
            n = n - 1
    endif
    n = n / 2
endwhile
```

Answers on p. 222

Algorithms for the main data structures

REVISED ●

For the exam you need to be able to:
+ push to and pop from a stack
+ represent a stack using an array and pointers
+ enqueue to and dequeue from a queue
+ represent queues (including circular queues) using an array and pointers
+ traverse linked lists
+ perform breadth-first traversal of trees
+ perform depth-first (postorder) traversal of trees.

These algorithms are covered in Chapter 4. You should ensure you are familiar with them as all can come up in the paper 2 examination.

Now test yourself TESTED ◯

8 A program contains a stack and a queue, both capable of holding integers.

The stack is represented by the array called `stack` and a variable called `top`.

The queue is represented by an array called `queue` and the variables `front` and `length`.

a) Write the function `pop()` for the stack.

b) Write the procedure `enqueue(data)` for the queue.

c) Write a program that reverses the order of the values on the stack.
   Assume:
   – Push, pop, enqueue and dequeue have been implemented.
   – The stack initially contains numbers and the queue is empty.
   Example

Answers on p. 222

Standard algorithms

Search algorithms

Two searching algorithms are covered here: linear search and binary search.

Linear search

Linear search involves methodically searching one location in a list after another until the searched-for value is found. The linear search algorithm starts at the beginning of a list and checks each item in turn until the desired item is found.

It can be expressed in pseudocode as follows:

```
pointer = 0

while pointer < lengthOfList and list[pointer] != searchedFor

      pointer = pointer + 1

endwhile

if pointer >= lengthOfList then

      print("Item is not in the list")

else

      print("Item is at location " + pointer)

endif
```

The order of the conditions in the `while` loop are important. That is because it makes use of short-circuit evaluation. This is when, given a condition made up of two parts linked by a Boolean operator, the computer only evaluates the second condition if it is necessary, having evaluated the first. For example:

```
Condition1 or Condition2
```

If `Condition1` is true there is no need to evaluate `Condition2` as the statement is true regardless of whether it is true or false.

```
Condition1 and Condition2
```

If `Condition1` is false there is no need to evaluate `Condition2` as the statement is false regardless of whether it is true or false.

This is used to our advantage in the line:

```
while pointer < LengthOfList and list[pointer] != searched
```

By checking the pointer first, `list[pointer] != searched` is never executed when the pointer is bigger than highest location in the list, preventing an out of bounds error.

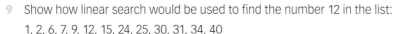

> **Now test yourself**
> TESTED
>
> 9 Show how linear search would be used to find the number 12 in the list:
>   1, 2, 6, 7, 9, 12, 15, 24, 25, 30, 31, 34, 40
> 10 Show how binary search would be used to find the number 12 in the list:
>   1, 2, 6, 7, 9, 12, 15, 24, 25, 30, 31, 34, 40
>
> **Answers on p. 222**

Binary search

Binary search works by repeatedly dividing a list in two and discarding one half until the item being searched for is found. For binary search to work, the list has to be in order.

```
lowerBound = 0

upperBound = lengthOfList - 1

midPoint = round((lowerBound + upperBound) / 2)

while list[midPoint] != searchedFor and lowerBound <= upperBound

        if list[midPoint] < searchedFor then

                lowerBound = midPoint + 1

        else

                upperBound = midPoint - 1

        endif

        midPoint = round((lowerBound + upperBound) / 2)

endwhile

if list[midPoint] == searchedFor then

        print("Item found at " + midPoint)

else

        print("Item not in list")

endif
```

Now test yourself

11 State which property of the list above makes binary search possible.

Answer on p. 223

TESTED

Exam tip

In an exam, questions about algorithms tend to fall into several categories:
+ Filling in the blanks: a version of the algorithm is given and you need to work out what statements or variables go in the blank spaces. Learning an algorithm is not like learning a script for a play. An algorithm is an idea that cannot be learnt word for word. Do not be put off if initially an algorithm looks unfamiliar, as the same idea can be expressed in different ways. Look through the code, and work through what it is doing.
+ Writing out an algorithm: often you will be given the option of writing out the algorithm in pseudocode or in the language of your choice. Pick whichever you are most comfortable with. If you are using a programming language, you should use comments to explain any code that might not be obvious. Assume the person marking is an experienced programmer, but not in the same language as you.
+ Tracing an algorithm: when tracing an algorithm, you are expected to show what changes are made to variables and what subroutines are called.
+ Demonstrating how an algorithm works on a data set: you are expected to show step by step how the algorithm works on the data. You are encouraged to draw out the data at each step.

When you encounter an algorithm question, take a moment to consider exactly what it is asking for. You will score no marks for writing out an algorithm when you have been asked to demonstrate it. If you have been given sample data, it is highly likely you are going to be asked to trace or demonstrate an algorithm acting upon it.

Sorting algorithms

Four sorting algorithms are covered here: bubble sort, insertion sort, merge sort and quicksort.

Bubble sort

A bubble sort works by:
+ Comparing the first item in the list with the second item and swapping them if necessary; then comparing the second item with the third item, and so on until reaching the end of the list.

Check your understanding and progress at **www.hoddereducation.co.uk/myrevisionnotesdownloads**

+ If any swaps were made in this first pass, then the list has to be examined again in a second pass, because some items may still be out of order.
+ If no swaps are made in a complete pass, then the sort is complete and no more passes are required.
+ We can keep track of the swaps by creating a Boolean variable (in this example called swapMade) and setting it to false at the start of each pass.

```
Set swapMade to true

while swapMade is true

        swapMade = false

        for position = 0 to listLength  -2 //i.e. the last but
one position

        if list[position] > list[position + 1] then

                temp = list[position]

                list[position] = list[position + 1]

                list[position + 1] = temp

                swapMade = true

        endif

endwhile
```

Example

FLAG=False

B	A	C	F	E	D

B and A are in the wrong order so are swapped and the flag set to true.

FLAG=True

A	B	C	F	E	D

B and C are in order so no change is made.

FLAG=True

A	B	C	F	E	D

C and F are in order so no change is made.

FLAG=True

A	B	C	F	E	D

F and E are out of order so they are swapped.

FLAG=True

A	B	C	E	**F**	D

F and D are out of order so they are swapped.

FLAG=True

A	B	C	E	D	**F**

The flag is set to false and starting at A the process is repeated.

When the algorithm gets to the last cell and the flag is false the list is in order.

193

Insertion sort

Insertion sort works by:

+ Splitting a list into two – a sorted sub-list and an unsorted sub-list.
+ During each pass, it takes the first item of the unsorted section and shuffles it down to the correct location in the sorted section.

```
for i = 1 to listlength - 1
        item = list[i]
        position = i
        while position > 0 and item < list[position - 1]
                list[position] = list[position - 1]
                position = position - 1
        endwhile
        list[position] = item
next i
```

A few things to note:

+ Initially the sorted sub-list is made up of one item at position 0. We start the for loop at 1 rather than 0 for this reason. A list of only one item is always sorted!
+ In the while loop, the position > 0 must be the first condition to make use of short-circuit evaluation (as we did in linear search).

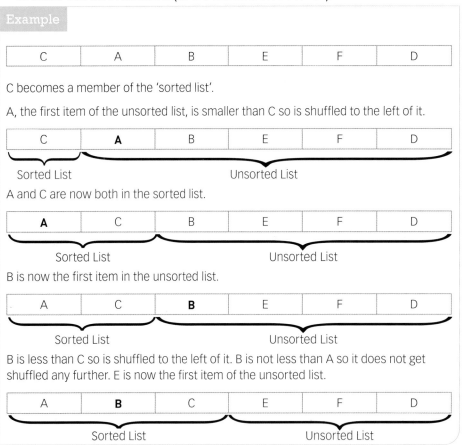

Example

| C | A | B | E | F | D |

C becomes a member of the 'sorted list'.

A, the first item of the unsorted list, is smaller than C so is shuffled to the left of it.

| C | **A** | B | E | F | D |

Sorted List   Unsorted List

A and C are now both in the sorted list.

| **A** | C | B | E | F | D |

Sorted List   Unsorted List

B is now the first item in the unsorted list.

| A | C | **B** | E | F | D |

Sorted List   Unsorted List

B is less than C so is shuffled to the left of it. B is not less than A so it does not get shuffled any further. E is now the first item of the unsorted list.

| A | **B** | C | E | F | D |

Sorted List   Unsorted List

This process continues until all the list is the sorted list.

Merge sort

Merge sort works as follows:

+ it splits a list of size n in half
+ the splitting is then recursively applied to the sub-lists
+ this continues until there are n lists of size 1
+ as the recursion unwinds, each pair of lists are merged with their items in order

Check your understanding and progress at www.hoddereducation.co.uk/myrevisionnotesdownloads

- each pair of newly merged lists are merged with another, with their items in order
- this is repeated until there is only one, sorted list.

The key to this algorithm is the way each pair of lists are merged together in order. The following merging algorithm is used:

```
Create an empty list called newlist

while list1 is not empty and list2 is not empty

        if the first item in list1 < the first item in list2 then

                Remove the first item from list1 and add it to
                newlist

        else

                Remove the first item from list2 and add it to
                newlist

        endif

endwhile

if list1 is empty then

        Add the remainder of list2 to newlist

else

        Add the remainder of list1 to newlist

endif
```

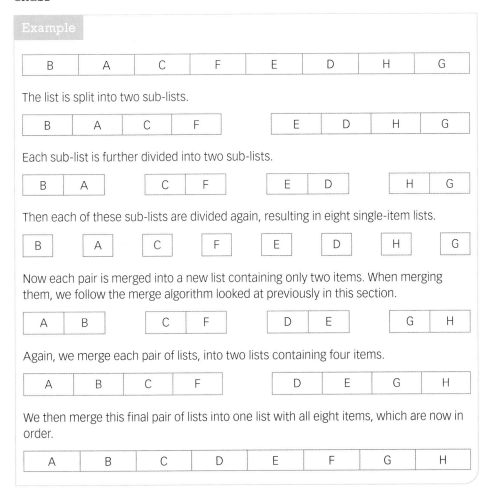

Example

B	A	C	F	E	D	H	G

The list is split into two sub-lists.

The list is split into two sub-lists.

| B | A | C | F | | E | D | H | G |

Each sub-list is further divided into two sub-lists.

| B | A | | C | F | | E | D | | H | G |

Then each of these sub-lists are divided again, resulting in eight single-item lists.

| B | | A | | C | | F | | E | | D | | H | | G |

Now each pair is merged into a new list containing only two items. When merging them, we follow the merge algorithm looked at previously in this section.

| A | B | | C | F | | D | E | | G | H |

Again, we merge each pair of lists, into two lists containing four items.

| A | B | C | F | | D | E | G | H |

We then merge this final pair of lists into one list with all eight items, which are now in order.

| A | B | C | D | E | F | G | H |

Quick sort

Quicksort works as follows:

1 Pick an item in the list and call it the pivot (it can be any item; we will always pick the first).
2 Split the remainder of the list into two sub-lists: those less than or equal to the pivot and those greater than the pivot.
3 Recursively apply steps 1 and 2 until all sub-lists are pivots.
4 The pivots can now be combined to form a sorted list.

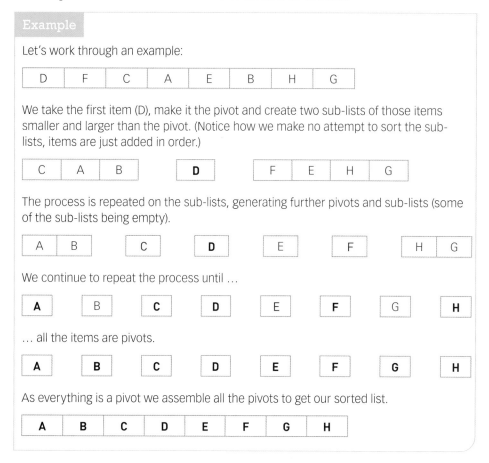

Example

Let's work through an example:

| D | F | C | A | E | B | H | G |

We take the first item (D), make it the pivot and create two sub-lists of those items smaller and larger than the pivot. (Notice how we make no attempt to sort the sub-lists, items are just added in order.)

| C | A | B | | **D** | | F | E | H | G |

The process is repeated on the sub-lists, generating further pivots and sub-lists (some of the sub-lists being empty).

| A | B | | C | | **D** | | E | | F | | H | G |

We continue to repeat the process until …

| **A** | | B | | **C** | | **D** | | E | | **F** | | G | | **H** |

… all the items are pivots.

| **A** | | **B** | | **C** | | **D** | | **E** | | **F** | | **G** | | **H** |

As everything is a pivot we assemble all the pivots to get our sorted list.

| **A** | **B** | **C** | **D** | **E** | **F** | **G** | **H** |

Exam tip

The examples above sort the lists in ascending order (0–9, A–Z). In the exam you may be asked to sort a list in descending order (Z–A, 9–0). To adapt an ascending sort algorithm to a descending sort algorithm, you simply switch what you do with the bigger and smaller value when comparing two locations.

For example, in an ascending bubble sort, when two locations are compared it is necessary to ensure the smaller value is on the left (i.e. if a location is bigger than the one to the right of it, they are swapped). In a descending bubble sort, the smaller value needs to be on the right (i.e. if a location is smaller than the one to right of it, they are swapped).

Making links

The space complexity is concerned with the memory we need in addition to the list in order to execute the sorting algorithms.

For instance, bubble sort and insertion sort both keep data in the original list and as such are known as in-place sorting algorithms. Regardless of the size of the list being sorted, they only require storage for the same set of variables. Therefore they have constant O(1) space complexity.

Merge sort, on the other hand, needs to make space for the sub-lists it creates. This extra space is proportional to the size of the list being sorted. Therefore a merge sort has linear O(*n*) complexity.

Check your understanding and progress at **www.hoddereducation.co.uk/myrevisionnotesdownloads**

Now test yourself

TESTED ◯

12 Demonstrate the stages of a bubble sort on the numbers 3, 5, 2, 4, 1
13 Demonstrate the stages of an insertion sort on the numbers 3, 5, 2, 4, 1
14 Demonstrate the stages of a merge sort on the numbers 9, 0, 1, 2, 5, 4, 3, 8, 7, 6
15 Demonstrate the stages of a quick sort on the numbers 9, 0, 1, 2, 5, 4, 3, 8, 7, 6

Answers on p. 223–24

Space and time complexity for standard algorithms

REVISED ◯

Below are the time and space complexities for the sorting and searching algorithms. You should commit these to memory. Two things to note:
1 The best and average case complexities are denoted with the Greek letters omega, Ω, and theta, Θ, respectively.
2 The complexity $O(n \log n)$ is known as linearithmic complexity, which is a cross between linear and logarithmic complexity. A discussion of its performance goes beyond the specification but you should be aware it scales worse than linear complexity but significantly better than polynomial complexity.

	Time complexity			Space complexity
	Best	**Average**	**Worst**	
Linear search	$\Omega(1)$	$\Theta(n)$	$O(n)$	$O(1)$
Binary search	$\Omega(1)$	$\Theta(\log n)$	$O(\log n)$	$O(1)$
Bubble sort	$\Omega(n)$	$\Theta(n^2)$	$O(n^2)$	$O(1)$
Insertion sort	$\Omega(n)$	$\Theta(n^2)$	$O(n^2)$	$O(1)$
Merge sort	$\Omega(n \log n)$	$\Theta(n \log n)$	$O(n \log n)$	$O(n)$
Quick sort	$\Omega(n \log n)$	$\Theta(n \log n)$	$O(n^2)$	$O(\log n)$

Shortest path algorithms

REVISED ◯

Dijkstra's algorithm

Dijkstra's algorithm finds the shortest path between two points. The algorithm goes as follows:
+ Mark the start node as a distance of 0 from itself and all other nodes as an infinite distance from the start node.
+ Carry out the following steps until the destination node becomes the current node:
  + Go to the closest unvisited node to the start node (initially this will be the start node itself) and call this the current node.
  + For every unvisited node connected to the current node:
    – Add the distance from the start node to the current node to the distance on the edge between the current node and the unvisited node.
    – If the newly calculated distance is less than the shortest recorded distance, then it becomes the new shortest recorded distance. Record the new shortest distance to that node, along with the label of the current node.
  + Mark the current node as visited.

Worked example

In this example, Dijkstra's algorithm is used to find the shortest path from A to J.

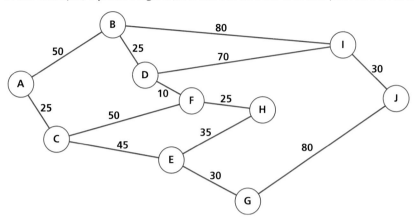

Figure 8.6 Nodes (1)

We start by assuming the distance from A to every node is infinity. (From there things can only get better!) The exception to this is A, which is a distance of 0 from itself.

We start with the closest node to A (which in this case is A) and mark it as the 'current node'.

Node	Shortest distance from A	Previous node
A (C)	0	
B	∞	
C	∞	
D	∞	
E	∞	
F	∞	
G	∞	
H	∞	
I	∞	
J	∞	

We then calculate the distance to A from all the nodes directly connected to A. If it is shorter than the currently recorded distance, then the new distance is recorded and a record is made of the current node in the previous node column so we know how we got to this node.

Node	Shortest distance from A	Previous node
A (C)	0	
B	∞ 50	A
C	∞ 25	A
D	∞	
E	∞	
F	∞	
G	∞	
H	∞	
I	∞	
J	∞	

Now we mark A as visited and repeat the process. C is now the closest unvisited node to A so we look at the nodes directly connected to C, namely F and E.

Check your understanding and progress at **www.hoddereducation.co.uk/myrevisionnotesdownloads**

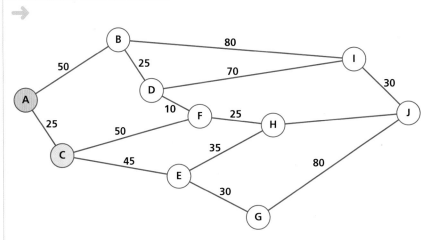

Figure 8.7 Nodes (2)

To update E and F, we add the distance of the current node C from A (in this case 25) to the distance from the current node C to the connecting nodes. In our example, the distance to F is 75 (that is, 25 + 50) and the distance to E is 70 (that is, 25 + 45).

We only update the values in the table if the values we have calculated are less than the values already in the table. In this case, the values in the table for E and F are infinity so we update them both and put the current node in the 'Previous node' column.

Node	Shortest distance from A	Previous node
A (V)	0	
B (V)	∞ 50	A
C (C)	∞ 25	A
D	∞	
E (V)	∞ 70	C
F (V)	∞ 75	C
G	∞	
H	∞	
I	∞	
J	∞	

B now becomes the current node and the process continues until J has been marked as the current node. We know the shortest distance from A to J is 160. Then, by following the previous nodes from J to A, the route can be determined. The node previous to J is I, previous to I is B and previous to B is A.

Node	Shortest distance from A	Previous node
A (V)	0	
B (V)	∞ 50	A
C (V)	∞ 25	A
D (V)	∞ 75	B
E (V)	∞ 70	C
F (V)	∞ 75	C
G (V)	∞ 100	E
H (V)	∞ 100	E̶F
I (V)	∞ 130	B
J (C)	**∞ 180̶ 160**	**G̶I**

A* Search

While Dijkstra's algorithm always finds the shortest path, it doesn't always go about finding it in the quickest way. A* search is a variation of Dijkstra's that uses a heuristic to try and get to the correct solution sooner. The heuristic we use is taking the straight-line distance from each node to the destination node.

> **Heuristic** A method or rule of thumb that quickly gives an estimated answer.

Worked example

As before, we start at A and work out the values for B and C. But this time, instead of assigning them the value of the edge, we use the distance from A (which we will call 'g') plus the heuristic value of the distance to J (which we will call 'h'). We will call their sum 'f'.

Node	Path distance (g)	Heuristic distance (h)	f = g + h	Previous node
A (C)	0	95	95	
B	50	80	130	A
C	25	90	115	A
D		75		
E		70		
F		65		
G		50		
H		45		
I		25		
3		0		

We then pick the unvisited node with the lowest value for f and make it the current node (in this case C).

Node	Path distance (g)	Heuristic distance (h)	f = g + h	Previous node
A (V)	0	95	95	
B	50	80	130	A
C (C)	25	90	115	A
D		75		
E	70	70	140	C
F	75	65	140	C
G		50		
H		45		
I		25		
J		0		

We repeat this until J is the current node. Just like Dijkstra's algorithm, we only update when the new value for f is better than the existing one.

The heuristic distance in the example is a simple guess as to how far each node is from J. The assumption is that the more nodes are traversed the closer we'll get to J. We can see from the diagram that while the details of the guess are not accurate, the general idea is correct.

Taking the straight-line distance between two locations is a common heuristic. For a heuristic to work with A* algorithm, it has to be admissible. This means it never overestimates the actual distance.

> **Admissible** The property of a heuristic that it never overestimates the actual value.

Both Dijkstra's algorithm and A* algorithm will find the shortest path between two nodes on a graph and as such will always give the same answer.

+ The advantage of A* algorithm is that it will potentially find the path in fewer steps.
+ The use of heuristics prevents A* algorithm exploring routes that will not offer an improvement over routes already checked.

> **Revision activity**
>
> Work through the example to confirm the number of steps taken by the A* algorithm.

Check your understanding and progress at **www.hoddereducation.co.uk/myrevisionnotesdownloads**

Making links

You can find out more about the use of heuristics in computational methods, Chapter 7.

Tree and graph data structures for looked at early in this chapter. A tree is a special example of a graph; it is a graph with no cycles (or loops). This means that the shortest path algorithms can be applied to trees just as they would be to graphs.

Now test yourself

TESTED

16 Explain the advantage of using A* search over Dijkstra's algorithm.

Answer on p. 224

Summary

Algorithms

+ Algorithms are sets of instructions for specific tasks.
+ Different algorithms can be used to perform the same task. They can be compared in terms of the time they take, the memory they require and how they perform on different data sets.
+ The complexity of an algorithm denotes how well it scales in terms of time or space needed to run.
+ We can represent algorithm efficiency/complexity using Big-O notation
+ Complexities can be constant, linear, logarithmic, polynomial and exponential.
+ Algorithms exist for: stacks, queues, trees, linked list depth-first and breadth-first tree traversal.
+ Linear search searches a list one item at a time until the element is found.
+ Binary search continually divides a list in two until the element is found.
+ Binary search performs better than linear search but requires the list to be sorted.
+ Bubble sort repeatedly passes through a list, swapping adjacent items.
+ Insertion sort takes each item from an unsorted list and shuffles it into a sorted list until it is in order.
+ Merge sort recursively splits a list in half until there are multiple lists containing one item. The single-item lists are recursively paired and merged in order. This is repeated until there is one, final, sorted list containing all items.
+ Quick sort picks an element from the list as a pivot and creates two sub-lists, one bigger and one smaller than this element. The same process is applied over and over to the sub-lists, until all elements are pivots and are thus in order.
+ The time and space complexities for sorting and searching algorithms should be committed to memory.
+ Dijkstra's algorithm finds the shortest path between two points in a graph.
+ A* algorithm improves on Dijkstra's algorithm by using heuristics.
+ A heuristic is an estimated value.
+ Dijkstra's algorithm and A* search will both always find the shortest path between two points and as such give the same result, but A* search can often come to this result in fewer steps.

Exam practice

1 Demonstrate how to perform a binary search for the letter E on the following list:

0	1	2	3	4	5	6	7	8	9	10
A	B	C	D	E	F	G	H	I	J	K

[2]

2 Show the steps of a merge sort on the following list:

D	A	B	F	E	C

[3]

3 Demonstrate how to perform a quicksort on the following list:

C	F	D	E	A	B

[3]

4 An algorithm can take up to $3n^3 - 4n^2 + 6n - 1$ steps to solve a data set with n items.

   a) Express the algorithm's complexity in Big-O notation. [1]

   b) State the complexity class of the algorithm. [1]

5 Using the graph below, use Dijkstra's algorithm to calculate the shortest path from:

   a) A to D [5]

   b) A to F [5]

6 Using the graph below, calculate the shortest path from A to F using:

   a) Dijkstra's algorithm [5]

   b) A* search (the heuristic value to F is given in red under each node) [5]

   c) Compare your answers to parts a) and b). [2]

7 Explain why bubble sort has a time complexity of $O(n^2)$ and a space complexity of $O(1)$. [3]

8 Eric is comparing bubble sort and quick sort and notes they both have a worst case time complexity of $O(n^2)$. He concludes, therefore, that it doesn't matter which of these algorithms he uses. Discuss to what extent you agree with Eric, justifying your answer. [9]

Answers available online

Glossary

Term	Definition	Page
1's complement	A simple process for a computer: it simply turns all 1s to 0s and 0s to 1s.	86
Abstraction	Hiding details or attributes when studying objects or systems to focus attention on the essential elements of the problem	150
ACID	Atomicity, consistency, isolation and durability are concepts that underpin database transactions.	64
Adjacency matrix	A table showing which nodes in a graph are connected and, if the edges are weighted, the weightings associated with those links.	112
Admissible	The property of a heuristic that it never overestimates the actual value.	200
Algorithm	A set of instructions explaining how to carry out a given task.	184
Applications software	Programs that allow a user to complete a task. Examples include word processors, spreadsheet packages and presentation software.	24
Architecture	When discussing computers, this refers to the approach taken in a computer's design.	11
Artificial neural network	A series of algorithms that tries to recognise underlying patterns and relationships within a set of data, through a process that mimics the way the human brain operates.	140
Assembler	A program that converts assembly code into machine code.	26
Assembly code	A low-level language that uses single words or mnemonics to represent instructions.	26
Asymmetric encryption	Encryption where one key (the public key) is used to encrypt data and another (the private key) is used to decrypt it.	47
Atomic	A field that cannot be broken down into multiple smaller fields.	57
Attribute	Variables contained within and associated to an object.	39
Backtracking	An approach to finding a solution that explores a possibility until it is no longer deemed feasible. At that point we backtrack to the last point at which it worked and follow a new path	178
Base case	A condition in a recursive subroutine that, when true, returns control to the subroutine that called it rather than running another recursive instance.	167
Big-O notation	A notation used to represent an algorithm's worst-case complexity.	185
Bitwise operation	A binary operation that takes two bit patterns of equal length and performs a logical operation on each pair of corresponding bits.	98
Boolean expression	An expression to which the answer is either true or false.	163
Bug	An error or mistake within program code that causes a program to behave in ways other than intended.	170
Cache	A temporary store where instructions or data an algorithm anticipates will be needed are stored, ready for fast access.	153
Cache memory	A fast memory that is built on or close to the CPU and is designed to reduce the need to access RAM, which has slower access speeds.	10
Central processing unit (CPU)	The central processing unit 'runs programs' by continually fetching, decoding and executing instructions.	8
Circuit switching	A pathway for the data is set up in advance of communication and then data is sent across it. The pathway is closed after transmission.	67
Class	A template used to define an object. It specifies the methods and attributes an object should have.	39
Closed source software	Software distributed as executable machine code, which means the source code is kept secret.	25
Collision resistance	The property that different inputs giving the same output occurs as infrequently as possible.	47

Compiler	A program that converts the entire highlevel source code into an executable machine code file that is then executed.	26
Complex instruction set computing (CISC)	This was a term retroactively coined for non-RISC processors. CISC processors tend to have a larger instruction set, including very specialised instructions.	13
Complexity	How well an algorithm scales in terms of time to execute or space needed as the size of the data upon which it operates increases.	185
Composite key	A primary key made of two or more fields. While on their own they may not be unique, each record's combination of them will be.	58
Computational methods	Any method that can be used to solve a problem by computational means. For example, searching, sorting, modelling and mathematical methods.	175
Computational thinking	A set of problem-solving methods that express problems and solutions in ways that a computer could execute.	150
Concurrent processing	Where several computations are carried out simultaneously.	160
Core	A core is a processing unit within the CPU.	10
Cyberbullying	Any form of bullying that takes place online.	144
Data controller	The individual whose data is being stored.	133
Data mining	Looking for patterns in large data sets	178
Data model	An abstract model that organises elements of data and how they relate to one another and to real-world entities.	151
Data packet	Data is broken down into chunks called packets when sent across a network.	68
Data redundancy	The unnecessary duplication of data in a database. When updates occur, all the instances of a data item must be changed. This leads to errors and also wastes storage space.	50
Data subject	The individual whose data is being stored.	133
Database	A structured, persistent store of data, organised so that it can easily be accessed, managed and updated.	49
Database management system (DBMS)	Software used to control a database, overseeing amendments to its structure, and used to access and amend the data itself.	55
Debugging	The process of finding and removing bugs (or errors in the behaviour) of a program.	174
Decomposition	Breaking down a complex problem into smaller parts that are easier to understand. The smaller parts are simpler to work with in order to find or develop solutions.	155
Denary	A term that describes the number system based on 10, often called decimal.	83
Denial of Service (DoS)	An attack meant to shut down a machine or network by overwhelming it with requests, making it inaccessible to its intended users.	136
Determinism	The property that a process with the same inputs will always give the same output.	47
Digital signature	A digital code (generated and authenticated by public key encryption) that is attached to an electronically transmitted document to verify its contents and the sender's identity.	135
Distributed computing	A collection of computers working together on a single task.	71
Domain name system (DNS)	A method that computers use to find the correct IP addresses given the URL	67
Edges	Links or lines between nodes in a graph.	112
Efficiency	A reflection of the amount of CPU time or memory an algorithm requires to execute.	184
Encapsulation	Ensures private attributes can only be amended through public methods. This prevents objects being manipulated in unintended ways.	40
Encryption	The process of making data unreadable to third parties.	45
Entity-relationship diagram	A diagram showing the tables, which hold the entities and their links, or relationships within a relational database.	52, 151

Check your understanding and progress at **www.hoddereducation.co.uk/myrevisionnotesdownloads**

Exponent	The power of two to which the number in the mantissa must be raised; the number of places the binary point should be moved.	91
Firewall	A network security device that monitors incoming and outgoing network traffic and permits or blocks data packets based on a set of security rules.	69, 136
First normal form (1NF)	Data after the first stage of normalisation. It must have a primary key, no repeating fields and all of them atomic.	57
Flat-file database	A database in which all data is stored in a single table.	50
Foreign key	The primary key of one table being used as a field in another table, creating a link.	51
Generalisation	Solving new problems based on previous problems for which we have an existing solution. This involves using an algorithm that solves a problem and adapting it so that it solves similar problems.	151
Graphics processing unit (GPU)	A type of processor designed with the purpose of drawing graphics on the screen.	13
Hacking	The process of gaining unauthorised access to a computer system.	69, 135
Hardware	The physical components of a computer system. For example the CPU, RAM, motherboard, mouse, monitor etc.	15
Hash function	A function that takes in data of any size and returns a fixed-length output.	47, 118
Hash table	Data structure where each item has its own unique index value.	118
Heuristic	A method or rule of thumb that quickly gives an estimated answer.	200
Heuristic solutions	An approximate, non-optimal, but sufficient solution – used when finding an exact solution is impractical.	179
Hex	We often use the shorter form to describe hexadecimal.	90
High-level languages	These are designed to be easily read by humans. They tend to use a combination of English keywords and mathematical notation. There are many high-level languages. Examples include C++, JavaScript and Python.	26
Index register	The index register holds a value that is added to the operand of an indexed addressed instruction, to give the memory address that is to be accessed.	38
Inference engine	Interprets and evaluates the facts in the knowledge base in order to provide a potential solution.	140
Inheritance	The ability for a class to inherit the methods and attributes of a parent class. Its 'child' class can have its own methods and attributes and override the methods of its parent class.	40
Integrated development environment (IDE)	A coding environment that incorporates numerous software tools to aid the writing, executing and debugging of code.	174
Internet service provider (ISP)	A company that provides access to the internet, for example BT, Virgin Media, Sky, Talk Talk, Hyperoptic and so on.	137
Interpreter	A program that reads and executes high-level source code line by line.	26
Interrupt	A signal sent to a CPU to signify another process is in need of processing time.	20
Interrupt service routine (ISR)	This is the program code that is called when an interrupt is triggered. Each interrupt will have a specific ISR associated with it. When the processor runs this ISR, it carries out the actions required to handle the situation that has triggered the interrupt.	20
Irreversibility	The property such that an output of a process cannot be used to derive the original input.	47
Key	A value that needs to be provided to encrypt/ decrypt data.	45
Knowledge base	A collection of information in a specific field of study.	140
Layering	The principle of dividing a complex problem into separate, independent sub-problems.	65
Layers	Organising programs into separate functional components that interact in a hierarchical way. Each layer usually only has an interface to the layer above it and the layer below it.	151
Least significant bit (LSB)	The smallest value bit in the number, or the rightmost bit.	89

205

Low-level languages	These are languages closely tied to the architecture of the CPU. They use the CPU's instruction set. The lowest level language is machine code, which is directly readable by the CPU. Assembly code is also considered a low-level language.	26
Machine code	Instructions and data stored in binary, directly readable by the CPU.	26
Magnitude	refers to the size of a value and does not take into account the sign, for example the magnitude of both 15 and –15 is 15.	85
Mantissa	The part of the floating-point number that represents the significant digits of the number.	91
Mask	A bit pattern that is used with the operand. The corresponding bits in the operand and mask are combined using a logical operator to produce a result.	98
Memory addressing	In assembly language there are different ways of referring to locations. We refer to these as different modes of memory addressing.	38
Method	A subroutine associated with an object. Additionally, **new** is a special type of method called a 'constructor'. Constructors define how an object is created. In pseudocode, constructors are always given the name **new**.	39
Method overloading	This is when a class contains two or more methods of the same name but that differ in the pattern of the arguments they take and/ or the type of data they return. The compiler then chooses the correct version according to the values being passed or being expected.	41
Mirror database	An identical instance of a database kept on a separate server.	64
Most significant bit (MSB)	The bit position in a binary number having the greatest value, or the leftmost bit. For an 8-bit binary number this will be the leftmost bit with value 128.	84
Node	A position in a data structure that can contain data or links to other nodes.	105
Normalisation	The process of changing the structure of a relational database to remove the potential for data redundancy.	57
Object	An instance of a class.	39
Object	An abstract data type used by a programmer.	150
Object code	When code is compiled but yet to be run through a linker, it is sometimes referred to as object code. In practice, you will often see the terms machine code and object code used interchangeably.	27
Open source software	Software that has its source code freely available and grants users the right to examine, modify and share it.	25, 136
Operand	The bit pattern being 'operated' on.	98
Operating system	Software that controls the computer, manages the computer's hardware and from which other programs can be run.	19
Optical character recognition (OCR)	A data input method that converts images of text to machine editable text.	54
Optical mark recognition (OMR)	A data input method that recognises the positions of marks made on paper.	54
Overflow	When a calculation produces a result that is too large to be represented accurately in the available space.	89
Overriding	This is when a subclass has a method of the same name (and pattern of parameters) as its parent class. The child class version is always used over that of the parent class: it is said to 'override' the parent's method.	41
Packet switching	Packets of data are sent across a network. They may take different routes and are reassembled by the receiver.	68
PageRank algorithm	An algorithm that determines the importance of web pages, taking into account the number of incoming links a page has and the PageRank of the pages those links come from.	79
Paging	Where programs are divided physically into equal-sized blocks called pages (typically several kilobytes).	19
Paradigm	A common set of ideas or ways of thinking.	146, 157

Check your understanding and progress at **www.hoddereducation.co.uk/myrevisionnotesdownloads**

Parsing	The process of analysing a string of symbols in a computer language to determine whether there are any syntax errors.	179
Peer-to peer streaming	Allows data to be shared directly between lots of different users/clients rather than downloading from a central server.	136
Pipelining	When discussing a CPU, it means different parts of the CPU performing different parts of the fetch– decode–execute cycle on a sequence of instructions.	11
Polymorphism	Meaning 'many forms', polymorphism is the ability for objects of different classes to be treated in the same way. For example, the same method may be applied to objects of different classes.	40
Preconditions	Requirements that must be met before a program can run.	153
Prefetching	Loading a resource before it is needed. This can refer to commonly used web pages being requested before they are used. For example, instruction prefetching is where the CPU caches instructions and data blocks before they are executed.	154
Primary key	A field that has a unique value for every record in a table.	50
Proprietary software	The owner of the copyright material retains intellectual property rights.	136
Protocol	A set of rules for communication between devices.	65
Prototype	An early version of a system, lacking full functionality but allowing a feel for what the final version will be like before large amounts of time are committed to its production.	29
Proxy	A server that sits between a network and the internet, through which internet data requests are made	69
Pseudocode	A way in which algorithms can be written using 'pretend' code. Unlike a real high-level language, there are no strict rules as to how pseudocode needs to look, but it should be understandable to someone familiar with programming (though perhaps in a different programming language to the writer).	32
Queue	A data structure that works the same way as, for example, a cinema queue. The first item into the queue is the first item out of the queue.	114
Random access memory (RAM)	A type of primary memory that the CPU uses for programs and data in use. It loses its contents when power is lost.	16
Read-only memory (ROM)	A type of primary memory that can only be read from. It retains its contents even when electrical power is lost. It is often used to store start-up instructions on a computer.	16
Recursive call	An instance of a subroutine calling itself (i.e. causing recursion).	167
Reduced instruction set computing (RISC)	A design approach where a CPU uses a small set of instructions. While this means a loss of some of the more specialised instructions, it allows for efficiencies in the processor design.	13
Referential integrity	Guaranteeing the consistency of a database by ensuring no record points to another record that doesn't exist.	63
Register	A discrete piece of memory built onto the CPU that holds a single piece of data.	8
Relational database	A relational database consists of multiple tables linked together. Each table usually represents a 'thing' or an entity and the links are their relationships.	50
Reserved word	A word put aside by the language as having a special purpose and so cannot be used as a variable name. Examples vary from language to language but may include: **if**, **else**, **for**, **while**, **return**.	174
Scheduling	The method an operating system uses to ensure all processes get sufficient processor time.	24
Scope (array)	When referring to an array, scope is the number of elements allocated to it when it is declared.	101
Scope (variable)	A variable's scope is the extent to which it can be seen within different parts of a program. Scope can be said to be global or local. A variable is said to be in scope at any particular part of the program if it can be used.	169
Search engine	A website used to find other websites. Users type in search terms and are given lists of web pages that match them.	78

Second normal form (2NF)	Data after the second stage of normalisation. In 2NF, all data is in 1NF and has no field depending on only part of the primary key.	58
Secondary key	A field by which records are likely to be searched and is therefore indexed.	52
Secure Sockets Layer (SSL)	A security technology for establishing an encrypted link between a server and a client.	135
Segmentation	Where programs are divided logically; they are split into blocks containing modules or routines.	19
Selection	Another term for branching.	163
Source code	The program code written by the programmer, usually in a high-level language.	25
Spider/web crawler	A program that visits websites adding terms from them to a search engine's index.	78
Stack overflow	When a stack runs out of space to store data.	167
Stack pointer	A register that holds the address of the top location in a stack.	108
Stalking	The use of the internet, or other electronic means, to harass and intimidate someone.	144
Structured Query Language (SQL)	A language used to find and manipulate data within a database.	54
Symmetric encryption	Encryption where the same key is used to encrypt and decrypt data.	46
Syntax error	An error in a program that breaks the rules of the language's structure. For example, **2 + 3 = a**	174
Third normal form (3NF)	Data in a relational database after the third stage of normalisation. In addition to being in 2NF, every field depends solely on the primary key and no other field.	59
Transaction	A group of actions in a database creating a unit of work.	64
Traverse	Travel through the list in the defined order.	107
Trolling	Deliberately upsetting people with social media posts in order to start an argument or offend someone.	144
Uniform resource locator (URL)	is the main part of a website address e.g. hodder.co.uk	66
User interface	The means by which the computer and user interact. This could be a command line interface, where operating system commands are typed in, or a graphical user interface, where programs run in windows and the user interacts using a mouse and icons. Graphical user interfaces are far more common now than command line interfaces.	19
Utility software	Small programs designed to help with the maintenance of a system. Examples include antivirus software, disk defragmentation and backup software.	24
Variable declaration	The point at which a variable is created.	170
Vertices	Nodes in a graph that contain data.	112
Virtual machine	A program that has the same functionality as, and can be used in place of, a physical machine.	24
Virtual memory	The use of secondary storage as an extension of a computer's physical memory.	19
Virtual server	A server that exists as a virtual machine, rather than a physical device dedicated to the task.	71
Weightings	Values applied to edges in a graph, for example distances.	112

Check your understanding and progress at **www.hoddereducation.co.uk/myrevisionnotesdownloads**

Now test yourself answers

Chapter 1

1 The control unit orchestrates the movement of data around the CPU and memory during the fetch–decode–execute cycle. During this process it decodes instructions.

2 Control bus, data bus, address bus

3 Arithmetic logic unit (ALU)

4 A calculation is carried out, meaning the results are stored in the accumulator.

A value is loaded from memory and stored in the accumulator.

5 Data bus

6 To ensure the next instruction in the program is fetched in the next cycle.

7 The time take to read from memory is significantly higher than the speed at which the CPU operates. Cache is faster than memory and closer to the CPU. This helps to reduce the bottleneck caused by memory's access speed.

8 Pipelining avoids the need for the CPU to have to wait until an instruction has been executed before fetching the next instruction. By splitting the fetch–decode–execute cycle into a pipeline of multiple stages, all parts of the CPU are continually being used, reducing time being wasted with them lying idle. In theory, the performance can be increased by almost as many times as there are stages in the pipeline. Because of issues such as overheads in the pipelining process and having to flush the pipeline, real-world improvements are never this high, but are still significant.

9 If a user has multiple programs open at once, these can be distributed across the CPU's cores, significantly improving performance over one core. In some cases, one program may be running but the task it's performing might have components that can be executed simultaneously (i.e. it is parallelisable). The cores can share the workload for such tasks, also improving performance.

10 In the Von Neumann architecture, data and instructions are stored together in memory, whereas the Harvard architecture has separate memory units for data and instructions, with their own buses.

11 Examples may include:
   - simultaneous multithreading
   - out of order execution
   - branch prediction
   - variable clock speed
   - power conservation features.

12 CISC has more addressing modes than RISC.

13 CISC processors tend to have more transistors than RISC processors.

14 RISC CPUs tend to use less power than their CISC equivalents. This is because their smaller instruction set means they can have simpler designs, with fewer transistors. Lower power consumption results in longer battery life, which is a desirable trait in a laptop.

15 A CPU has a very general instruction set; a GPU's instruction set is specialised for the maths used in the rendering of 3d graphics. (Consequently, CPUs are able to run programs GPUs cannot.)

A GPU will have many more cores than a CPU. The cores in a GPU can all only perform the same instruction at the same time. A CPU has fewer cores but these can independently execute different instructions.

16 – scientific/engineering modelling
   - code breaking
   - crypto currency mining
   - video encoding
   - machine learning

17 Multiple processing units executing different instructions on different pieces of data simultaneously (multiple instructions multiple data).

18 Multiple processing units executing the same instruction on different pieces of data simultaneously (Single instructions multiple data).

19 Examples include:
   - keyboard
   - mouse
   - joystick
   - scanner
   - microphone
   - touchscreen
   - trackpad
   - webcam
   - barcode scanner
   - fingerprint scanner

20 Examples include:
   - monitor
   - projector
   - speaker
   - motor
   - LED
   - printer
   - plotter
   - 3D printer
   - headphones
   - laser cutter

21 Most schools will use a combination of tape drives, Redundant Array of Inexpensive Disks (RAID) and offsite storage.

22 Optical

23 Backups often involve a large amount of data. Magnetic media tends to offer higher capacities (at a lower price) than other storage media. The slower read/write speed compared to flash storage is not an issue when it comes to backing up.

24 DVDs are light, durable and easy to transport. They are also significantly cheaper than USB memory sticks.

25 RAM is volatile; ROM is non-volatile.

RAM can be written to; ROM is read-only.

26 RAM is volatile (ROM is not).

27 Virtual storage can be accessed from multiple devices.

It is easier to upgrade the size of virtual storage.

If the device is lost, the data isn't lost with it.

Chapter 2

1 Any three from:
  - provides a user interface
  - memory management
  - management of CPU time
  - manage peripherals
  - manage system's security
  - file management
  - allows the installation and removal of applications.

2 To allow memory to be mapped across the physical memory and secondary storage, allowing the amount of memory locations available to the operating system to be extended.

3 Paging divides memory by physical amounts (typically 4KB), whereas segmentation divides memory according to logical divisions within its content.

4 An interrupt service routine provides the code to be executed when its corresponding interrupt is generated.

5 The priority of an interrupt signifies how critical it is. An interrupt can only stop a process of a lower priority than itself.

6 The scheduler ensures the CPU executes processes in the order they arrive. When a process is generated it is added to a queue. The CPU repeats the cycle of taking the process at the front of the queue and executing it to completion.

7 Each process is given an equal time slice (and is placed in a circular queue). When its time is up, the CPU moves onto the next process, returning back to the first process when it has spent equal time on every other process. Completed processes are removed from the queue.

8 An operating system (i.e. systems software that manages a computer's hardware and applications) that guarantees responses within a given, short period of time.

9 Accept any reasonable examples such as:
  - running an email client for downloading/composing emails
  - running a media player, playing music/videos
  - running a web browser for accessing websites
  - running a word processor for document creation
  - running a virus checker to prevent malware.

10 The BIOS sets up the computer to the point it is able to load up the operating system.

11 The driver provides instructions to the operating system, allowing it to interact with the printer. It shows the device how data is to be sent to the printer and how to interpret signals back from it (such as being low on paper or ink).

12 A virtual machine can run an operating system. This allows one operating system to be run within another one. A Windows user could run an application with a virtual machine running Linux.

13 A utility. It has one purpose: to make files smaller, which helps with system maintenance (by potentially freeing up space).

14 An application. It allows the user to make leaflets/posters/flyers and so on.

15 For software to be classed as open source, the program's source code has to be available with permission to do anything with it.

16 If source code is freely available for others to amend, recompile and redistribute, there is less incentive for people to pay for the software.

17 Interpreters can be useful when debugging software as there is no need to wait for compilation after every amendment, and the interpreter can continue running up to the point it encounters an error.

18 A high-level language is designed to be human readable and usually consists of a mix of English words and mathematical statements. High-level languages cannot be read directly by a computer and therefore need translation software (i.e. a compiler or interpreter).

19 Lexical analysis, syntax analysis, code generation, optimisation

20 The symbol table stores information such as the data type and scope of variables within the program being compiled.

21 Libraries allow programmers to use code other people have written, saving them time and enabling them to draw upon the expertise of others. They will likely have been tested and refined over time, meaning they will contain more efficient code than the programmer could write and (unlike the programmer's code) won't need debugging.

22 A linker combines the object code generated when a program is compiled along with any libraries used, generating an executable machine code file.

23 The prototype is used for evaluation by the user at the end of each iteration. This evaluation is used to feed into the next iteration. By the end of the process, the prototype has become the final product.

24
  - requirements definition
  - analysis
  - design
  - coding
  - testing
  - maintenance.

Check your understanding and progress at **www.hoddereducation.co.uk/myrevisionnotesdownloads**

25 The spiral model is a risk-focused software lifecycle. It is iterative. Each iteration involves determining objectives; identifying and resolving risks; developing and testing; and planning the next iteration.

26 – size and complexity of the project
   – the amount of interaction that will be possible with the end user
   – the expertise and experience of the software development team
   – whether the software team are situated together or in geographically remote locations
   – how well suited the product is to prototyping.

27 – less documentation during the process
   – can be hard to set milestones and plan for time and budget
   – can be hard to ascertain progress being made.

28 The program prints the highest number in an array, along with its position.

29

```
word = input("Enter a word").lowercase()

vowelCount = 0

consonantCount = 0

for i = 0 to word.length-1

    vowels = [a","e","i","o","u"]

    vowelFound = false

    for j = 0 to vowels.length - 1

        if word.substring(i,1) == vowels[j]
then

            vowelFound == true

        end if

    next j

    if vowelFound = true then

        vowelCount = vowelCount + 1

    else

        consonantCount = consonantCount + 1

    endif

next i

if consonantCount > vowelCount then

 print(word + " has more consonants than
vowels.")

else if vowelCount > consonantCount then

    print(word + " has more vowels than
consonants.")

else

    print(word + " has an equal number of
    vowels and consonants.")

endif
```

30 Some programs are more easily solved with different approaches. Different paradigms allow different approaches.

31 In a declarative language, the programmer states the conditions of the result, but not how to get the result. This is the case with SQL. For example `SELECT forename FROM Employee WHERE surname = 'Smith';` states what is needed but not how to get it.

32 Full details will depend on the language studied.

The language will almost certainly be possible to be considered as procedural as its programs are described through a sequence of steps that can then be grouped into subroutines.

Many languages adhere to more than one paradigm. For example, Java/C++/C# allow for procedural programming but are primarily designed to be object oriented. Many languages also allow an element of functional programming.

33 Loads the contents of the given memory location into the accumulator.

34

```
INP

STA num

ADD num

ADD num

OUT

HLT

num    DAT
```

35

```
        INP

        SUB one

        OUT

        HLT

one    DAT 1
```

36

```
number = int(input("Enter a number"))

if number < 10 then

        print(0)

else

        print(10)

endif
```

37

```
            INP

            STA num

            SUB oneHundred

            BRP double

            LDA num

            ADD num

            ADD num

            BRA end
```

```
double      LDA num

            ADD   num

end         OUT

            HLT

onehundred  DAT 100

num               DAT
```

38 All three branch to their given label depending on the value in the accumulator.

BRA always branches regardless of the value in the accumulator.

BRZ branches if the value in the accumulator is 0

BRP branches if the value in the accumulator is >= 0

39

```
loop        INP

            SUB eleven

            BRP end

            BRA loop

end         HLT

eleven DAT 11
```

40 Write an LMC program that takes in a number and outputs the number 1 that many times.

```
            INP

loop        STA num

            LDA one

            OUT

            LDA num

            SUB one

            BRZ end

            BRA loop

end         HLT

one         DAT 1

num         DAT
```

41 With direct addressing, the operand represents the address being used. With indirect addressing, the operand represents the memory location that holds a value representing the memory location to be used.

42 Immediate addressing is quicker as the operand represents the absolute value, meaning that, unlike direct addressing, no time has to be spent getting a value from memory.

43 A class is a template that specifies state (through attributes) and behaviour (through methods). An object is an instance of a class.

44

```
class Mansion inherits House
    private fountain
    public procedure new(givenDoorColour,
givenGarden, givenFloors, givenFountain)
        fountain = givenFountain
        super.new(givenDoorColour,
givenFloors, givenGarden)
    endprocedure
    public procedure changeFloors
(givenFloors)
        if floors >= 2 then
            floors = givenFloors
        endif
    endprocedure
endclass
```

Chapter 3

1 File compression is the process of making files take up less storage space.

2 Lossy: JPEG

Lossless: PNG

3 JPEG can achieve very high compression ratios on photographs, allowing them to be quickly transmitted across the internet.

PNG stores a perfect representation of the image (the same pixel for pixel) while still achieving a respectable amount of compression.

4 3A5B11A2B1A6B

5 The quote is better compressed using dictionary coding. Run-length encoding only performs well on data with large amounts of consecutively repeating data. This is not the case in natural language. Dictionary coding performs well when sequences of data repeat throughout a file. This works well here, for example the phrases 'the end' and 'the beginning'.

6 Symmetric encryption requires a key to be agreed by both parties in advance. This is not practical when transmitting data, making symmetric encryption unsuitable. (Note that this issue can be circumvented by agreeing a key over asymmetric encryption then moving to symmetric encryption.)

7 Keeping files stored on a computer/saved in database protected in case anyone gains unauthorised access.

8 Deterministic (always gives the same output)

Irreversible (input cannot be determined from output)

Low levels of collision (two different inputs are unlikely to give the same output)

9 A hash of the document can be taken and shared between all parties (and if necessary publicly shared).

At any point in the future, another hash can be taken. If it matches the original, the data has not been changed.

10 – records
   – fields
   – tables

11 A flat-file database stores all data in a single table. In a relational database, data is stored in multiple tables that are linked.

12 require less space for large databases

   easier to maintain and use when storing complex data

13 A primary key needs to be unique, whereas it is possible (and indeed likely) two people in the database will have the same surname.

14 Tables are linked using primary and foreign keys. The primary key of a record appears in another table as a foreign key, creating a link.

15 It would be a common action to search for bookings on a given date. Making the booking date a secondary key means it would be indexed, and these searches would be faster.

16 Indexing a field reduces the time it takes to be searched. The disadvantage of this is that the index itself needs to be stored, taking up extra storage space.

17 `Manufacturer` and `CarModel` are likely to have a one-to-many relationship.

18

19 The school can have sheets with all student names in a class printed on them, with boxes alongside that can be shaded in. The teacher shades in the boxes of all those present and then these are centrally scanned.

   This was a common method of registering students prior to computers being more common in all classrooms and electronic registration being used.

20 CSV, or comma separated values, files store different pieces of data separated by commas. In the case of a database, it stores the value of each field separated by a comma (and starting a new line for each record).

21 – Data must already be in 1NF
   – All fields must depend on the whole of the primary key. In other words, if a table has a composite key, every field that is not part of the key must depend on all of the fields within the composite key.

22

Table Stock

`stock_number, stock_name, number_in_stock, supplier_ref`

Table Order

`order_number, order_date, order_quantity, stock_number`

Table Supplier

`supplier_ref, supplier_name, supplier_email`

23 a) `SELECT Forename,Surname FROM Customer;`
   b) `SELECT Forename,Surname FROM Customer WHERE TelephoneNumber LIKE '0121%' AND BonusPoints > 1000;`
   c) `SELECT RoomNumber,BookingDate FROM Customer JOIN Booking ON Customer.CustomerID = Booking.CustomerID WHERE Surname = 'Smith';`
   d) `INSERT INTO Customer (Forename, Surname, TelephoneNumber, BonusPoints) VALUES ('Joshua', 'Stevenson', '029 2018 0606',0)`

   NB answer can include `CustomerID` but usually this is set to auto-increment by the DBMS, preventing duplicate values occurring.

   e) `DROP TABLE Customer;`

24 A customer could be deleted while they still have bookings. This would mean that there would be rooms booked out but no person allocated to those bookings.

25 A group of operations that are designed to carry out a single task within a database. The transaction itself must be:
   – Atomic: it either completes or fails but cannot partially complete.
   – Consistent: it won't put the database into a state inconsistent with its rules.
   – Isolated: it won't run alongside any transactions that may impact it
   – Durable: once it has made changes, those changes remain.

26 Two identical copies of a database provides an element of redundancy for the bank. If the database being used fails, it can switch to the other without losing any data or having downtime.

27 HTTPS (Hypertext Transfer Protocol Secure) is used for transferring data over a network, usually web pages over the World Wide Web. It is designed to be secure so that third parties cannot read the data if intercepted.

   DHCP (Dynamic Host Configuration Protocol) is used to allocate IP addresses to devices when they join a network.

   UDP (User Datagram Protocol) is used to send data across a network when it's important that it is sent at a constant, fast rate but there is no need to ensure every packet is received. An example of its use is video streaming.

28 The link layer obtains data from the internet layer and places it as signals on the physical connections. It also receives signals from the physical layers and passes them as data to the internet layer.

29 HTTPS belongs to the application layer
   DHCP belongs to the application layer
   UDP belongs to the transport layer.

30 – LAN: one limited area; WAN: covers a large area.
   – LAN: owned in total by the operating organisation; WAN: communication links owned by communication company.

213

31

32 Packet switching prevents segments of the network being tied up at any given time by two devices communicating. This means all users experience a more consistent quality of service.

33 When two devices communicate over a network using circuit switching, they have exclusive use of that connection over the time they are communicating. This means that while these two devices will have an excellent quality connection, those parts of the network will be unusable over this time to other users. Packet switching avoids this by allowing connections to be shared by multiple devices at the same time.

34 A firewall monitors traffic going from the internet into and out of a network. It then allows packets through if they meet its set of rules.

35 A network interface card (NIC) allows a computer to connect to a network. It will usually have an Ethernet port or have a built-in wireless antenna. These days it is common for NICs to be built into the motherboard.

36 A switch connects multiple devices on a network. When data comes in through one port it sends it out the port to which the device with the data's destination address is connected. Typically, a switch uses MAC addresses to identify devices.

A router can also connect multiple devices and can connect two networks (in a home network, your home's LAN to the internet). It identifies devices by their IP addresses. Using routing tables, it is able to determine the most efficient route to send data.

37 Advantage: Wi-Fi allows devices to be used from anywhere within range of a signal.

Disadvantage: signals can vary according to obstacles such as walls and distance from the wireless access point.

Wireless traffic can be easily intercepted and so must be encrypted.

38 Material is spread across multiple computers in multiple jurisdictions, with different laws. This made it hard for regulators, as they were dealing with many people across multiple countries.

39 A client–server model centralises all the network's functionality. This makes it much easier to identify issues and maintain hardware. Having a central point means security can be focused on that area, rather than having data stored across multiple machines.

40 <div> tags are used to set dividers. These are areas of a page to be treated as one block.

41

```
border-color: red;
border-style: dashed;
border-width: 5px;
```

or

```
border: 5px dashed red;
```

(#FF0000 can be used instead of red)

42 A class is a group of elements on a page that are to be formatted the same way.

An identifier is a specific element on a page to be formatted. Elements can belong to both a class and an identifier. In this case, the formatting of the identifier overrides that of the class.

43 HTML sets out the structure of the page using tags.

CSS determines the formatting of the page.

JavaScript provides any functionality on the web page (such as validation or interactivity).

44

```
var lowerBound = 0;
var upperBound = list.length - 1;
var midPoint = Math.
round((lowerBound+upperBound) / 2);
while(list[midPoint] != searchedFor &&
lowerBound <= upperBound)
{
      if(list[midPoint] < searchedFor)
      {
            lowerBound = midPoint + 1;
      }
      else
      {
            upperBound = midPoint - 1;
      }
      midPoint = Math.
round((lowerBound+upperBound) / 2);
}
if(list[midPoint] == searchedFor)
{
      document.write("Item found at "
+midPoint);
}
else
{
      document.write("Item not in list");
}
```

Check your understanding and progress at **www.hoddereducation.co.uk/myrevisionnotesdownloads**

45 A search engine spider is a program that travels from web page to web page indexing their contents. It visits a page, adds words on that page to an index, then uses one of the links on that page to travel to its next page.

46 The search engine would look at the words *computer* and *mice/mouse* in its index and select pages where the index shows the word computer directly precedes the words mouse or mice.

47 PageRank determines the significance of a site. By looking at how many sites already link to a site, it is able to determine those sites that are likely to be of more use, so they can be presented in order to the person searching.

48 Site A may have fewer outgoing links than site B. The sites linking to Site A may have a higher PageRank themselves.

49 Client-side scripting puts the processing demands on the browser and as such the client's computer. This reduces the work the server has to do, saving the owner extra hardware requirements and expenses.

50 Scripts running on the client can be circumvented or amended. Therefore the owner cannot rely on them being run on the client's browser. They can also be viewed by the user and code could be copied/duplicated

Chapter 4

1 a) 130
   b) 193
   c) 216
   d) 22
2 a) 10001100
   b) 1000100
   c) 11001000
   d) 10010100
3 a) 00101101
   b) 01111101
   c) 11111101
   d) 11000100
4. a) 00111000
   b) 10111000
   c) 11111101
   d) 10110000
5 a) 40
   b) −68
   c) −49
   d) −121
6 a) 01010000
   b) 01001001
   c) 01010110
   d) 01100101
7 a) 10110
   b) 11
   c) 100
8 a) 1A   b) 5C   c) AF

9 a) 1010 1011 1100
   b) 1010 0101 1101
   c) 1011 1011 1100 0011
10 a) 165
   b) 95
   c) 734
11 a) 83
   b) C7
   c) ED
12 a) 1.25
   b) −2.5
   c) 0.375
13 a) 5.5
   b) −0.3125
   c) −0.125
14 a) 0110100000 000001
   b) 1011000000 000010
   c) 0110000000 111110
15 a) 01110 010
   b) 01110 001
   c) 01000 001
16 a) 0111010000 000010
   b) 0110111000 000011
   c) 0100100000 000010

17

Operand	0	0	1	1	0	1	1	0
Mask	1	0	1	0	1	0	1	0
AND	0	0	1	0	0	0	1	0
OR	1	0	1	1	1	1	1	0
XOR	1	0	0	1	1	1	0	0

18 10010001 with XOR
19 01001001 with AND
20 a) i) 68   ii) 71   iii) 100
   b) i) E   ii) x   iii) d
21 a) Jane assuming row/column
   b)

names	0	1	2	3	4	5
0	Alan	Kuldeep	Li	Sarah	Harry	Mary
1	Jane	Navdeep	Charles	Joe	Jane	Irina
2	Wendy	Deborah	Dillip	Umar	Johan	Hua

   c) Navdeep, Charles, Joe
22

Data item	Vehicle manufacturer	Start (3) Alpha pointers
1	Ford	5
2	Vauxhall	0
3	Alfa	4
4	Fiat	1
5	Mercedes	2

As a table

a)

		Start (3)
Data item	Animal	Alpha pointers
1	Monkey	4
2	Lion	1
3	Cheetah	5
4	Zebra	0
5	Gorilla	2

b)

		Start (3)
Data item	Animal	Alpha pointers
1	Monkey	4
2	Lion	
3	Cheetah	5
4	Zebra	0
5	Gorilla	1

c)

		Start (3)
Data item	Animal	Alpha pointers
1	Monkey	6
2	Lion	
3	Cheetah	5
4	Zebra	0
5	Gorilla	1
6	Tiger	4

a) As a diagram (examples).

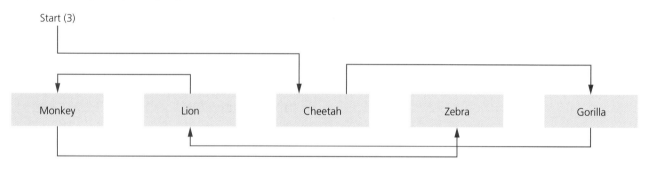

b)

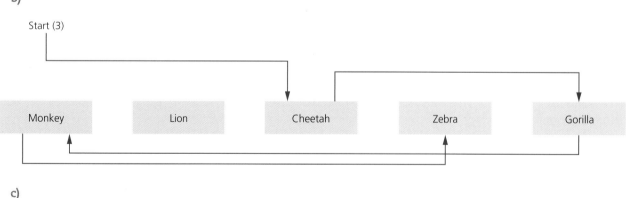

c)

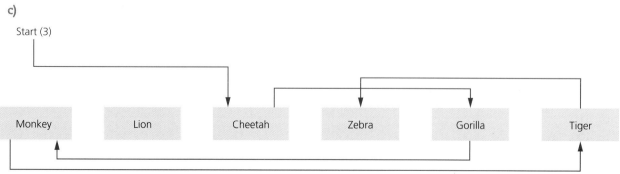

Check your understanding and progress at **www.hoddereducation.co.uk/myrevisionnotesdownloads**

24

Initial	PUSH 9	POP	POP	PUSH 17	POP	POP
	9					
12	12	12		17		
7	7	7	7	7	7	
3	3	3	3	3	3	3

25

Initial	PUSH 12	POP	POP	PUSH 9	POP	PUSH 6
5	5	3	7	7	12	12
3	3	7	12	12	9	9
7	7	12		9		6
	12					

26 Example

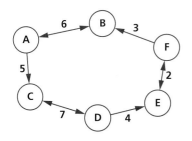

27 a)

ABCDE

Stack				D		E	
			C	C	C	C	
		B	B	B	B	B	
	A	A	A	A	A	A	
Visited	A	B	C	D		E	

b)

ABCED

Queue		B	B	B	C	E	D	
			C	C	E	D		
			E					
Visited	A	B	C	E	D			
Current	A	A	B	B	C	E		

28 a)

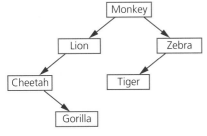

b) Monkey Lion Cheetah Gorilla Zebra Tiger

c) Gorilla Cheetah Lion Tiger Zebra Monkey

29 a)

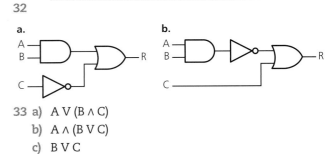

b) / + 3 12 – 7 2

c) 3 12 + 7 2 – /

30 a) 101 * 104 = 10504

10504 MOD 251 = 213

b) 52 * 55 = 2860

2860 MOD 251 = 99

31 a)

R = (A ∧ B) ∨ ¬ C

A	B	C	A∧B	¬C	R
0	0	0	0	1	1
0	0	1	0	0	0
0	1	0	0	1	1
0	1	1	0	0	0
1	0	0	0	1	1
1	0	1	0	0	0
1	1	0	1	1	1
1	1	1	1	0	1

b)

R = ¬ (A ∧ B) ∨ C

A	B	C	A∧B	¬(A∧B)	R
0	0	0	0	1	1
0	0	1	0	1	1
0	1	0	0	1	1
0	1	1	0	1	1
1	0	0	0	1	1
1	0	1	0	1	1
1	1	0	1	0	0
1	1	1	1	0	1

32

a.

A, B, C → R

b.

A, B, C → R

33 a) A ∨ (B ∧ C)

b) A ∧ (B ∨ C)

c) B ∨ C

34 a)

CD\AB	00	01	11	10
00	1	1	1	1
01	1	1	0	0
11	0	0	0	0
10	0	0	0	0

The blue block is ¬C ∧ ¬D
The green block is ¬C ∧ ¬A
(¬C ∧ ¬D) ∨ (¬C ∧ ¬A)
Simplifying to ¬C ∧ (¬D ∨¬A)

b)

CD\AB	00	01	11	10
00	0	0	0	0
01	0	1	1	0
11	1	1	1	1
10	1	0	0	1

The blue block is C ∧ ¬B
The green block is B ∧ D
(C ∧ ¬B) V (B ∧ D)

35

CD\AB	00	01	11	10
00	0	1	1	1
01	0	1	1	1
11	0	1	1	0
10	0	1	1	0

The blue block is A ∧ ¬C
The green block is B
(A ∧ ¬C) V B

36

A	B	S	C
0	0	0	0
0	1	1	0
1	0	1	0
1	1	0	1

37

Clock pulse	0	1	0	1	0	1	0	1
Input	0	0	0	1	1	1	1	0
Output Q	0	0	0	1	1	1	1	0

Chapter 5

1 Examples:
   - an inaccurate record of payments may show missed payments that are not correct and affect access to credit
   - inaccurate name and address details will prevent access to credit because the lender cannot verify the home address or individual
   - an inaccurate record of outstanding credit or past credit can affect the rate at which credit is offered or the amount offered and rate for a mortgage application.

2 Data is held for a specific purpose and must not be used for any other purpose. Once the reason for keeping the data is over there is no necessity to keep the data and it should be deleted. Data kept beyond the limit for necessary use, therefore, can only be used illegally for a purpose that was not agreed by the data owner.

3 There are seven provisions:
   - **Lawfulness, fairness and transparency** – valid reason, not breach any other laws, processed fairly, clearly identified use of data.
   - **Purpose limitation** – clear purpose for collecting data and only used for that purpose.
   - **Data minimisation** – relevant data only and limited to what is necessary.
   - **Accuracy** – data stored must be accurate and kept up to date.
   - **Storage limitation** – data should only be kept for as long as necessary for the stated purpose.
   - **Security** – data must be kept securely.
   - **Accountability** – the data holder is responsible for how the data is used and for compliance with all the regulations of the DPA.

4 Hacking is when a computer system is accessed without authorisation.
This is using technical skills and know-how to bypass the security in a system.

5 Hacking can be authorised by the owner of a computer system to test for vulnerabilities in the security. Since it is authorised, it is not illegal.

6 – digital signatures or certificates that use encrypted messages to confirm the identity of the sender.
   - Secure Sockets Layer (SSL), a protocol that enables encrypted links between computers to ensure the security of a transaction.
   - user IDs, passwords and access rights, used for basic identification of users and their legitimate rights to access specific data.
   - anti-malware software such as antivirus and anti-spyware applications used to identify and remove suspicious software on a computer system.
   - firewalls, which can be software applications or hardware, that sit between the system and external networks to prevent certain types of data and users accessing the system; firewalls can also be set to simply deny access to all external users.

7 It makes it illegal to make unauthorised access:
   - to computer materials
   - with intent to commit further offences such as stealing money
   - with intent to damage or impair the operation of a computer, for instance distributing malware.

8

Open-source software	Proprietary software
Access to the source code	No access to source code
May be free of charge or very cheap	Almost always some cost involved
Users can modify the software	Copyright law means users cannot modify the software
Can be installed on as many computers as necessary	Extra licences must normally be obtained before installing on additional computers
No one is responsible for any problems with the software	Full support from the software developer – fully tested before release, regular updates to fix bugs and improve features, faulty software replaced
Usually only community support	Commercial and community support available
Often of very high quality because of the community of highly skilled developers	High-quality software because a lot of money is spent developing it
Updates are often provided by a community of highly skilled developers, to fix bugs and improve features	Updates provided by the developer, sometimes with extra costs involved.

Check your understanding and progress at **www.hoddereducation.co.uk/myrevisionnotesdownloads**

9 – full support for the product by the developers
   – regular updates to fix issues or add improvements or new features
   – often high-quality software
   – often includes tutorial guides and training support.

10 Peer-to-peer streaming allows data to be shared directly between computers. There is no or limited monitoring possible for this process, allowing the illegal sharing of files.

The illegal sharing of files is an offence under the Copyright, Design and Patents Act and is illegal.

Under the Act it is illegal to copy, modify or distribute any copyright material, including software, without the relevant permission.

11 Some rights reserved: less restrictive than proprietary software.

May be no restrictions on use but the developer might require attribution or that the software cannot be used for commercial purposes.

12 The Act is intended to allow suitable authorities (e.g. GCHQ, MI6) access to communications to prevent criminal or terrorist activities.

The Regulation of Investigatory Powers Act provides certain public bodies, such as the police and other government departments, with the right to:
   – demand internet service providers (ISPs) provide access to a customer's communications
   – allow mass surveillance of communications
   – demand ISPs fit equipment to facilitate surveillance
   – demand access be granted to protected information
   – allow monitoring of an individual's internet activities
   – prevent the existence of such interception activities being revealed in court.

13 Examples:
   – high street shops are expensive to maintain; the cost of the premises, staff, displayed stock
   – high street shops require people to travel to the high street in order to select and purchase items – with the associated time and travel costs
   – high street shops will only be able to hold a limited range of items, for example fewer options/sizes for clothing.
   – large out of town warehouses are cheaper to run, have significantly less idle stock, require fewer workers
   – the internet provides the customer with immediate 24/7 access to a wide range of items with no time or travel costs
   – online shopping baskets and payment systems allow easy and safe purchasing
   – efficient logistics, provided by computer software for stock retrieval and distribution, route planning and customer contact make delivery of these items cost-effective.

14 Computers are able to look at huge amounts of data very quickly and can analyse patterns in that data

to determine potential solutions. These potential solutions can be tested by the software to identify the most effective solution.

By using algorithms that apply statistical analysis to patterns within the data, computers can generate mathematical weightings for particular patterns and match these to known solutions to similar problems to formulate a potential solution. These weightings are used to test the proposed solution, and any differences between the predicted and actual result are used to adjust the weightings.

15 Driverless cars are able to communicate with each other to co-operate effectively. With the unpredictable behaviour of human drivers eliminated, driverless cars can co-operate to avoid collisions. This means they can move more quickly, more fuel efficiently, managing routes to avoid congestion and there is no need for traffic management, such as roundabouts, traffic lights and so on.

16 Examples include:
   – Speech recognition systems that identify key words and patterns in the spoken word to interpret the meaning, for example Siri or Alexa.
   – Medical diagnosis systems used to self-diagnose illness from the symptoms and to support medical staff in making diagnoses.
   – Control systems that monitor, interpret and predict events to provide real-time process control, for example chemical plants. Tesla and other driver support and self-driving cars, Amazon and others use artificial intelligence to predict what products might be of interest to consumers.

17 – online meetings reducing the need for travel
   – electronic documents replacing paper ones
   – better logistics, reducing energy use in delivery systems

18 Access to apps for communication may not be available, limiting access to friends and family, particularly those who are living in another country.

Access to news items may be limited, meaning people cannot stay informed about issues within the country or the wider world.

Ideas and opinions cannot be shared or discussed widely.

Political opinion and news coverage may be limited to a centrally sanctioned version only.

19 Data mining is an automated process that searches for patterns in large data sets to predict events.

20 – track how long people take to complete tasks
   – how many tasks are completed in a set time
   – how many and how long people take for breaks
   – internet activity while at work.

21 – Throwaway devices: people constantly updating tech and throwing away old tech – devices that cannot be repaired economically.

- Hazardous waste: computers use some toxic materials that should be recycled carefully; they are often simply disposed of in the environment.
- Rare elements: computer devices use some rare elements that can be expensive and environmentally problematic to source.
- Energy use: data centres use a lot of energy.

22 Examples: to limit access to socially unacceptable material, extreme politics and ideas, dangerous information such as advice on creating products that can harm or contribute to terrorist activities, or terrorist propaganda.

23 – product keys to ensure that only one user with the decryption key can access the material
- watermarks that are visible on the product to show that it is not a legitimately obtained copy
- shut down websites that are offering pirated material.

24 Established concepts about the messages that different colours send, and how colours can work together within a design.

25 Under the Communications Act 2003, it is a criminal offence to send indecent or offensive communications and if traced the offender may end up with a criminal record.

The Act is in place to deal with communications that contain credible threats of violence, such as trolling or stalking, or communications that contain material grossly offensive to identified individuals and intended to cause harm.

Those who repeat the messages are also subject to the provisions of this Act, and re-sharing or re-posting an offensive message may be illegal.

Governments have pressed social media providers to put into place systems to deal with offensive communications.

Chapter 6

1 Hiding details or attributes when studying objects or systems, to focus attention on the essential elements of the problem. This process is used to identify what is important in a problem, and then formulate it to create an algorithm.

2 Grouping together items with similar features in order to develop a general solution by using an algorithm that solves a problem and adapting it so that it solves similar problems. This is often based on looking at similar existing problems for which there is a solution.

3 A representation of reality by taking a real-life problem and building a model of it. The purpose is to identify what is important by removing unnecessary detail, leaving only the key elements of the problem.

4 Examples:
- inputs: PIN, choice of transaction, amount of cash to withdraw
- outputs: greeting, instruction to enter PIN, choose transaction, cash withdrawal amount,

any error messages, messages about process, for example waiting for bank, entering new PIN, balance if requested. Also verbal messages provided via headphone socket for those with impaired vision.

5 Requirements that must be met before the program can run.

Examples:
- device specification, software requirements, operating system, additional software, input requirements and validation.

6 – they are reliable and bug free, having been tested and used many times
- they save time for the programmer
- they save on development costs for a project
- often optimised for computational efficiency.

7 Loading a resource before it is needed, for example commonly used web pages being requested before they are used.

Algorithms can also be used to prefetch instructions by predicting which instructions or data are likely to be required by a program. The data likely to be needed next is fetched and stored in a cache ready to be used by the program, minimising delays waiting for data or instructions to be fetched from storage.

8 Breaking the complex problem down into smaller more manageable parts. Dealing with each small part of the problem is much simpler than trying to deal with a complex problem. Breaking the problem down allows us to work on each sub-problem individually, then combine those individual solutions into a solution for the whole problem.

For very large problems, a team of programmers can work on individual parts of the problem.

9 The components of a problem can be solved individually; many may already have existing, tested and robust solutions or an existing solution that can be modified. For large problems, individual components can be allocated to members of a team of programmers.

Each component represents a single, self-contained solution module that can be developed and tested independently, before being assembled into a solution for the main problem.

10 As the output from one module may be required as input for another, it makes sense to develop the solution in that order.

The data flow through a program may determine the order, for example a module gathering input data may be required before one that processes that data.

11 Examples:

Is it feasible:
- Can it be done?
- Is it cost-effective?
- Can an effective solution be developed within a realistic time frame?

If yes:

- Programming paradigm required.
- Choice of programming language, that is, does it have the necessary features to create the solution?
- System requirements including peripheral requirements.

12 Programs have to be written specially to take advantage of parallel processing and can be much longer and more complex. Only if a significant number of processes can be completed simultaneously is this an advantage.

13 – in more complex programs, there may be delays while other parts of the program complete
- organisation of the separate tasks and switching between processes can cause delays in processes starting and slow the program
- some problems just cannot be broken down into tasks that can be completed simultaneously
- problems with large sections that need to be completed sequentially will not benefit from other parts being processed simultaneously.

Chapter 7

1   a) Any two statements, for example:
```
temp = list[position]
list[position] = list[position + 1]
```
b) `if list[position] > list[position + 1] then`

c) `for position = 0 to listLength-2`
or
`while swapMade is true`

2   a) Any two statements, for example:
```
lowerBound = 0
upperBound = lengthOfList – 1
```
b) if list[midPoint] < searchedFor then
or
`if List[midPoint] == searchedFor then`

c) while list[midPoint] != searchedFor and lowerBound <= upperBound

3   For bubble sort:

If the `while` loop has been chosen, it is condition controlled.

If the `for` loop has been chosen, it is count controlled.

For binary search:

The `while` loop is condition controlled.

4   a) False
b) True
c) Determines if a number is even.
d) The program will never reach the base case of `n == 0`, meaning it would continue making recursive calls until the computer runs out of stack space, at which point a stack overflow error is generated.

5   A global variable can accessed from any point in the program. A local variable can only be accessed from the part of the program in which it is declared. This

is usually a subroutine, although in some languages a local variable can be local to the structure (e.g. `if`, `while`, `for`) in which it is declared.

6   a) As we only see n declared in `foo()`, we can assume it is local to that procedure.
b) n is local to `foo`, which means it is not in scope when the line `print(n)` is called. As the program is trying to print a variable that doesn't exist, it generates an error.

7   When a program is modular, it's easier to split work between the programming team, with modules assigned to different people.

Testing becomes easier as each module can be tested individually, and then once it is determined that it works, it can be confidently used within the whole program.

Modules from previous projects can be reused, and modules from the current project can be reused in future projects.

8   The program would output

10

15

9   – breakpoints
- watches/watchpoints
- stepping
- stack traces

10 IDEs tend to consume a lot more system resources than text editors, and as a consequence they can take longer to load. Writing a program often results in a number of additional project files. All this may be overkill for very simple programs that won't benefit from the advantages of the IDE.

11 It must be able to be represented:
- in a structured, algorithmic form.

It must be feasible to solve it:
- within the time available
- at a realistic cost
- using the available resources

12 – stakeholder requirements identified
- information available used to clearly define the problem and system requirements
- features of current or existing solutions or solutions to similar problems identified
- data requirements and structures identified.

13 A problem-solving technique used to divide the problem into sub-problems repeatedly until all sub-problems can be solved. The solution is then built recursively by solving and merging the sub-problems into a single solution.

14 Excessive details are removed or hidden leaving the basic requirements for a solution. This clarifies the requirements and makes complex problems more manageable. By removing unnecessary detail the programmer can:
- focus on the important aspects of the problem
- identify pre-existing solutions to parts of the problem.

15 An approximate solution identified by looking at existing but similar problems and their solutions.

16 Performance modelling is used to test how well a solution functions under a range of conditions. This will test the robustness of the solution when under stress and is particularly useful when it is potentially dangerous to test in real situations.

17 Problems can often be better understood if presented as a visual model. A visual model will often identify key features and trends in a complex situation that cannot be seen from the data alone.

Chapter 8

1 An algorithm is a set of instructions that, when followed, carry out a process. A program is the algorithm implemented into a form that can ultimately be run on a computer.

2 – pseudocode
  – flowcharts

3 – time taken to run
  – space required to run

4 $O(n^2)$

5 $O(1)$

6 Linear, $O(n)$. The time taken grows proportionally to the size of the list.

7 Logarithmic, $\log(n)$. Each time the size of n doubles, the loop requires one further iteration.

8 a) The pop function

```
//Assumes top points to the item on top of the
// stack
function pop()
        if top >= 0 then
                result = stack[top]
                top = top - 1
                return result
        else
                print("Stack is empty")
                return null
        endif
end function
```

  b) The enqueue procedure

```
procedure enqueue(item)
        if length < queue.length then
                queue[front + length] = item
                length = length + 1
        else
                print("Queue is full")
        endif
end procedure
```
  Note:
```
queue[front + length] = item
```
  could also be

```
queue[(front + length) MOD length] = item
```
  if the queue is considered circular.

  c) Reversing the stack

```
//Note: a cleaner solution is to have two stacks
//and pop from one and push onto the other.
//As we don't have two stacks, we shall use the
//queue
lastPopped = pop()
while lastPopped != null
        enqueue(lastPopped)
end while
//Assuming dequeue also returns null when empty
lastDequeued = dequeue()
while lastDequeued != null
        push(lastDequeued)
end while
```

9 First location is checked

1	2	6	7	9	12	15	24	25	30	31	34	40
↑												

then the next

1	2	6	7	9	12	15	24	25	30	31	34	40
	↑											

and the next

1	2	6	7	9	12	15	24	25	30	31	34	40
		↑										

and the next

1	2	6	7	9	12	15	24	25	30	31	34	40
			↑									

and the next

1	2	6	7	9	12	15	24	25	30	31	34	40
				↑								

until 12 is found

1	2	6	7	9	12	15	24	25	30	31	34	40
					↑							

10 In the example below, when an odd number is divided by two the result is always rounded down (i.e. 5 / 2 = 2). Rounding down is often used in practice as it works easily with integer division. Rounding up or down is acceptable but should be done consistently.

Check your understanding and progress at www.hoddereducation.co.uk/myrevisionnotesdownloads

LB = lower bound; MP = midpoint; UB = upper bound

0	1	2	3	4	5	6	7	8	9	10	11	12
1	2	6	7	9	12	15	24	25	30	31	34	40
LB						MP						UB

(0 + 12) / 2 = 6

15 at location 6 is too high so UB becomes MP – 1 (i.e. 5)

0	1	2	3	4	5	6	7	8	9	10	11	12
1	2	6	7	9	12	15	24	25	30	31	34	40
LB		MP			UB							

(0 + 5) / 2 = 2

6 at location 2 is too low so LB becomes MP + 1 (i.e. 3)

0	1	2	3	4	5	6	7	8	9	10	11	12
1	2	6	7	9	12	15	24	25	30	31	34	40
			LB	MP	UB							

(3 + 5) / 2 = 4

9 at location 4 is too low so LB becomes MP + 1 (i.e. 5)

0	1	2	3	4	5	6	7	8	9	10	11	12
1	2	6	7	9	12	15	24	25	30	31	34	40
					LB							
					MP							
					UB							

(5 + 5) / 2 = 5

12 at location 5 is the target so the value has been found at 5.

11 The numbers in the list are in order.

12 The first pass …

3, 5, 2, 4, 1

3, 2, 5, 4, 1

3, 2, 4, 5, 1

3, 2, 4, 1, 5

After the second pass …

2, 3, 1, 4, 5

After the third pass …

2, 1, 3, 4, 5

After the fourth pass …

1, 2, 3, 4, 5

After the fifth pass the sort finishes …

1, 2, 3, 4, 5

13

3 is assumed to be in place

3, 5, 2, 4, 1

5 is already in place

3, 5, 2, 4, 1

2 gets inserted in its position

2, 3, 5, 4, 1

4 gets inserted in its position

2, 3, 4, 5, 1

1 gets inserted in its position

1, 2, 3, 4, 5

14

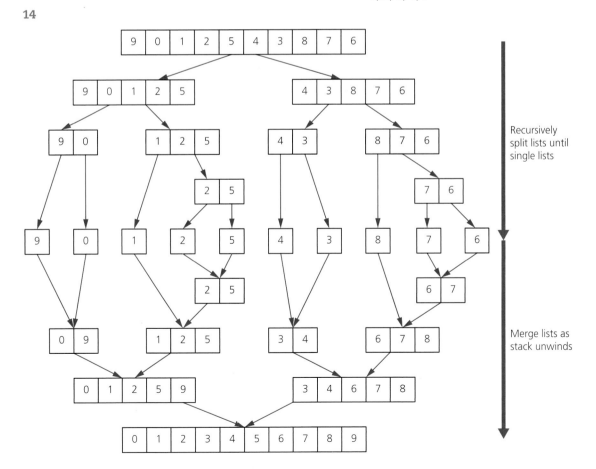

Recursively split lists until single lists

Merge lists as stack unwinds

My Revision Notes OCR A-level Computer Science Second Edition

15 A pivot is picked and two sub-lists created. This process is recursively applied to each sub-list until the lists are one item big.

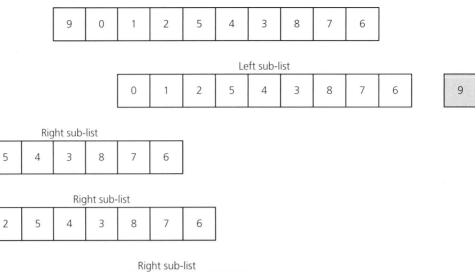

| 9 | 0 | 1 | 2 | 5 | 4 | 3 | 8 | 7 | 6 |

Left sub-list

| 0 | 1 | 2 | 5 | 4 | 3 | 8 | 7 | 6 | | 9 |

Right sub-list

| 0 | | 1 | 2 | 5 | 4 | 3 | 8 | 7 | 6 |

Right sub-list

| 1 | | 2 | 5 | 4 | 3 | 8 | 7 | 6 |

Right sub-list

| 2 | | 5 | 4 | 3 | 8 | 7 | 6 |

Left sub-list

| 4 | 3 |

| 5 |

Right sub-list

| 8 | 7 | 6 |

Left sub-list

| 3 | | 4 |

Left sub-list

| 7 | 6 | | 8 |

Left sub-list

| 6 | | 7 |

16 Both A* search and Dijkstra's algorithm will find the shortest path between two points but A* search avoids exploring paths that will not find a better solution, meaning it finds the shortest path in a quicker time.

Check your understanding and progress at **www.hoddereducation.co.uk/myrevisionnotesdownloads**